Devolution and Globalisation

IMPLICATIONS FOR LOCAL DECISION-MAKERS

OECD

ORGANISATION FOR ECONOMIC CO-OPERATION AND DEVELOPMENT

ORGANISATION FOR ECONOMIC CO-OPERATION AND DEVELOPMENT

Pursuant to Article 1 of the Convention signed in Paris on 14th December 1960, and which came into force on 30th September 1961, the Organisation for Economic Co-operation and Development (OECD) shall promote policies designed:

- to achieve the highest sustainable economic growth and employment and a rising standard of living in Member countries, while maintaining financial stability, and thus to contribute to the development of the world economy;
- to contribute to sound economic expansion in Member as well as non-member countries in the process of economic development; and
- to contribute to the expansion of world trade on a multilateral, non-discriminatory basis in accordance with international obligations.

The original Member countries of the OECD are Austria, Belgium, Canada, Denmark, France, Germany, Greece, Iceland, Ireland, Italy, Luxembourg, the Netherlands, Norway, Portugal, Spain, Sweden, Switzerland, Turkey, the United Kingdom and the United States. The following countries became Members subsequently through accession at the dates indicated hereafter: Japan (28th April 1964), Finland (28th January 1969), Australia (7th June 1971), New Zealand (29th May 1973), Mexico (18th May 1994), the Czech Republic (21st December 1995), Hungary (7th May 1996), Poland (22nd November 1996), Korea (12th December 1996) and the Slovak Republic (14th December 2000). The Commission of the European Communities takes part in the work of the OECD (Article 13 of the OECD Convention).

FOREWORD

Scotland is at the forefront of processes of devolution in the United Kingdom. Following a referendum, a new Scottish Parliament was opened on 1 July 1999. The Parliament and its partners now have the challenge of developing the institutions and economic development approach that will deliver economic growth and social inclusion in a globalising economy. However, devolution and globalisation are important developments not just for Scotland but also for many other countries across the OECD. Our governments are looking for devolution to deliver real benefits for economic and social development in a changing environment. The policies pursued by devolved governments and agencies at city and region level can have a major impact on economic adjustment, competitiveness and social cohesion in our economies. But it is fundamental that the policies and institutional structures that are adopted can respond to the new globalising environment.

This is why the OECD and Scottish Enterprise collaborated to hold a pioneering conference on 'Devolution and Globalisation - Implications for Local Decision-makers' in Glasgow on 28-29 February 2000. Some 130 delegates from twenty countries debated common challenges and compared and contrasted their approaches. This book publishes the main papers, discussions and conclusions of the conference. It was prepared by Jonathan Potter of the OECD LEED Programme and Scottish Enterprise participated in its funding. Robert Pollock from Scottish Enterprise collaborated closely with OECD in organising the themes and content of the conference.

The principal messages of the book are that:

- A more devolved economic development paradigm is required to respond to rapid restructuring and change in the globalising economy.

- New institutional structures are needed in order to promote policy innovation, tailoring and flexibility, based on networking and stakeholder participation.

3

- Devolved development strategies should focus on building competitiveness and social cohesion in the face of increased restructuring and change.

- City and region governments and development agencies wield important policy tools, for example for entrepreneurship promotion, human capital development and regeneration.

- Devolution provides an opportunity for institutional and policy innovation that should be seized. Cities and regions that develop strong institutional capital and distinctive development policies are more likely to be successful in the globalising economy.

TABLE OF CONTENTS

Boxes

INTRODUCTION

This book deals with two very important trends, namely devolution and globalisation. People often think of devolution and globalisation as two opposing phenomena, if not contradictory terms. One is a process of increasing localisation of decision-making. The other is a process of increasing internationalisation of economic interactions. Nonetheless these two trends are interdependent, because in order to compete successfully in a globalising economy, territories increasingly need policies that help build and exploit endogenous capabilities. Devolved governments are best placed to design and deliver such policies.

The economic development policies pursued by devolved governments also help to fill a gap being created as globalisation reduces the capacity of central governments to direct economic and employment growth in certain traditional ways. Thus, macroeconomic policy tools that were relied on heavily in the past are now more difficult to use, such as exchange rate movements or changes in money supply, because of international agreements and increasing international finance flows. In addition, the increased competition associated with globalisation is calling into question the effectiveness of sectoral industrial policies that attempted to support declining industries or create national champions. Furthermore, many governments have been reducing their use of conventional regional policies that attempted to redistribute investment from prosperous to poorer regions within a country, because of concerns about the zero-sum game and limited impacts on long-term capacity building in recipient areas. Central, or nation-state, government and its institutions clearly still have a significant role to play in the spatial distribution of economic activity, but in the globalising economy, endogenous development policies designed and implemented by city and region governments are also becoming critical.

The main concern of this book is to examine how city and region governments need to redesign their institutions and development policies in order to respond to the twin trends of devolution and globalisation. It examines what policies city and region governments and development agencies should develop in the context of devolution and globalisation and what governance structures they need to put into place in order to deliver these policies.

In terms of policies, it is argued that cities and regions need to develop flexible, tailored and integrated strategies to compete in an increasingly rapidly-moving and internationally-open economic environment. Critical to this are policies for entrepreneurship and human capital development, which both have pervasive impacts on long-run rates of economic growth. It is also argued that cities and regions need policies to support social cohesion in order to counteract problems of exclusion of people and places from growth processes in the globalising economy.

In terms of governance structures, it is argued that devolved governments have a fundamental role to play in successful policy, because more than national governments, cities and regions are able to ensure that what they put in place is well adapted to the needs and opportunities of their own area. But it is also argued that devolution should not be seen as a simple transfer of powers from central to city and region level, but rather as a process that requires multi-level partnership and networking as well.

The debate about the devolution of economic development powers within the context of globalisation is closely linked to the emergence of a new territorial development policy paradigm that emphasises the promotion of endogenous growth rather than redistribution. The focus of this new paradigm is on building long-term local development capacities, for example in terms of entrepreneurship, human capital and local institutions. This paradigm should be constituted by four pillars:

- Encouraging devolution of responsibilities for economic development policy to local level and the creation of a series of local partnerships for policy design and delivery between governments, the social partners and civil society.

- Improving the competitive environment of cities and regions by building human and social capital and providing appropriate institutional infrastructures, including technological institutes.

- Stimulating entrepreneurship and inward investment in cities and regions by supporting the creation of enterprises and self-employment, by improving the investment environment for attracting inward direct investment and by strengthening networks and clusters.

- Fighting social exclusion and improving quality of life.

City and regional governments have a clear role to play developing measures in all of these areas. Therefore regional policies should no longer be seen as the domain of nation-state government alone, they have to involve city and regional governments as well.

The book is structured as follows. Section one provides an overview of the issues and trends associated with devolution and globalisation and identifies some of the main challenges and trends for economic development policy. Section two examines in more detail the issue of institutions and governance and puts the case for a new model of networked institutions. Section three examines the policy strategies and instruments that cities and region governments and development agencies should use in the globalising economy. It includes chapters on policies for entrepreneurship, human capital and social cohesion. Section four sets out the conclusions and key policy messages from the book.

SECTION ONE

OVERVIEW

CHAPTER 1

KEY TRENDS AND CHALLENGES

Public attention has been drawn to the issue of devolution by a programme of reforms undertaken by the United Kingdom Labour government during the 1997-2001 parliament. This programme included the inauguration of a new Scottish Parliament and a new Welsh Assembly, the creation of a series of Regional Development Agencies in England in 1999 and the establishment of a new city-wide government and mayor for London in 2000. These bodies have major responsibilities for developing policies for economic development and social cohesion.

The United Kingdom is just one of many OECD governments involved in recent years in transferring economic development powers to cities and regions or creating new arrangements for sharing powers between the nation-state and devolved governments. Since the 1970s, other OECD countries introducing significant measures include Australia, Belgium, France, Italy, the Netherlands, Spain and Sweden. In addition, Federal structures have been established for some time in Austria, Canada, Denmark, Germany, Mexico and the United States, with many of the same issues arising for economic development management. Whilst it must be recognised that city and region structures and powers vary significantly between different OECD countries, and that there are further differences within countries, there is a clear call for international comparison and exchange of ideas on best practices in agency structures and development strategies.

Devolution opens up new possibilities and challenges for economic development policymakers because it gives them the capacity to develop their own distinctive approaches to economic development and to develop new institutional relationships suited to their own city or region. In doing so, they must adapt to a new economic environment, characterised by globalisation of competition, markets, technologies and finance.

This chapter provides an overview of the implications for local policy-makers of the two inter-related forces of devolution and globalisation in order to set a context and framework for subsequent chapters. The chapter starts by examining what is meant by devolution and globalisation and how they are interlinked. This is followed by discussion of what new institutional frameworks are required in this new environment. Discussion then turns to the policy instruments that devolved governments should employ for economic development. Finally, some issues are raised about devolution of economic development policies that imply the need for a continued framework for co-operation within nation-states to co-ordinate and balance city and region actions.

The concepts of devolution and globalisation and their interlinkage

Devolution

A generally acceptable basic definition of devolution is that it is a process of transfer of powers between central, nation-state, government and lower levels of government, principally operating at city and region levels. It is important to emphasise that devolution must involve some real transfer of powers and not just a deconcentration of policy formulation and implementation from central government offices in the national capital to central government offices in the cities and regions. Furthermore, although it is easy to conceive of devolution as a linear process of transfer of powers from central to local, this view is too simplistic. Processes of devolution usually involve the need for co-operation between many different levels of government, requiring each level of government to work with new partners.

It is useful to consider further the distinction between devolution to city and region governments and deconcentration to local and regional offices of central government departments. The aim of deconcentration has been to increase the local input to policy design in order to increase policy efficiency. It responds to a concern that policy design at the centre has suffered in the past from being removed from information on the needs of the target group, leading to a poor diagnosis of problems and lack of innovation in traditional public policies. Deconcentrating parts of the design process to local offices helps overcome these problems by shortening the process of decision-making and providing more information to the central level. Devolution goes further than this. Its aim is to increase policy effectiveness by developing entirely new policies as well as to improve governance by bringing decision-making closer to the people affected. The challenge for devolution, therefore, is not only to improve decisions about how to implement traditional policies, but also to change the system. One of the main consequences of adopting the devolution approach rather than deconcentration is that the central level needs to operate as a partner with the local level and no longer as its controller. In the long-run this approach is likely to lead to more innovative and effective policies than simple deconcentration.

The logic for devolution is closely tied to the principle of subsidiarity in governance. This articulates the notion that governance is most effective and democratic when decisions are made as close as possible to the population affected. By devolving appropriate powers to city and region level, decisions can be rendered more responsive to the needs and preferences of local people, democracy can be strengthened and the effectiveness of the public sector can be improved by helping to ensure that the right public services are provided in the right way. Indeed, in certain cities and regions with a strong independent identity each of these arguments have been used to justify demands for increased political autonomy.

Peters and Pierre (2001) identify five key reasons why multi-level governance arrangements have emerged in recent years involving new co-operations between nation-state and city and region governments:

- The nation-state has been weakened by the fiscal crisis that has affected most Western countries in the past two decades.

- The nation-state is being challenged by transnational institutions such as the European Union and at the same time subnational governments are becoming more assertive.

- The decentralisation implemented in most of Western Europe during the 1980s and 1990s strengthened regional and local governments, making them less dependent on the state.

- Recent public administration reform has focused on enabling each level of government to separate the political-democratic element of government from the managerial-service-producing sector of government and this has tended to relax the previous command-control nature of intergovernmental relationships.

- The overall nature of the political project pursued by contemporary Western states has changed significantly over the past 10-15 years. Previously the emphasis was on expanding the political sphere in society, whereas the current main objectives are to increase efficiency in public service delivery and delivering more customer-attuned services.

It was highlighted in the introduction to this book that important steps towards devolution have recently been taken within the United Kingdom and other OECD countries. There are nevertheless important differences in forms of devolution between countries and whilst many countries are pursuing devolution, some are embracing the concept more enthusiastically than others. In particular, the precise nature of the institutional arrangements put into place in different countries reflects their specific history and existing institutional arrangements. Le Galès (1998), who reviews some of the differences in the development and performance of devolved region governments in Europe since the 1970s, argues that there has certainly not been a uniform shift towards a single new form of regional governance across Europe.

For example, in Italy five 'special regions' were set up between 1945 and 1963. These five special regions (Valle d'Aosta, Trentino-Alto Aldige, Friuli-Venzia Guilia, Sardinia, Sicily) have more powers and more autonomy and were set up earlier than the other 14 (now 15) ordinary regions that came into being in the 1970s. Italy is therefore an example of asymmetric devolution. Further important developments have occurred at the level of local authorities and municipalities. In particular, the principle of statutory autonomy of local authorities was established in 1990 and new competencies were transferred, whilst in 1993 the Italian parliament voted for the direct election of mayors and presidents of provinces. This is an important change that has given more power and stability to city government in Italy. Following its perceived success, the direct election of regional presidents was decided in 1999.

Spain is another case of 'asymmetric devolution'. Following the end of the Franco administration in the late 1970s, the new Spanish constitution provided for the transfer of powers from central government to 17 autonomous regional communities and guaranteed the autonomy of the municipalities. Regions were created following referendums, starting with special regions in Calatonia and the Basque Country in 1979 and Galicia in 1981 followed by 14 autonomous regional communities created between 1981 and 1983. The latter were given increased powers in 1992. As well as Catalonia, the Basque Country and Galicia, relatively greater autonomy has now also been granted to Andalucia, the community of Navarro, Valencia and the Canary Islands. Powers for economic development policy are shared between central and regional governments. There are significant differences among regions in their government structures and powers.

In Germany, the federal law of 1949 established the constitutions of the Länder (regions) and their autonomy over the competencies they control. Following reunification, there are now 16 Länder, which have joint responsibility with the federal government to develop economic policies. The Länder are also

18

represented in nation-state government through the Bundesrat, which consists of representatives from each region. This body has the power to veto national legislation affecting the Länder. In their turn, the Länder have sometimes devolved further, by working more with local bodies, and there has been a tendency for some local governments to become more autonomous vis-à-vis state and federal authorities. Wollman (2001) nonetheless argues that recent administrative reform in Germany has not had major inter-government consequences overall, partly because in the German system each tier of government largely conducts its own processes of institutional change.

In France, the main devolution initiative was taken in 1982 with what are known as the decentralisation reforms. These reforms introduced directly-elected regional assemblies in the 22 existing planning regions. The regional assemblies now have significant competencies for economic development as well as a general competence to intervene in any area that affects the region, unless specifically excluded. More recent devolution has been limited to the promotion of voluntary groupings of local authorities in 'pays' and 'agglomerations', proposals to devolve significant powers in the special case of Corsica and moves to transfer powers to other regions in limited areas (training, nature reserves, managing industrial waste and managing certain ports and airports). However, even with relatively limited devolution, as Reigner (2001) argues, there are important negotiated exchanges between different tiers of government, for example with the 'contrats de plan' between national governments and the regions.

In countries like Sweden and Ireland, devolution is much newer. So for example in Ireland, whilst there has been strong national government and a long tradition of local government, it was only in 1994 that the eight regions were put into place, followed by the creation of two regional assemblies in 1999. Recently new pressures have emerged in Ireland to create a regional tier of government and strengthen local authorities. Similarly, in Sweden four 'pilot' regions were only put into place in 1999. Moreover, the trend towards devolution is not inevitable. A recent referendum in Portugal in 1998 led to the rejection of a proposal to create a new regional layer of government there.

These European examples demonstrate how far devolution to cities and regions differs between countries. Other European countries and countries elsewhere in the OECD area clearly have different histories and institutional structures. Stoker et al (1996) attempt a classification of different governance systems, focused again on the European Union states. The following main governance types are identified:

- *Classic unitary states* have subnational government only at the local level. Regional structures exist in administrative form and they are strictly subordinated to the central state.

- *Devolving unitary states* have undergone a process of reform to establish elected regional authorities above the local level. The regional tier enjoys a certain degree of constitutional protection and autonomy.

- *Regionalised states* are characterised by the existence of a directly-elected tier of government with constitutional status, wide-ranging autonomy and legislative powers. These powers have gone furthest down the road of regional devolution of the unitary states in the European Union.

- *Federal states* involve a constitutional sharing of powers and the co-existence of sovereignties. The regional tier exists in its own right and could not be abolished or restructured by the federal or central government.

Stoker et al placed the European Union states in the following categories in 1996 although, as noted above, there have been some changes since then in Ireland, Sweden, the United Kingdom and Portugal, and possible new categorisations have therefore been added in parentheses.

An updated Stoker et al typology of regional government in European Union states

Classic Unitary	Devolving Unitary	Regionalised	Federal
Denmark	France	Italy	Germany
Finland	The Netherlands	Spain	Austria
Greece	Portugal		Belgium
Ireland	(Ireland)		
Luxembourg	(Sweden)		
Sweden	(United Kingdom)		
United Kingdom			
(Portugal)			

Original source: Stoker et al (1996)

It should also be recognised that there can be intermediate steps between full devolution and increased co-operation between nation-states and bodies working at sub-national level. A good example is where central governments work directly with local partnerships of voluntary bodies, public sector bodies, the private sector, without this necessarily being controlled by intermediate levels of government at the region or city level. One such initiative, the Irish Area Based Partnerships for combating unemployment, is studied in OECD (1996a). Ireland is a relatively small country in OECD terms and this has facilitated the direct link from national government to local communities.

One lesson that can be drawn from the co-existence of different forms of devolution is that it is not necessary to have the same model everywhere. Furthermore, devolution does not necessarily stop at the level of city and regional governments, but may extend to networking arrangements with many further partners. But there are also dangers that need to be avoided when pursuing devolution, which will be discussed later in the chapter, namely of deepening territorial disparities and competition.

Globalisation

Globalisation can be seen as a process of expansion of cross-border networks and interactions leading to profound changes in how economic management and other policies need to be implemented. Globalisation is not entirely new, since goods, technologies and capital have been exchanged between countries for centuries. Furthermore, globalisation is not an already-achieved state, in which national borders have disappeared and capital, labour and resources are fully mobile. Many networks remain national, regional and local. International connections are strongly uneven, with leading regions and cities and leading firms. And whilst there are important migration flows, most labour remains tied to place. This is why we refer to the 'globalising economy' rather than an already globalised economy in this book.

Nonetheless, the huge interest in globalisation as a process reflects well-documented trends towards greater and greater international interactions across an increasing range of fields, supported by new technologies and government co-operations that did not exist in the past. The key implication of this increasing interconnectedness across borders is that the future of regional and city economies is closely related to their emerging role in international and no longer just national contexts.

Globalisation also needs to be seen not as a single phenomenon, but rather as a series of inter-linked trends. In the economic dimension these trends include increased trade, foreign direct investment, cross-border inter-firm alliances, internationalisation of finance, wider and more rapid diffusion of technology and fragmenting and increasingly customised markets. Each of these main trends is discussed briefly below. They are each woven deeply together in ways that change the possibilities and objectives of policy.

Increased international trade. One of the key characteristics of globalisation is the increase in international trade. For example, export volumes from the OECD countries increased steadily between 1983 and 1999, with an average annual growth rate of some 6% (OECD, 2000b), and imports have also increased. Regulatory changes in trade relations, such as deregulation, privatisation and the liberalisation of trade and investment regimes have played a part in increasing these trade links (OECD, 1997b). Newly-industrialising countries, particularly from East Asia, have added to the growth in trade. Moreover, as well as trade in final products, intra-firm trade through the international sourcing of components and inputs has increased strongly, linked to the increase in foreign direct investment. Overall, increased international trade is associated with greater exposure of enterprises to increased competition as well as new opportunities to exploit external markets. In particular, city and region economies have become more open.

Increased foreign direct investment. The recent increases in flows of foreign direct investment (FDI) have been even stronger than for trade. Flows are increasing between OECD Member countries and new emerging countries are beginning to participate actively in both inflows and outflows. FDI flows have been growing much faster than GDP in OECD countries. OECD data show average annual FDI inflows in OECD countries increased from approximately US$19.1 billion in the 1971-80, to US$87.1 in 1981-90 and US$223 billion in 1991-98. This rapid expansion has been driven by (OECD, 1997b):

- increased market entry and competition as leading firms establish operations in the main triad areas (Europe, North America and Asia);

- liberalisation of financial flows, related both specifically to FDI and more generally to deregulation of financial markets;

- improved communications and technology, which have assisted in the internationalisation of both large and small firms;

- firm-specific advantages, which give foreign affiliates a competitive edge over domestic firms in adopting new technologies, raising finance, developing and testing new products etc.

With the growth in FDI, cities and regions find themselves competing for new investment capital. They are also competing to attract and retain high quality investment, in terms of those subsidiaries with the sorts of roles in the functional system of the multinational firm that are associated with good jobs and high spin-off potential (such as research and development facilities or operations with a product mandate).

Increased cross-border inter-firm alliances. There has also been a marked increase in cross-border strategic alliances between firms in technology, outsourcing, distribution and marketing. As Vickery (1996) shows, they take a variety of forms, including nonequity agreements in development, production and marketing, minority equity participations and jointly-owned subsidiaries. They tend to involve large firms in research and development-intensive industries. However, small firms may also be involved in alliances, particularly where they have a strong innovation capacity. They have often been motivated by the search for technological complementarities, reductions in the innovation time-span and increases in efficiency and by market access and restructuring in mature technologies and slow-growth industries. Firms often need to develop such alliances to stay competitive.

Internationalisation of finance. In addition to FDI, international portfolio investments play an important role in the globalisation of investment capital. Leyshon (1996), for example, discusses the growing power of those financial institutions that operate beyond and across national financial spaces, leading to a new 'post-national' financial geography. At the heart of this geography sits a handful of increasingly powerful and influential financial centres that are made up of a dense networks of financial institutions and markets, which increasingly radiate power on a global scale. It is important that regions and cities, and indeed distressed areas and disadvantaged people within them, are not excluded from their circuits. Where there is financial exclusion (i.e. where viable projects cannot find funding), public intervention may be required.

Wider and more rapid diffusion of technology. Another key aspect of current globalisation processes is the great advance in new technologies, which is having a strong and pervasive effect on all industries and services. The massive improvement in the capacity of the information and communications technologies and the large reductions in their cost is one key measure of this technological change. This is playing a critical role in the development of the New Economy. However, there is increasing product and service and process innovation in all areas of the economy. It is therefore increasingly recognised that city and region economic development strategies need to focus strongly on building innovative environments.

Fragmenting and increasingly customised markets. This change is often seen as part of a shift from a traditional 'Fordist' economic model to a model based on 'Flexible Specialisation'. Whereas the Fordist period from the end of the Second World War to the mid-1970s was characterised by mass production of standardised products, the period of Flexible Specialisation that seems to have emerged subsequently in advanced economies is characterised by flexible production for niche markets. In this environment, the ability of firms to adjust rapidly to changing markets is one of the critical factors in their competitive success. Again, cities and regions need to create environments that facilitate rapid adjustment by local firms, which can sometimes be supported through initiatives for clusters and local enterprise networks.

More rapid and cheaper transport and communications have been one set of factors facilitating these globalisation processes. Another set of facilitating factors, which are more directly influenced by the policies of OECD governments, involve regulatory reform, regional integration and liberalisation of investment and markets, reflecting the current dominance of 'neo-liberal' political thinking in OECD countries. Thus recent years have seen the emergence and strengthening of the role of various multinational institutions in economic organisation, including the World Trade Organisation and regional blocs such as the European Union, Mercosur, NAFTA and ASEAN, which have favoured increasing economic integration.

All these trends are leading enterprises, workers and places to take on more specialist roles as part of systems stretching across borders. For example, what are known as global cities are increasingly concentrating corporate headquarters, financial and business services functions and cultural amenities of international importance whilst multinational branch plants are increasingly specialising in particular functions within their wider parent company. Our economies are becoming much more open than in the past and hence both more exposed to competition and better able to exploit external markets. And the competitive environment is much more dynamic and rapidly-moving.

Globalisation is therefore leading to profound changes in the objectives and methods of economic management policies. A globalising economy is associated with the potential for more rapid restructuring and change, whilst our economies are also becoming more open. One of the major concerns of today's governments is therefore to facilitate structural adjustment and innovation in order to bolster competitiveness. In addition, globalisation is associated with uneven development and the emergence of new winners and losers, both in terms of people and places, with certain groups of people and places being more closely-bound to processes of wealth creation whilst others are increasing excluded. Policies are therefore needed both to support innovation and to combat exclusion.

The importance of devolved governments in the response to globalisation

The contemporary importance of the two trends of devolution and globalisation, which might be considered to be opposed, is often described as a paradox. In the recent wave of work on globalisation, many authors have pointed to the idea that locality should matter less for economic development in a period of globalisation because of cheap transport, rapid communications, and mobility of goods, capital and labour. They point to the increasing importance of international networks and the increasing 'footlooseness' of capital. At first sight, devolved policies would therefore seem to be unrelated to the economic imperatives of the globalising economy.

However, it is also true that local environment continues to make a difference to the competiveness of firms located in any territory and that most capital is still far from 'footloose'. Firms depend on local labour markets and often tap into local subcontracting networks or innovation networks. They also have sunk costs that tie them to an area. Therefore, as globalisation levels out access to basic markets and inputs, there needs to be more emphasis on providing the sort of local environment (strong local supplier base, technological institutions, skill pools and so on) that will allow local firms to establish high productivity and innovation, especially in a territory's key export-base activities. This points to the link between devolution and globalisation in terms of economic development, because it is devolved governments, operating at local and regional level, that are best placed to influence the quality of the local environment that is taking on more importance in the globalising economy.

There is also a second key link. Much of the discussion of globalisation also points to the social divisions that are associated with economic restructuring in a globalising economy. Devolved governments have a range of policies they can use to help counter problems of exclusion within their territory.

The key contribution of devolved governments to the response to globalisation is therefore to use their micro-level policy instruments, and their capacity to tailor, mobilise and co-ordinate policy, in order to create favourable city and region environments for competitiveness and to counter social exclusion. This role would appear to be becoming even more important since globalisation seems to be reducing the effectiveness of some of the policy tools traditionally wielded by nation-state governments. In particular, macro-economic policy instruments such as exchange rate adjustments and changes in money supply are now more constrained because of international agreements and increasingly important international finance flows. For example within the Euro zone, European integration and European Monetary Union have made macro-economic policies more uniform. Member countries have less flexibility to differentiate their macro-economic policy in order to promote growth or respond to asymmetric shocks. In this context micro-policies, territorial policies, take on a new importance.

The following benefits are often attributed to the devolution of policy powers in the field of economic development, which are all associated with promoting locally-based, bottom-up policies:

- The devolution of policy design and delivery helps tailor policy more to local circumstances and thus increases effectiveness. Cities and regions are at a more appropriate level than nations for identifying economic development needs and opportunities because they are in close contact with local realities and the local environment. City and region governments and development agencies can identify and tackle problems, exploit opportunities and encourage the best long-term conditions in their area. They can find the type of development strategy best suited to their conditions and preferences.

- Devolved arrangements can better co-ordinate the range of different policies and agencies that are acting together in any local area. For example, in the past central government sectoral initiatives, for example for business development, social exclusion, education and training and sustainable development, have often been run separately and not linked together. The city or region is often at the right scale to 'join-up' the planning and management of initiatives in these areas and to help ensure effective co-ordination between them.

- Devolution can help bring out local participation, increasing the leverage of policy. There are many actors operating at local level that could be brought in to support policy initiatives from the private sector and the non-profit sector. At the city or region level it is often easier to identify and mobilise the actors who could support new initiatives and invest their knowledge and resources.

One further benefit of devolution is that it allows for more time to be focused on the particular economic development issues of cities and regions than would be possible with central government.

The widespread emergence of a new devolved type of approach to economic development seems to represent a shift in policy thinking towards a new paradigm that can be referred to as an endogenous development paradigm. Under this paradigm, city and regional economic development policy is being fundamentally reshaped around the exploitation and improvement of endogenous capacities and competitive advantage rather than around national macroeconomic and sectoral policies.

The notion of endogenous development stresses the localised nature of economic development, focusing on the importance of developing and exploiting local resources for growth and the existence of local social interactions and external effects that promote growth. Traditional economic development theories have tended to underestimate the importance of the local environment to economic growth, concentrating instead on factors operating at the national level. But the critical role of local environment is clearly evident when we consider the uneven nature of development within OECD countries. Some areas, like the north east of Italy or Cambridge in the UK have emerged as new industrial spaces. While other traditional rural regions or heavy manufacturing regions have declined because of inadapted firm structures, institutions and cultures. Notions of endogenous development help to explain why some regions and localities grow faster than others and suggest how to reinforce development in weaker areas.

Endogenous development, based on resources existing within the local area, contrasts with exogenous development, which is dependent on investments by external agents. In the past, regional economic development has often tended to stress exogenous development. Thus there has been major support for branch plant investments by large firms and frequent attempts to implant high technology industry in lagging areas. But the exogenous development model has often been criticised for stimulating only weak connections between external investments and local firms and capabilities. Endogenous development, by contrast, stresses local linkages and exploitation of local resources and capabilities. It implies that cities and regions should seek to specialise in sectors where they can build a comparative advantage in the globalising economy, for example by developing the right infrastructures and externalities, recognising external opportunities and threats and adapting the local economy accordingly. This is at the heart of ideas about the local-global linkage and the sorts of economic development policies that devolved governments should pursue (Stöhr, 1990).

Endogenous development strategies help local economies to adapt to the new economic environment of globalisation in two ways. Firstly, by building a basis for an internationally competitive regional economy that is dynamic and innovative and capable of capture market niches in the global economy. Secondly, by facilitating structural adjustment to cope with rapid technological and market change and new competition.

It is important to get this right at a city or regional level, because these territories are increasingly exposed. OECD statistics analysed and prepared by the Territorial Development Service show that there are marked economic disparities between regions and whilst some of these have reduced during the past 15 years, this convergence is slow and disparities remain. Thus, some regions are being successful in competing in these new conditions, but others are being less successful. On certain measures and in certain countries there actually appears to be divergence. In terms of employment, work by Blanchard and Katz (1992) show for the United States that employment has grown at different rate, with demand and other shocks having largely permanent effects. Similarly, Martin and Tyler (2000) demonstrate that regional employment growth paths have also been divergent in the European Union from 1975 to 1998. Some authors, such as Ohmae (1995), point to the idea that we have moved to an economy where regions are in competition with each other, just as we used to think in terms of competition between nation-states in the past.

A recent Nobel prize winner, Robert Barro, has produced some very interesting work on the determinants of economic growth in different nations and territories (Barro, 1998). He addresses the paradox that whilst neo-classical economic theories would suggest that different regions and territories may be expected to converge towards the same level of growth in the long run, we actually witness important and persistent differences in growth rates. His explanation is that differences in growth rates are mainly dependent on the initial capital that territories benefit from, in terms of physical capital, human capital and financial capital and on how this capital is mobilised. In terms of cities and regions, it would appear that the most successful areas will therefore be those that have a lot of initial capital on various dimensions - the educational system, the technological system, the communication system and so on - and that have systemic advantages for making this capital productive, such as the presence of firm and institutional networks, high mobility of capital and labour and an important capacity for innovation and entrepreneurship. The presence of devolved institutions capable of developing distinctive and tailored policies can be part of this initial capital of a city or region - its institutional capital.

In a globalising economy, then, which is characterised by increasing competition amongst cities and regions, devolved governments have a key role in developing distinct and tailored policies to create the right local environment to exploit niche opportunities that will drive their growth. But at the same time devolved governments contribute to the response to the social inequalities associated with economic restructuring.

Devolution and new institutional structures

Devolution requires changes in institutional structures. One important aspect of this is developing appropriate relationships between devolved city and region governments and central government at the nation-state level. Clearly, devolution calls for new co-ordination mechanisms between the city and region governments receiving devolved powers and central governments within the nation-state. Whenever power is devolved, there tends to some tension between the responsibilities and objectives of the central and the local levels. Central government often retains some controls on the actions that cities and regions can take, for example by regulating competition between areas for new investment or by imposing limits on local tax adjustments. Appropriate arrangements are therefore needed so that there is an appropriate central framework where required but that devolved governments also have the flexibility they need to design effective policies that respond to the demands of local people.

A further important aspect of devolution and new institutional relationships concerns how different levels of government are bound together in multi-level governance arrangements, or vertical co-ordination. For cities and regions, the need for vertical co-ordination across levels of government relates in part to vertical co-ordination upwards, between devolved governments and national and international governments and institutions. It also relates in part to vertical co-ordination downwards, between devolved governments and governments and partners operating within the devolved territory.

It has been argued above, that devolved governments offer key advantages for responding to globalisation because of their greater capacity to deliver endogenous development approaches whilst at the same time some of the capacities of the nation-state, notably in the area of macro-economic management, are being undermined. This should not be taken to mean, however, that we are witnessing what has been called the 'end of the nation-state' and its replacement by supranational and subnational governments (Ohmae, 1995). Neither should it be taken to mean that the shift to devolved government is inevitable, because essentially it is still nation-states that make the decisions about the degree and type of devolution within their territory. Nation-states, or groupings of nation-states at international level, are still the principal decision-makers on the regulation of globalisation processes, such as trade policies, investment policies, competition policies and environmental policies. They also continue to provide many services, like defence, which are best organised at national and international scales. And they are well-placed to co-ordinate horizontally the policies of different cities and regions. In consequence, what we are witnessing is not the replacement of the nation-state by city and region governments, but transformations of how different levels of government relate to one another and changes in the policies each level of government pursues.

Hirst and Thompson (1996) make a strong case for the continued role of the nation-state within systems of multi-level governance in a globalising economy. They argue that nation-states still have a significant role to play in economic governance at the level of both national and international processes. However, they see this role as shifting away from direct intervention in certain areas of economic management, where the nation-state is no longer able to impose outcomes, towards the provision of legitimacy for and ensuring the accountability of supranational and subnational governance mechanisms. They see nation states as key pivots between international agencies and subnational activities because they provide legitimacy as the exclusive voice of a territorially-bounded population. Thus in a system of governance in which international agencies and regulatory bodies are already significant and growing in scope, nation-states are crucial agencies of representation. Nation-states ensure that, indirectly, international bodies are answerable to the public and that decisions made in international agencies can be enforced through domestic laws. Cities and regions are currently a long way from being able to play this role themselves.

Clearly, then, whilst many countries are devolving important economic development powers to cities and regions, the central state remains powerful and continues to fulfil important roles in a globalising economy. Thus we are not witnessing a shift from nation-state to wholly independent city and region governments, but the emergence of multi-level government that requires co-ordination between cities and regions, nation-states and international agencies.

Whilst there has been significant discussion of the issues of co-ordination between cities and regions and nation-states and international agencies, there has been much less attention given to the need for co-ordination downwards with local governments and partners that can support economic and social development within a city or region. However, paradoxically, one of the effects of devolving powers from the nation-state to the region or the city is to create a set of new centres at the region or city level. These new centres need to develop linkages with the various local bodies involved in economic development within the region or city. Rather than attempting to work independently of such local organisations, regions and cities should work with them so that they can tailor policy to local needs and make it responsive to local conditions.

There are a number of mechanisms that can be used to achieve vertical and horizontal co-ordination of economic development policies across different levels of government. With these arrangements, regions and cities need to achieve a certain flexibility of policy and tailoring of policies to local needs and at the same to ensure a certain accountability and efficiency of policy. Some of the most frequently used mechanisms include performance targets, output related funding, partnerships, flexible resource management and reporting of performance to a wider set of public and private stakeholders. However, it is not always straightforward to make such arrangements work.

Current thinking on internal relationships within a city or region tends to stress the importance of local networks and partnerships between different public sector agencies, between the public and private sectors and with organisations from the non-profit sector. Local partnerships can bring such benefits as a co-ordinated approach to multi-dimensional problems and local participation in policy decisions and implementation. But it is also important that the right structures and processes are in place to permit such partnerships to work effectively. City and regional authorities with devolved powers may therefore need to rethink the nature of their linkages within their local area and how partnerships might be developed with other local agencies and the private sector.

Recent devolution processes in OECD countries have increased the need to improve governance at city and regional level in order to create structures and policies that can resolve the complex economic, environmental and societal problems that these areas are now facing. The recent OECD publication, *Cities for Citizens: Improving Metropolitan Governance* (OECD, 2001a) examines the governance question for large urban regions in OECD countries, based on detailed evaluations of governance experiences in various OECD cities and on the identification of good practices. The work suggests that great scope exists for the adjustment and reform of institutional, financial and fiscal frameworks in metropolitan areas. It proposes governance principles which will help Member countries to reap the benefits which good governance and 'smart growth' offer and to achieve more sustainable forms of urban development.

Key conclusions are that reforms in metropolitan governance can help in:

- developing long term strategic planning which is critical to sustainable development;

31

- enhancing local democracy through improved election procedures, and strengthening the level of identification of citizens with the metropolitan area in which they live;

- developing more 'people-centred' demand-driven strategic policies and better access of the public to information and public services;

- adopting measures to improve transparency and accountability in decision-making processes;

- improving the level and quality of services across the metropolitan region through more cross-sectoral approaches to infrastructure, transport, housing and environmental services.

However, there still exist shortcomings in current governance arrangements in metropolitan areas, such as:

- Urban sprawl, arising in part from competitive pressures within metropolitan areas. Sprawl necessitates the provision of major infrastructures and poses serious problems for strategic planning, often weakening the urban core.

- Social integration, which is difficult to achieve in metropolitan areas due to socio-spatial fractures which concentrate certain groups in 'distressed areas' and require multi-sectoral metropolitan wide strategies.

The report concludes that even if no one uniform model of metropolitan governance can be generally applied, the changes recently introduced share some common principles which, when brought together, constitute a solid benchmark for assessing the adequacy of the systems of governance of large cities. The Principles, which have been developed in conjunction with national and sub-national governments and in consultation with associations of municipal authorities, are reproduced in Box 1.

The Council of the OECD formally welcomed the Principles of Metropolitan Governance in June 2001 and has invited Member countries to facilitate the diffusion of these principles and facilitate exchange of experience. The OECD Territorial Reviews of Metropolitan Areas are a further important vehicle for evaluating the extent to which these governance improvements are being taken up by OECD Member countries.

Box 1. OECD Principles of Metropolitan Governance

There is no one model of metropolitan governance. It is clear that (in addition to the broad principles which underlie any adequate system of democratic government – transparency, accountability, accessibility, representativeness, constitutionality, and protection of fundamental freedoms) a number of principles can also be applied in order to define the adequacy of systems of governance for metropolitan regions in the 21st century.

Cities for Citizens: Cities should be developed, not only to meet the needs of the economy, but also to help fulfil the aspirations of people for a higher quality of life through measures that can also maintain and enhance the attractiveness and liveability of cities.

Coherence in Policy: The objectives and institutional frameworks of metropolitan governance should be adapted to and focused on key local problems such as economic development, affordable housing, congestion, sprawl, safety, environmental quality, and the regeneration of older areas, which should be tackled simultaneously, taking into account linkages and trade-offs.

Co-ordination: Metropolitan governence must reflect the potential and needs of the entire urban region. The roles and responsibilities of each level of government in respect of metropolitan areas should be clearly defined in order to facilitate policy coherence and cross-sectoral integration. Given the administrative fragmentation of metropolitan regions, co-ordination is also necessary among local authorities across jurisdictions, and between elected authorities and various regional boards or agencies with functional or sectoral responsibilities.

Endogenous Development: Rather than basing economic development mostly on attracting investment through financial and fiscal incentives, emphasis should be put on investment in infrastructures and human development to take best advantage of local resources. Metropolitan governance can help to set priorities, taking a coherent approach to development based on the strengths and opportunities of a region.

Efficient financial management: Metropolitan governance should allow for the costs of measures to be reflective of benefit received and assure complete transparency, accountability and monitoring. It should also guarantee that all parts of the urban region are considered in assessments of the appropriate level for and of the costs and benefits of, public services.

Box 1 (continued)

Flexibility: In order to adapt as necessary to economic and social trends, technological innovation, and spatial development, institutions have to be open to changes. A forward-looking, prospective approach is also indispensable to allow for flexibility as well as sound strategic planning.

Particularity: Except where the case for standardisation is justified, policies and institutions of government must be crafted to fit the unique circumstances of various parts of the country and to achieve the best cost efficiency of measures.

Participation: Given the growing diversity and size of metropolitan regions, governance must allow for the participation of civil society social partners and all levels of government involved in the metropolitan area. New technologies and methods of communication can encourage and support more inter-active policy environments, bringing government closer to people.

Social cohesion: Metropolitan governance should promote a mix of population, non-segregated areas, accessibility and safety, and the development of opportunity, and facilitate the integration of distressed urban areas.

Subsidiarity: Services must be delivered by the most local level unless it has not sufficient scale to reasonably deliver them, or spill-overs to other regions are important.

Sustainability: Economic, social and environmental objectives must be fully integrated and reconciled in the development policies of urban areas, as reflected in the concepts of the healthy city and the ecological city; in the context of the wider bio-region, this implies greater co-operation between urban and rural areas.

Devolved city and region governments should bear in mind these principles when seeking to develop new governance arrangements and policies.

The policy instruments of devolved governments in the globalising economy

Devolved cities and regions have the flexibility to introduce a range of micro policies that respond to the challenges of globalisation. For city and region policymakers these challenges fall in two main areas.

The first major challenge is to build competitive city and regional economies to respond to the increased economic openness and rapid economic restructuring associated with globalisation. The recent OECD Growth Study has examined what causes differences in growth rates between OECD countries in the emerging 'New Economy'. It found that the main causes of different national growth rates in the 1990s were different levels of ICT investment, different levels of employment growth and labour productivity growth, differences in labour skill levels and innovations in how capital and labour are combined. In response, as well as stressing the importance of maintaining sound framework conditions in the form of flexible and competitive markets, the work identified four major policy areas that should be the focus of particular attention in the New Economy. These are policies for information and communications technologies (ICT), innovation, entrepreneurship and human capital. These policy areas are clearly just as relevant at the city and region level as at the national level. There are many actions that can be taken at city and region level that can help to help achieve national objectives for competitiveness in these areas. This book focuses in particular on the latter two policy areas, covering entrepreneurship and human capital. However, policies to foster the use of ICT and to build and maintain a conducive environment for innovation and the application of new technologies are also important at the regional and local scales.

The second major challenge is to combat the problems of poverty and social exclusion that can be brought about by the economic restructuring associated with globalisation. Globalisation tends to create winners and losers, with the losers tending to be those people with relatively low skills and those places with declining traditional economic bases. In examining how city and region governments may respond, this book places a particular emphasis on policies to regenerate distressed areas, which is where problems of exclusion are most visible, although it must be recognised that not all problems of exclusion are found in these areas.

Building competitive city and regional economies through entrepreneurship

It is now widely accepted that success in stimulating entrepreneurship, i.e. in generating new businesses and helping small businesses to grow, is an important factor contributing to economic growth in the globalising economy through supporting structural adjustment and job creation. Reynolds et al (2000), for example, provide strong international empirical evidence of the association between the level of entrepreneurship and national economic growth rates. In terms of structural adjustment, entrepreneurship has an important role in promoting the use of local resources, improving efficiency and productivity and encouraging innovation. In terms of job creation, although the data analysis issues are complex there is strong evidence that small businesses have substantially increased their share of employment in developed economies in recent years. And the impression of relative small firm job dynamism has also tended to be confirmed by studies of net job creation by different sizes of enterprise. For example, in the United States it has been estimated that small firms with less than 100 employees were responsible for about 85% of all net new job creation (Birch, Haggerty and Parsons, 1997). Devolved governments have an important contribution to make in stimulating entrepreneurship by developing appropriate programmes and policies to create a healthy local entrepreneurial environment.

The OECD LEED Programme has been promoting local initiatives for entrepreneurship for many years (see for example OECD, 1990a). The role of entrepreneurship in job creation has also been recognised by the European Commission, which has introduced entrepreneurship as one of the 4 pillars of the European Employment Strategy agreed with Member States in 1997 and updated yearly. This is not just a European and national level strategy. The Commission also wishes to mobilise actors at the regional and local levels to implement the European Employment Strategy by identifying the potential of job creation at local level and strengthening partnerships to this end.

The Global Entrepreneurship Monitor (Reynolds et al, 2000) highlights a range of conditions that are important in stimulating entrepreneurship at national level, many of which are also relevant for those seeking to create competitive city and region economies. The main factors they identify are:

- The availability of finance.
- Government policies designed to support start-ups.
- Government programmes designed to support start-ups.
- Education and training for entrepreneurship.
- R&D transfer.
- Commercial and professional infrastructure.
- External market openness.
- Access to physical infrastructure (including information technology)
- Cultural and social norms (including the social legitimacy of entrepreneurship).

Two other key factors are also important. Firstly, the entrepreneurial opportunity (the existence and perception of market opportunities available for exploitation). Secondly, the degree of entrepreneurial capacity (the motivation of individuals to start new firms and the extent to which they posses the skills required). Together, these represent areas where city and region policymakers may choose to intervene to encourage entrepreneurship.

A number of workers have also stressed the importance of the local competitive environment for business success in the globalising economy. The importance of local environment is underlined by the fact that we find strong concentrations of industrial output in certain core regions as well as the common occurrence of agglomerations of firms in the same or related industries in certain 'hotspots' of entrepreneurship. In these localities, agglomeration economies help to reduce transaction costs, increase positive externalities and increase innovation. There is a range of factors at play that reinforce the competitiveness of firms in these areas, such as the presence of social capital, institutional thickness, technological infrastructure and so on (Saxenian, 1994; Storper, 1997; Scott, 1998).

Porter (1990, 1998a) is one of the leading authors stressing the importance of the role of local competitive environment to business success in local clusters. He argues that in the context of rapidly changing markets and technologies, the success of firms in industry clusters depends on four inter-related influences, depicted in a diamond: factor conditions (the cost and quality of inputs); demand conditions (the sophistication of local customers); the context for firm strategy and rivalry (the nature and intensity of local competition) and related and support industries (the local extent and sophistication of suppliers and related industries). Diamond theory stresses how these elements combine to produce a dynamic, stimulating and intensely competitive business environment. Porter sees the cluster as being the manifestation of the diamond at work (Porter, 1998b).

There are many examples of local enterprise clusters, in various sectors, with various internal governance systems and in different states of development, for example the financial services and media sectors in London, film-making in Los Angeles, cut flowers in the Netherlands and opto-electronics in Arizona. Increased access to world markets allows larger concentrations of such clusters to develop but also increases the chances that established clusters may collapse.

The strength of these clusters derives from locally-based agglomeration economies - or synergies - such as specialised local labour markets, a thick bed of associated suppliers, customers and competitors and supporting institutions such as specialised research, education and financial institutions. The flow of knowledge within clusters is critical to their competitiveness because it supports innovation, adaptation and the shift to higher value-added. It is often argued that social capital and supporting institutions play a major role in the success of clusters. In addition, the concentration of firms in clusters may lead to an increased differentiation of products and a greater division of labour between firms in the cluster, associated with increased entrepreneurship and competitiveness.

A key issue for local policy-makers is therefore to establish whether there is a role for policy in supporting clusters and if so, what is that role. There is a feeling amongst certain commentators that policymakers are sometimes seeking to apply cluster policies in cases where the critical mass and interactions are not present. Others are concerned that policy-makers are showing too little inventiveness in their approaches to clusters, that they are in effect seeking to apply the same 'off-the-shelf' strategies and selecting the same, often 'high-tech', industries to support. Such a lack of tailoring to local circumstances may lead to destructive competition between areas. What is clear, is that any approach to supporting clusters must be based on correcting specific market failures and enabling innovation. Thus cluster policy may seek to improve the flow of information (e.g. by fostering networking and co-ordination), correct under-provision of public goods (e.g. by investment in sector relevant infrastructure and training) and release positive externalities (e.g. by supporting research and development activity and new technology based firms).

Policies to support entrepreneurship and local enterprise clusters will be examined in more detail in chapters 5 and 6, including a presentation of the comprehensive and innovative strategy that Scottish Enterprise has introduced to support clusters and evidence on the internationalisation of clusters in Italy.

Building competitive city and regional economies through human capital

In the era of globalisation, knowledge-intensive industries are becoming increasingly important as drivers of economic growth. OECD economies are being affected by a wave of pervasive technological innovations and new industries are emerging such as biotechnology and microelectronics. Furthermore, competition in all sectors is increasingly based on innovation and customer responsiveness. In this new environment, cities and regions with a highly-skilled workforce are more likely to be competitive and successful.

The trends towards the 'knowledge economy' call for people to acquire more skills within large sections of the workforce. Moreover, the new type of competition is associated with a need not just for more skills, but also for new types of skills. In a modern economy, new attributes like flexibility, entrepreneurship and technological competencies are at a premium. These changes in the demand for skills suggest that a new policy approach is therefore required, based on the concept of lifelong learning. People will need new attitudes to learning, easier access to learning, better guidance and counselling and access to new technologies. City and region governments and development agencies clearly have an important role to play in delivering training given these requirements for human capital development.

It is helpful to formulate and deliver training policy at city and region level rather than nationally for a number of reasons. Specifically, as Greffe argues in chapter 8 of this book, city and region governments have a role to play in funding appropriate training, in encouraging employers to train, in improving the quality of training available and in making sure that it is adapted to the emerging needs of local businesses. The locality provides a focus for partnerships and projects, it creates a relatively easy link between practical and classroom activities, and it is a place where other barriers, such as social problems, can be identified and tackled so that they do not prevent training from being effective. Thus, in comparison with past initiatives, effective policies are likely to require greater local decision-making in determining appropriate training, greater partnership between the public and private sector and new ways of delivering training.

Chapters 7 and 8 address in more detail the question of the design and implementation of policies for human capital development in city and region economies. A key issue for local policy-makers is to establish how best to collaborate with partners to create a comprehensive strategy for lifelong learning.

Supporting social cohesion at city and region level

Globalisation of the economy is imposing powerful forces of restructuring on OECD Member countries which have important social as well as economic consequences. These forces include rapid technological change, a secular decline in the contribution of manufacturing to economic output and employment, the deregulation of certain key industries and services and the internationalisation of competition through a rapid increase in both trade and foreign direct investment. Whilst bringing undoubted benefits for OECD economies in terms of the stimulation of economic growth, there have also been winners and losers in the restructuring process, demonstrated by substantial socio-economic disparities between different localities and an increasing polarisation of society. Although city and region governments and agencies cannot tackle all aspects of these problems on their own, they do have important instruments they can use to help counter the problems.

The disparities arise because the new jobs often do not arise in the same locations as the old jobs are lost and do not involve the same skills and occupations. The barriers that exist to the ability of people to move to new places of work and to move between occupations have also contributed to the emergence of disparities. There has been considerable discussion of the phenomenon of deindustrialisation in OECD countries which has been a marked trend in employment terms since the 1960s. In Europe, for example, between 1980 and 1993 some 18 million additional jobs were created in services but in the same period 15 million jobs were destroyed in manufacturing (Dicken, 1998). Moreover, even within given industries there has been displacement of traditional jobs by technological change. Much of the explanation for the increase in disparities among people and among places relates to a decline in traditional industries and the emergence of new ones. There is a lively debate about the extent to which loss of traditional unskilled manufacturing jobs in OECD countries has been caused by increased trade from and increased foreign direct investment to developing countries, and the extent that it instead reflects technological change. In either case the consequences are clear to see. The adverse impacts of these processes have fallen on particular segments of the workforce, and most importantly the unskilled and semi-skilled.

It is possible to think about the winners and losers from the restructuring processes associated with globalisation in two key ways. Firstly, there is a spatial divide between rich and poor areas. Thus the job loss with de-industrialisation has been concentrated in manufacturing-dominated cities and regions and also in inner city areas where a lot of the manufacturing was concentrated in the past. These areas have often been faced with plant closures or long-run decline in their economic base. Secondly, there is a social divide between relatively low-skilled and relatively high-skilled people. In terms of the social divide, people with relatively few qualifications and skills have seen a reduction in the employment opportunities available to them. In addition, women, youth, ethnic minorities and older people tend to experience relatively high rates of unemployment. This is preventing significant groups of society from participating fully in the basic social structures and activities enjoyed by the rest of the population, such as housing, transport, health, education and training.

A key challenge is therefore to hold our societies together in the face of these pressures and build a socially-just and sustainable economy. Provision of employment is a critical factor in establishing social cohesion and indeed economic efficiency. Although employment creation depends in part on macroeconomic actions at national and international levels, city and region policy-makers also have much to contribute to this in micro-economic terms. On the one hand this can be achieved by the measures highlighted above for promoting economic growth and competitiveness in the city or region. But in many localities this alone will not be enough to tackle poverty and exclusion from work. In addition, measures explicitly targeted at excluded people are required, which help to create job opportunities, to ensure that excluded people have access to them and to assist people to move up a ladder towards higher quality, more stable and better remunerated work. Appropriate initiatives may take many forms, for example schemes to encourage self-employment and the creation of small individual or community enterprises, training and work experience to attach excluded people to the labour market, the creation of networks for mutual assistance, retraining and job matching strategies to respond to plant closures and the provision of finance to potential entrepreneurs from disadvantaged groups by supporting micro-credit organisations and solidarity funds. Often these initiatives can be particularly effective when targeted on distressed areas, where there is the greatest concentration of exclusion.

There is much evidence that city and region initiatives can help in the battle against exclusion, together with nation-state policies. Chapters 9 and 10 of the book tackles this question in more detail, with a particular focus on policies to combat exclusion in distressed localities.

Limiting territorial disparities and territorial competition

Without proper co-ordination mechanisms there is a danger that devolution might aggravate territorial disparities and intensify territorial competition to a degree that would be counter to the overall well-being of a nation. This section examines these two issues and their implications for how devolution should be managed.

Territorial disparities

There are large income disparities across the territories of the OECD area, both among cities and regions in different countries and among cities and regions in the same country. For example, within the European Union (EU), Boldrin and Canova (2001) note that in 1995-7 the richest region, Inner London, had a GDP per resident of 229% of the EU average, followed by Hamburg with 198% whilst the two poorest regions (excluding the French overseas departments and territories), Ipeiros in Greece and the Portuguese Azores, had only 43% and

50% of average GDP respectively. Furthermore, the concern is often expressed that the increasing economic integration that comes with globalisation may exacerbate these disparities. Economic restructuring has led to the emergence of some highly visible success stories like Silicon Valley in the United States or the north east of Italy, which can exploit increasingly large markets to continue their growth, whilst other mainly traditional rural or industrial 'rustbelt' areas face decline. With barriers to the mobility of people, these disparities imply major inequalities of opportunity and likely economic inefficiencies.

It can be argued from neoclassical economic theory that the poorest regions stand to gain from increased international integration, because investment will flow towards regions with the lowest costs and to activities in which the region has comparative advantage. However, in reality, territorial disparities have not been reducing markedly in OECD countries in recent years. As detailed in the OECD Territorial Outlook (OECD, 2001g), although there has been some convergence on certain measures, this convergence has been very slow and on other measures there is no sign of convergence. Moreover, the 'new growth theories' (see for example Fujita, Krugman and Venables, 1999) provide a counter-view. Essentially, new growth theories argue that positive externalities at the local level generate increasing rather than decreasing returns on investment, such that capital and other factors of production are likely to flow to the most advanced regions, leaving poorer regions further behind. In particular, territorial disparities may be exacerbated by globalisation if increasingly mobile capital and labour flows towards the more advanced regions to exploit externalities. If the problems are not addressed there is a risk of setting into motion dynamic processes of cumulative causation.

A key issue that therefore has to be addressed when pursuing devolved economic development strategies in a period of globalisation is how to avoid an increase in disparities, given that not all cities and regions have the same growth prospects. In most countries there is a political imperative to reduce disparities, both to overcome inequalities of opportunity and to reduce the economic inefficiencies associated with having high levels of congestion in one area alongside underused resources in another. A variety of arrangements to support investment in poorer regions are possible, whether organised at international level (like the European Union Structural Funds), at national level (like traditional national government regional policies) or through inter-regional co-operation arrangements (like the arrangements between Länder in Germany). The aim of such transfers is to ensure that even lagging regions have the necessary levels of technological infrastructures, education and training, communications and business development capital to permit economic development.

The uneven nature of regional development in Ireland over the last 10 years or so provides one illustration of the problems of spatial disparities that can emerge within the context of overall national economic growth. In Ireland, the central belt has attracted a relatively large share of recent employment growth, with the remoter rural areas left behind. OECD Territorial Development Service figures show that the Mid-East region, which immediately surrounds Dublin, saw an increase in employment of 51% between 1991 and 1998, compared with a national average of 32%, whilst population increased by 13.5% during the same period compared to a national increase of 5.1%. The Mid-East region is absorbing a lot of the pressure associated with Ireland's strong national growth despite efforts to promote the more peripheral areas. Underlining these concerns about uneven development, the Industrial Development Agency is reported as having introduced an internal target to try and direct one-half of all new jobs in greenfield inward investment projects to the Border, Midlands and West regions (Irish Times, 4/7/01).

Another problem, that of supplying the basic infrastructure necessary for growth in disadvantaged regions, is illustrated by the Highlands and Islands of Scotland. Major public investment in high-bandwidth telecommunications infrastructure was required, in collaboration with the private sector, at the end of the 1980s and in the early 1990s in these remote rural areas. The purpose of the public sector involvement was to ensure that firms located or wishing to locate in remote areas were not disadvantaged with respect to firms operating in the central parts of Scotland. Without public investment, such areas may be excluded from participating equally in the globalising economy.

In the past, national governments have operated regional policies that attempted to redistribute investment, in particular industrial investment, from richer regions to poorer ones in order to combat the territorial disparities discussed above. However, policies should attempt to do more than simply redistribute income, because if this is the only outcome of policy, then transfers will always be required. Instead, policies need to build the endogenous development capacity of poorer territories.

The recent OECD Territorial Outlook (2001g, p. 182) identifies some of the dangers of pursuing policies that simply redistribute resources without genuinely building local capacities. It is argued that policies based on redistribution mechanisms involving direct assistance to enterprises, technocratic approaches to heavy infrastructure, or support to declining economic activities do little to stimulate growth and employment in the territories concerned and may even be costly blind alleys. In particular, the publication highlights the following lessons from the setbacks or partial setbacks that countries have experienced in pursuing these policies in the past:

43

- The inadequacy of pouring massive amounts of assistance through bureaucratic channels into lagging territories, if programmes do not address the real reasons for lagging development.

- The limits of artificial interventions such as growth pole strategies combining large-scale infrastructure and expensive tax incentives, which have often created only small islands of development.

- The unused capacity that can be created when major infrastructure projects are launched without taking local demand into account.

- The delayed adjustment associated with maintaining direct assistance to declining sectors in order to protect local economic activities.

It is argued that bottom-up, endogenous development policies should be pursued in order to avoid such problems.

There is a dual message here then. Firstly, policies for transfer of resources between territories are still necessary because convergence cannot be expected to be either automatic or rapid and because there are barriers to the mobility of labour to richer areas. Secondly, however, in order to avoid the mistakes from the past, transfers should seek to support genuine endogenous development in lagging territories. Thus, the nature of new territorial policies to support poorer areas is likely to be different from those operated in the past. In particular, a modern territorial development policy is likely to focus on creating a good environment for economic development in less favoured cities and regions, for example through support of entrepreneurship and human capital development, and to be designed and managed by city and region administrations. Where the underdevelopment is mainly intra-regional or intra-urban, devolved governments themselves have a role to play in correcting inequalities within their own regions and cities.

Territorial competition

With globalisation, city and region economies increasingly find themselves competing with each other for resources, such as investment, skilled labour, markets and technological infrastructure, as well as for markets (Keating, 1998; Ohmae, 1995). Without effective co-ordination of their policies, devolution to cities and regions could lead to the further development of zero-sum game policies or territorial competition, for example through competitive bidding or incentives wars.

44

Storper and Scott (1995) illustrate this issue with reference to the United States. They point to the implications of a decision by a region that hopes to become the dominant focus of a new technology and plans to invest significant amounts of public money in fostering an infant industry. If other regions also move in the same direction, there is likely to be considerable wastage of resources. Similarly, they argue that competitive and uncontrolled subsidies or competitive reduction of wages may be undertaken by one region, with dramatic effects on the efforts of another to develop technology or to upgrade skills and productivity. Equally, the predatory poaching by one region of another region's industrial firms may result in reductions in national wealth, especially where those firms have important synergistic relations to others in their region of origin. In each case, inter-regional co-ordination will be needed to ensure that each region's actions and plans harmonise with the wider interests of the national economy as a whole.

This issue of competitive bidding is particularly visible in the attraction of foreign direct investment, where it is often argued that competition between cities and regions for a limited volume of investment projects has inflated the subsidy cost of inward investment attraction. Such competition for inward investment has become an increasingly important issue as the scale of international investment has increased with globalisation. Schweke et al (1994) go as far as referring to a 'new civil war' between states in the USA, quoting the recent large automobile projects in the USA as examples of the escalation of costs. Thus the attraction of a BMW plant to South Carolina in 1992 is estimated to have cost US$68,000 per job, whilst the attraction of Mercedes-Benz to Alabama in 1993 was estimated to have cost between US$150,000 and US$200,000 per job. They argue that these sorts of tax breaks and other incentive costs are excessive and that their main effect is to entice employers to locate in one territory rather than another. For them, part of the solution is at local level, where incentives should only be used judiciously (when capable of generating more development and fiscal benefits than costs), but federal government may also need to intervene to curb wasteful competition between states.

A related danger is that, in the absence of co-ordination, devolution and globalisation will lead to a 'race to the bottom' in tax and regulatory environments that could leave cities and regions unable to provide the social conditions that people demand. With more highly mobile capital and labour, cities and regions may be afraid to apply stricter conditions than competing locations. Thus, those cities and regions prioritising social well-being, for example through spending on job creation and active labour market policies, may feel threatened by those pursuing more aggressive market-friendly policies for inward investment attraction and innovation in high-technology.

Finally, with devolution there is also the possibility that 'territorial protectionism' could emerge, whereby cities and regions seek to protect their production, their resources and their fiscal revenue from other areas. In particular, the poorer territories need some resource transfers for development and income support, but richer territories, if they are raising and spending tax revenues locally, may begin to resist calls to finance other areas. In many devolved countries there are 'solidarity funds' that assure certain transfers between regions, including countries where devolution has been asymmetric, such as Spain and Italy, as well as federal countries such as Germany. However, we have seen recently in Italy, for example, the emergence of political forces (such as the growth of the Forza Italia party) opposed to continued subsidies from the north to the south.

Whilst some degree of competition between public authorities may be justifiable and healthy, public authorities at all levels need to be aware of the danger that excessive competition could develop between cities and regions, to a level where overall mutual interests are no longer served. Various forms of national, international and inter-regional co-operation mechanisms can be envisaged to curb problems. These could involve regulations brought in by nation-state governments or supra-national organisations or new forms of co-ordination organised among cities and regions themselves.

Summary

This chapter has described devolution as a shift towards multi-level governance involving new partnerships between nation-states and devolved governments at city and region levels. There is no one single model of devolution, since structures vary considerably between countries, and the trend towards devolution is not inevitable. But devolved structures do offer key advantages for flexibility, tailoring, integration and innovation in economic development policies, which help respond to the rapidly-moving and increasingly complex nature of economic development problems in a globalising economy.

Globalisation creates a more rapidly-changing and complex environment for economic development policy because of a process of expansion of cross-border networks and interactions built up from a series of interlinked trends including increasing international trade, foreign direct investment, cross-border inter-firm alliances, internationalisation of finance, wider and more rapid diffusion of technology and fragmenting and increasingly customised markets. Economic development policies therefore need to focus on facilitating economic adjustment and innovation and on counteracting problems of uneven development or the exclusion of people and places from wealth creation processes.

Devolved governments, through influencing the local competitive environment, can strengthen their area's capacity to adjust to economic change and exploit new opportunities. This idea is behind a widespread shift in economic development thinking towards a new policy paradigm based on bottom-up or endogenous development. This paradigm stresses the localised nature of many economic development levers and focuses on developing and exploiting local linkages and local skills and resources and local infrastructures and on building sectors where the territory can find a comparative advantage in global markets.

Devolution clearly requires changes in institutional structures. This does not mean that sub-national governments are replacing the nation-state, but that there are transformations in both of their roles and in how they relate to each other. Devolution therefore calls for new co-ordination mechanisms between the city and region governments receiving devolved powers and central governments within the nation-state. Devolution also calls for new internal relationships within a city or region between devolved governments and its civil society partners. Devolved governments should not attempt to create new centres at city and region level, but should work with other relevant partners within their territory to identify development needs and solutions. The OECD Principles of Metropolitan Governance provide useful guidance on the issues and appropriate responses.

One of the central points in the chapter has been that devolved city and region governments have the flexibility to introduce a range of micro-policies that respond to two major challenges of globalisation: building competitive city and region economies and countering social exclusion. Whilst nation-states also continue to have a critical role in these areas, devolved governments can contribute. For competitiveness, it is argued that devolved governments need to develop local policies for Entrepreneurship and local policies to strengthen and exploit human capital. Entrepreneurship and human capital are widely recognised to be two fundamental drivers of territorial competitiveness in the globalising economy, although exploitation of information and communication technologies and policies for innovation also need to be addressed. In order to counter the social exclusion associated with recent economic restructuring it is argued that devolved governments need policies to tackle poverty and exclusion from work, especially in distressed areas within their territory.

Finally, it has been argued that in order for devolution of economic development management to cities and regions to be successful, attention needs to be paid to curbing territorial disparities and potential problems of territorial competition between devolved authorities. Various forms of co-ordination mechanisms can be envisaged, whether organised by international agencies, nation-state governments or between cities and regions themselves.

SECTION TWO

INSTITUTIONS AND GOVERNANCE

CHAPTER 2

TERRITORIAL GOVERNANCE IN A DEVOLVED CONTEXT

A network model of devolution

As highlighted in chapter 2, devolution of economic development management in the context of multi-level governance raises some key governance issues about reforming institutions and organising institutional co-ordination and financial flows. This section outlines some of the main issues and describes in more detail one model of governance, based on devolution to city and region networks and partnerships. This model appears to be well suited to managing economic development policies in the increasingly rapidly moving and complex environment of a globalising economy.

One of the key characteristics of the globalising economy is that economic development is increasingly stimulated by good networking among institutions and firms. Indeed, just as we can talk of the 'networked enterprise' we can also talk of the 'networked state' (Castells, 1996a, 1996b). Networking between firms takes place through channels such as subcontracting and strategic alliances, requiring the building of trust in order to reduce costs, increase flexibility and increase innovation. Collaboration and trust is also important between governments and their partners from civil society. Thus in many OECD countries, policy is not only influenced by traditional partners such as labour unions, but also by lobbies, non-governmental organisations and interest groups representing various economic, social or political interests. These interest groups form a network in which government is just another, albeit a powerful, player (OECD, 2000c).

The European Commission has recently been undertaking a major review of governance issues as an input to its 2001 White Paper on governance. In its preparatory work, the Commission has very much adopted the vision of the network model of governance (European Commission, 2001). This model is seen as being better suited than traditional hierarchical models to the current socio-economic context, which is characterised by rapid change, fragmentation and complex and interconnected policy problems, because networks permit more flexibility and adaptability to change. In announcing the White Paper to the European Parliament, the President of the European Commission, Romano Prodi, underlined this by arguing that

'We have to stop thinking in terms of hierarchical layers of competence separated by the subsidiarity principle and start thinking, instead, of a networking arrangement with all levels of governance shaping, proposing, implementing and monitoring policy together.' Romano Prodi, 2000.

This networked approach does not apply only to the European Union and national governments, it is also being adopted by cities and regions. For example, Eurocities, an association of politicians from Europe's major cities, wrote in its contribution to the consultation for the White Paper that:

'In our cities we have experimented with the devolution of power and the decentralisation of service provision. We have been developing partnerships between the public, voluntary and private sectors on a more systematic basis than hitherto. In a phrase, we have been breaking from a top-down model of government. In its place we are evolving more participative models of governance engaging, involving and working much more with citizens, local groups, businesses and associated agencies.' Eurocities, 2000.

However, introducing networked governance implies the development of appropriate mechanisms for managing co-ordination between devolved and other levels of government and between devolved governments and other partnership within their territory. Box 2, based on OECD (1997a), identifies a number of instruments of control, co-ordination and accountability that can be used.

Box 2. Mechanisms for managing networked governance systems

Performance-based and administrative controls. Two basic types of control can be used in the context of networked governance involving sub-national governments: performance-based and administration- or rules-based.

Performance-based controls focus on output and process. Specific earmarked grants are becoming less common in favour of general grants that can be used more flexibly by the recipients. This shift provides the incentive and opportunity for increased consultation between funders and recipients on appropriate guidelines and minimum standards.

Box 2 (continued)

Administrative controls are generally evolving away from detailed central interference in local affairs and towards broader policy orientation. Jurisdictional controls are also changing so that as well as checking the 'regularity' of actions, increasingly there is also a concern for results and performance. Less hierarchical forms of monitoring, which are often informal and sometimes encouraged by joint financing, also exist in many countries.

Formal and informal co-ordination and consultation. There are various forms of co-ordination and consultation that can be used among different levels of government or between sub-national governments and their partners. These may be:

- Horizontal and/or vertical;

- More or less formal (based on informal practices or more formal 'understandings' or conventions).

- Structural or procedural (using special co-ordinating bodies or achieved through procedural means).

- Institutionalised versus ad hoc (in principle either open-ended or limited in duration).

- Mandatory (legal requirements) or voluntary.

- Binding or non-binding.

- Primary or subsidiary (inter-institutional co-operation may be the primary mode of policymaking or only come into play under certain conditions).

Institutions charged with accountability. All levels of government are obliged to perform the tasks and manage the resources allocated to them as efficiently and effectively as possible, and there are institutions in all OECD countries charged with ensuring that this is the case, although their mandate does not always range across all levels of government. There has been a shift away from accountability for compliance with procedures towards accountability for performance or results. This is putting more emphasis on evaluating the efficiency with which resources are used and the extent to which targets have been achieved. It implies defining common goals and setting performance standards.

Source: OECD (1997a)

The Sabel and O'Donnell paper presented in the next chapter of this book also advocates a network model of devolution. They argue that during the last decade or so, we have been witnessing a profound innovation in public sector governance. It is an innovation that has devolution at its heart, since in order to ensure co-ordination, flexibility, innovation and adaptation to city and region needs, the centre is relying much more on local networks and partnerships for policy design and implementation. In their view, this innovation makes it possible for public administrations to overcome previously encountered limits to their capacity to solve the complex and differentiated problems of economic development policy in a globalising economy. They also argue that through new forms of relationships between the centre and the local, democratic societies are adapting their decision-making processes to become much more inclusive, accountable and responsive to local and territorial realities in a rapidly changing world economy.

Sabel and O'Connell present the recent history of governance in terms of three main governance phases. Their first phase corresponds to the great institutional innovation of the 19th century, namely delegation to the administrative state of responsibilities for co-ordinating and providing services and security to citizens. In the Whitehall parliamentary form delegation was to a professional civil service, in the European corporatist form delegation was to industrial interest organisations and in other countries, such as the United States, delegation was to some combination of both. However, in the view of Sabel and O'Donnell, none of these early forms of delegation produced real accountability or effective co-ordination because various interest groups or the civil service were allowed to influence policy design in ways that favoured the protection of their own interests.

According to Sabel and O'Donnell, we entered a second major phase from the early 1970s. During this phase, governments sought responses to the problems of accountability and co-ordination that had afflicted traditional administrative delegation, using what is known as 'the new public management' or the principal-agent movement. Key features of the new approach were a switch from broad programmes to narrowly-defined programmes and a separation of policy conception from execution. This included an increased degree of devolution to local participants, whether civil servants or third party providers, using management by results emphasising broad indicators of performance.

However, Sabel and O'Donnell argue that the new public management or principal-agent movement itself has important limits to its capacity to restore accountability and effectiveness in governance. The first weakness they identify relates to the difficulty of genuinely separating policy conception from execution. It is difficult in practice to distinguish between conception and execution, or between the principal and the agent, because policymakers cut themselves off from information they need. Furthermore, separation of conception and execution interferes with traditional channels of accountability since it becomes more difficult to identify whether responsibilities for problems lie with those concerned with policy design and target setting or with those concerned with execution.

The second weakness that Sabel and O'Donnell identify with the new public management is that devolving authority through narrow programmes within administrative structures generates problems of co-ordination between different levels and units of administration. Management by results encourages a narrowing of the scope of programmes and a narrowing of the tasks undertaken, hindering the ability to find a more global answer to the more global problem that the policy initiative aims to address. Thus the new public management, or principal-agent movement, appears to be susceptible to the creation of what are referred to as 'wicked problems', which have the double characteristic of information generation and co-ordination failures. In particular, the new public management is seen as creating obstacles to taking the sort of cross-cutting and integrated approach that is required in the complex and changing field of economic development in a globalising economy.

One response has been to introduce teams of civil servants at the centre of government that try to ensure that an integrated approach is taken to policy formulation through the exploration of cross-cutting problems and the implementation of connected solutions. However, even this response relies on the capacity of central teams of civil servants to identify and respond to cross-cutting problems, and is therefore likely to face limits, particularly when these teams are cut off from local knowledge about the realities of implementation on the ground.

In the view of the authors, a new third phase of public sector governance reform is now beginning to take hold, based on the 'pragmatist institution'. This mirrors in the public sector changes that are occurring in private sector firms. The pragmatist institution can be seen as operating somewhere between the formal bureaucracy and the informal network. It has the advantage of creating a locally-integrated cross-cutting approach and tapping into local knowledge, at the same time as providing some overall co-ordination from the centre. At the heart of the innovation is a mechanism of collaboration between central policymakers and local networks and partnerships of stakeholders from local government, the social partners and civil society. Under this mechanism, local stakeholders have a role in the definition of tasks and targets whilst the centre assists the process by pooling information and benchmarking local initiatives against one another. It is argued that this stimulates a process of continuous trial and error. Thus the key difference between the new public management and governance through the pragmatist institution turns around the devolution of responsibilities for policy design and implementation to local networks of stakeholders. They are encouraged to experiment and innovate within a broad co-ordinating and benchmarking framework provided by central policymakers. These new relationships between the centre and local networks are seen as representing not just a more efficient method of organising public policy but also as being part of a shift from a representative democracy to a form of more participative democracy, referred to as 'democratic experimentalism'.

Sabel and O'Donnell argue that through introducing this type of governance innovation, governments can begin to better address the wicked problems that they have experienced in areas such as social exclusion, small business development and environmental protection, releasing greater innovation and responsiveness to local needs. They highlight the case of school governance reforms in Chicago, Kentucky and Texas, where 'pragmatic' public administrations have developed systems that encourage experimentation, 'by defining broad problems, setting provision of standards, pooling measurements of local performance, aiding poor performers to correct their problems and revising standards and overall goals according to the results'. In these areas, the central education department at the state or city level has given local schools the autonomy to plan for themselves how to meet centrally-established general standards, with the input of citizens as teachers and parents. The authors also suggest that economic development structures in Scotland may be operating in line with some of the key features of the pragmatist model. Certainly, the Scottish Executive and its principal economic development agencies, Scottish Enterprise and Highlands and Islands Enterprise, co-ordinate centrally with networks of Local Enterprise Companies responsible for adapting policy design and delivery to local conditions. Sabel and O'Donnell advocate a wider shift towards this form of devolved and networked governance in order to improve the management of complex economic development problems in the globalising economy. The model proposed is one where broad frameworks are established centrally and services are adapted to local conditions through partnerships and networks at city and region level.

Two key implications would appear to emerge from the analysis of Sabel and O'Donnell. The first is that national governments in OECD Member countries should put into effect devolution programmes in order to exploit the potential of this organisational innovation to increase the effectiveness of their economic development policy frameworks. The second is that in order to release many of the potential benefits in terms of better co-ordinating programmes, taking better account of local conditions and increasing democratic participation by citizens, governments may have to implement a model of devolution that resembles that proposed by Sabel and O'Donnell. This is a model that requires both a central framework to co-ordinate, set objectives and benchmark performance and a series of local networks and partnerships of economic development agencies and other stakeholders.

These observations also raise the important question of the level at which central-local relations should be organised. It can be argued that as nation states devolve more economic development powers to cities and regions, they are in a process of creating new centres in these cities and regions. But if these cities and regions are to be successful in creating innovative, tailored, comprehensive and co-ordinated policy responses, they may have to resist using their newly-acquired powers to recreate the traditional forms of delegated governance that central governments arc now moving away from. Instead they may have themselves to adopt more flexible forms of governance through which they co-operate with local partnerships and networks at a lower level within their city or region.

Overall, the analysis of Sabel and O'Donnell provides a clear argument for putting in place devolved forms of policy making and also advocates a type of devolution based on working with local networks and partnerships. However, these reforms are still at an early stage and there is a need for information on how widespread they are and how well they are working. In particular, a number of questions still need to be addressed about how to make such arrangements work efficiently and about whether this type of framework is more adapted to the provision of certain economic development services rather than others. It is therefore interesting to test Sabel and O'Connell's notions against the unfolding situation in OECD countries.

New developments in this area are currently flourishing. In an increasing number of countries, governments create or support partnerships aimed at a better co-ordination of policies and adaptation of local needs. These networks of partnerships are assigned various goals, ranging from promoting social inclusion to stimulating economic development and improving the quality of life. The OECD has led a cross-national study of partnerships to identify how these partnerships improve co-ordination and adaptation of policies to local conditions, thus improving governance. The study has shown that partnerships at local or regional level cannot be taken as the unique answer to the 'wicked problems' referred to by Sabel and O'Donnell. In order to maximise the effectiveness of partnerships in improving governance, adjustments must also be made to the policy and accountability frameworks of the constituent partners, including government departments at national level. Mechanisms should allow for co-ordination problems encountered at local level to be fed up to the top and for facilitating the necessary trade-offs at national level. Partnerships should also operate in a strategic framework which makes it possible for civil servants and local officials to use this co-ordination tool as a way to improve the effectiveness of their action at local level. Accountability relationships in partnerships are complex (simultaneously directed to governing organisations, to the public and between constituent partners), and their strength is a central condition for effective co-ordination. Flexibility in programme management ensures the good functioning of partnership in practice (Box 3).

Box 3. OECD Strategy to Improve Governance through Partnerships

The OECD Study on Local Partnerships proposes a strategy to improve governance through partnerships. This strategy is based on the experience of partnerships evolving across a wide institutional spectrum and in a broad range of policy areas. It can be applied to, or inspire improvements in, a range of governance instruments, such as tripartism, decentralisation, national-regional contractualisation, and public service agreements, all of which promote better collective actions and solutions.

1. Make policy goals consistent at central level. The creation of a network of partnerships should be accompanied by an exercise at central level to facilitate the necessary trade-offs between government departments (and social partners) in order to achieve full consistency among national policy objectives related to the goals assigned to partnerships. Partnerships should not be accountable to one single central agency, but rather to all the partners needed to fulfil their missions. The partners should agree on the role to be given to partnerships in policy implementation and improving governance.

2. Adapt the strategic framework for the partnership to the needs of the partners. Programming exercises should enable public service officers and local officials to achieve their own policy objectives through participation in the partnership strategy. This will encourage them to use the partnership as a tool to improve the quality of their own action locally. To foster a co-operative climate, the terms of the contribution of each partner to the implementation of the common strategy should be explicit and transparent. Services should normally be delivered by individual partners rather than by the partnership itself.

Box 3 (continued)

3. Strengthen the accountability of partnerships. Partners from all sectors should have a clear policy on the issues addressed by the partnerships. They should, accordingly, define mandates and reporting mechanisms for their delegates. Partners should agree on appropriate representation mechanisms for each sector, and on a clear distribution of responsibility when public programmes are implemented with the partnership's involvement. They should seek to separate the functions of strategic planning, project appraisal and assistance provision. These measures will ensure efficient co-ordination and secure partners' commitment.

4. Provide flexibility in the management of public programmes. The needs of local public service offices for more flexibility in the management of programmes should be addressed in a way to ensure that their participation in the definition of a local joint strategy can be followed by involvement in its implementation. Partnerships should be involved in the targeting of public programmes related to common goals, whilst the responsibility for delivery should remain with public services.

Source: OECD (2001b)

During the conference, Ging Wong, a Canadian delegate to the OECD LEED Committee, described recent devolution processes in Canada with particular reference to the federal employment ministry, Human Resources Development Canada. Canada is a country with a Whitehall tradition, but it is also a federal state operating through collaboration between the centre and the provinces and territories in a number of fields. As with any country, Canada has a range of different forms of governance arrangements according to the policy field, the provinces and territories involved (Canada operates asymmetric devolution), the history of service provision and so on, and there are significant differences between government departments in particular (see Aucoin, 1995). It is nonetheless interesting to compare the example of recent devolution of powers in one of the largest Canadian federal departments, Human Resources Development Canada (HRDC), with the Sabel and O'Donnell model. This is a department which alone represents some 60% of the total federal budget (approximately C$60 billion per year expenditure) and delivers a broad range of policies.

HRDC has been involved in devolution processes in the following ways.

–   Firstly, it has increased the autonomy of selected local offices. Thus, in 1994 the service delivery network of some 400 HRDC offices across Canada was redesigned in order to give increased importance to 100 principal Human Resources Canada centres. The managers of these centres were given increased discretion and flexibility in order to adapt policies to conditions on the ground and build community capacity with local partners.

–   Secondly, it developed a series of bilateral agreements between the federal government and nine provinces for the design and delivery of new employment benefits and active labour market policy measures. There are several different forms of agreement, based around either co-management by federal and provincial authorities or fully provincial delivery. In each case there is a binding commitment to evaluate jointly the results. Targets, performance measurement frameworks and reporting mechanisms are agreed between HRDC and each province.

–   Thirdly, involvement of third party service providers in employment programmes has increased, typically through performance contracting, although this is not the type of devolution seen recently in New Zealand and Australia, where there is a very strong contractability and contestability challenge to the monopoly of public administration.

–   Fourthly, it has promoted 'social union initiatives', where certain social programmes have been organised as co-ordinated activities involving both provincial and federal levels of government. This has included the very successful launch and development of joint initiatives to provide better benefits through the tax system to poor children and people with disabilities, whilst at the same time reforming the system for federal health and social transfer payments to the provinces.

–   Fifthly, in order to improve accountability, HRDC has been subject to the Canadian federal government's 'controllership initiative'. The primary focus of this initiative is to improve the reporting of policy outcomes to parliamentarians and to the Canadian public in general. Policy outcomes are anticipated, measured and reported in relation to the overall government policy agenda.

These reforms would appear to be more consistent with the second phase of governance innovation outlined by Sabel and O'Donnell (the new public management or principal-agent form) than with their third phase of 'democratic experimentalism', which they argue is only now beginning to emerge. Thus the HRDC reforms have involved the separation of policy conception from execution and devolution of decision-making to local participants. Policy conception is shared between the federal and provincial governments and execution is carried out by provinces, local offices or third parties with a focus on management by results (set by agreement between the federal and the provincial government). It is less like the democratic experimentalist phase in that local stakeholders (such as third party providers and civil society organisations) have only a very limited role in the definition of tasks and targets.

Sabel and O'Donnell advance two main arguments as to why the principal-agent movement is likely to fail to deliver effective policy, firstly the impracticality of distinguishing between the conception and execution of policy and secondly the lack of co-ordination that arises between different levels and units of administration. HRDC has been aware of these potential problems and the possibility of duplication and inefficiencies arising through devolution of powers and has put in place certain measures designed to block them. In particular two key innovations were introduced in the 1990s, both related to the identification of cross-cutting policy issues.

Firstly, HRDC policy-makers have started to formulate policy with reference to the concept of 'silos' of government activity or policy, in other words broad policy fields within which cross-cutting policy issues become evident. In social policy, for example, civil servants have been working with cross-cutting policy issues related to youth employment, displacement of older workers, lifelong learning, dealing with the voluntary sector, aboriginal communities and so on. Their responses provided the foundations of a major strategic rethink of social policy. Secondly, a major medium-term policy research agenda has been developed across the federal government in partnership with research communities in order to identify the policy gaps when looking forwards over five years in respect to these cross-cutting issues.

Although there are likely to be a number of examples of other initiatives in Canada that are similar to the sorts of collaboration through local networks advocated by Sabel and O'Donnell, it is not clear that there is a strong trend to adopt that type of approach. Indeed, in some cases actual governance arrangements appear to be going in the other direction. For example, in Ontario important recent education and health reforms have involved recentralisation rather than increased devolution to local networks. In that province, some 160 local education boards were amalgamated to form just 60 boards in 1997, whilst at the same time provincial-wide tests were introduced to the elementary high school system. Similarly Ontario's hospital sector was recentralised to create just one hospital board for each major city, centralising all the administrative functions of all hospitals in the area. In both cases centralisation was considered by the Ontario government to have the advantages of avoiding duplication and increasing efficiency. The Canadian evidence therefore suggests that there is nothing inevitable about moving to new central-local relationships based on increased devolution to partnerships and local networks of agencies.

Box 4 gives the example of how the state of North Rhine Westphalia in Germany has organised the devolution of power from the centre to the local level within the region. The NRW model has involved the creation of fifteen sub-regions within the state, within which local government authorities and social partners have been included in economic development decision-making. One of the keys to their success is the strong co-operation and communication between different local actors, which has generated a much increased level of trust among the important stakeholders.

Box 4. Devolution of policy design in North-Rhine Westphalia, Germany

The economic development context

The state of North-Rhine Westphalia (NRW) is located in the west of Germany. It has approximately 18 million inhabitants and contains the important cities of Cologne, Düsseldorf and Dortmund. The region has been through a process of deep structural change during the last 40 years, recording job losses between 1960 and 1998 of more than 400,000 in the coal sector and 350,000 in the iron and steel sector. The state government has therefore placed considerable emphasis on implementing an effective and efficient regional policy combining its own state financial resources with funding from the federal government in Berlin and the European Union.

Box 4 (continued)

What does the NRW devolution approach involve?

NRW was the first state in Germany to devolve decision-making for economic development planning and projects towards networks of local government authorities and other partners operating at sub-regional level. The aim was to increase the flexibility and local adaptedness of policy, which previously had been dominated by initiatives designed at state level, targeted mainly at restructuring the two sectors most affected by economic change; coal and iron and steel. Devolution was introduced in 1989 through an initiative called the 'Zukunftsinitiative für die Regionen Nordrhein-Westfalens' (ZIN). This created 15 new ZIN sub-regions operating below the level of the Land but above the level of the existing 5 Regierungsbezirke and the 54 municipalities and districts. At this new level the relevant players from different local government authorities and social partners from different sectors are brought together to design a jointly-agreed economic development strategy and to propose projects for funding by the state government.

How does it work?

The main innovation has been the introduction of sub-regional 'conferences' and working group meetings bringing together representatives from local and regional government authorities, the chambers of commerce and industry, trade unions, local labour offices, universities and research institutes and the private sector. These sub-regional 'conferences' have the task of adjusting and co-ordinating state and partner policies and have had a particularly important role in promoting the growth of enterprise clusters. Within this framework, local decision-makers design and approve an economic development strategy that responds to the potential strengths and weaknesses of each ZIN sub-region.

They also make a prioritised list of proposals for major development projects for approval for state funding. By making the final decisions on the projects that will be funded, the NRW state government retains the ability to co-ordinate policies across the region and to ensure that they are in line with state-wide economic development objectives. An important pre-condition for the effective working of the regional conferences is that each is chaired by someone who is accepted by all of the stakeholders.

Box 4 (continued)

What are its objectives?

The principal reasons for introducing this devolved networking approach are:

♦ To strengthen self-responsibility and empower local and regional stakeholders.

♦ To better tailor policies to local conditions in terms of local potential and the special resources available in each local area.

♦ To design a sub-regional profiles that will make strengths more transparent and attractive, in particular for foreign investors.

♦ To improve co operation and co-ordination among stakeholders through networking and the division of labour.

♦ To promote co-ordinated strategic development that will make it easier to plan and carry out economic development measures.

What are the strengths and weaknesses of the approach?

The NRW approach provides a good model of how to avoid the risk of recentralisation within devolved regions by ensuring that mechanisms exist for mobilisation and co-ordination of local actors and for taking account of local circumstances. It has been very successful in improving co-operation and communication among localities and among stakeholders and introducing a systematic and locally-tailored approach to strategic planning. Furthermore, the regional conferences have provided the basis for further more informal networking that has contributed to an atmosphere of increased co-operation and trust among the important stakeholders.

Wanieck (1993) points to four remaining challenges related to the details of the ZIN process:

Definition of the regions: The flexibility was given to local players to constitute their own regional boundaries. However, the outcome has been that the ZIN sub-regions correspond as much to pre-existing administrative boundaries as to functional economic regions.

> **Box 4 (continued)**
>
> *Degree of decentralisation*: There is some tension between the stated objective of devolution and the state government's retention of the right to take the final decisions on project funding.
>
> *Legitimacy of the regional conferences*: The regional conferences are made up of a combination of representatives of public bodies and private interest groups and are not directly elected. Much attention therefore has to be paid to the choice of participants to try and minimise the chances of deviation from the public interest.
>
> *Co-ordination by the Land*: A large part of the funding for ZIN projects comes from existing state programmes. However these have broadly retained their original aims and eligibility conditions. This limits the ability of the regional conferences to develop a fully independent and locally-tailored approach.
>
> These sorts of issues arise in any devolution context and need to be resolved through careful attention to the detailed arrangements, with proper regard to need to find the right balance between central co-ordination and local flexibility.

The North Rhine Westphalia approach provides a further illustration of how new institutional partnerships can be implemented in order to respond to current governance challenges. Cities and regions will therefore need to consider carefully what type of governance arrangement is likely to be best in their circumstances, recognising that there are different models and possibilities. Nonetheless, some clear arguments have been put forward as to why devolution to cities and regions using a network and partnership model may be particularly well suited to managing economic development policies in a complex, globalising environment.

Summary

This chapter argued that devolution should not be limited to a simple transfer of power between central and local or regional governments, but that in order to respond to the dynamic and complex policy challenges of a globalising economy there is a need for greater interaction and networking between different levels of government and its civil society partners. These more co-operative relationships tend to involve mechanisms like joint definition of targets and objectives and accountability techniques such as output measurement and measurement by results.

The 'democratic experimentalist' model put forward by Sabel and O'Donnell in the next chapter is one approach to increasing networking and interactions. At the heart of this innovation is a mechanism of collaboration between central policymakers and local networks and partnerships of stakeholders from local government, the social partners and civil society. Under this mechanism, local stakeholders have a role in the definition of tasks and targets, whilst the centre assists the process by pooling information and benchmarking local initiatives against one another. This is argued to generate continuous innovation, experimentation and adaptation of policy that is likely to be more effective than traditional hierarchical arrangements in providing the sort of flexibility, tailoring and integration of policy that is required in the globalising economy. There is nevertheless clearly a variety of different possible models of governance and not all areas are implementing the devolved, networked and experimental approach outlined here.

City and regional governments need to consider carefully what institutional arrangements are likely to be best in their circumstances. There is still a need for assessment of how well such arrangements work compared with other approaches and for an exchange of information on best practices on how to make horizontal and vertical collaboration work well. The OECD LEED Programme and the Territorial Development Service are undertaking ongoing work in this area. What is clear, however, is that city and regional governments receiving new devolved powers should avoid replicating the previous centralism practised by the nation-state. Instead, strong interaction with social and economic partners is required in order to address the complex problems of economic development in a globalising economy.

In the next chapter, Sabel and O'Donnell describe in more detail the 'democratic experimentalism' model that has been referred to here.

CHAPTER 3

DEMOCRATIC EXPERIMENTALISM:
WHAT TO DO ABOUT WICKED PROBLEMS AFTER WHITEHALL

by

Charles Sabel, Columbia Law School, United States of America and
Rory O'Donnell, University College Dublin, Ireland

Why reform of democratic governance is on the agenda

Quietly, without the raucous clash of party and programme that mark even lesser stirrings, democracy is on the move. The economic turmoil and political revolts of the 70s and 80s together with the globalisation of world markets that continues today have brought renewal as well as disruption. At the local level citizens in many countries are directly participating with government in solving problems of economic development, schooling, policing, the management of complex ecosystems or drug abuse. Their successes, though manifestly fragile, already suggest possibilities of public co-ordination that even recently seemed beyond reach. Central governments of nearly all political colours at times encouraged these developments by devolving authority to lower levels and loosening the grip of public bureaucracies on the provision of some services while wholly privatising others. At times they simply tolerated local experimentation by waiving formally, or through inaction, their statutory rights to specify how programmes are administered. Viewed from the centre government seems reformable (surprisingly so, given recurrent fears that the modern state would prove a new feudal overlord), but more in its capacities for self-limitation and dis-entrenchment than its positive abilities to co-ordinate and construct. Viewed from the local problem-solving units, the central government seems indispensable as an ally in the consolidation of nascent innovations, but capriciously unreliable in its ignorance of local circumstance and its own potential to foster development. Both perspectives take government as disjointed and fragmentary, not formative and framing. In this they invite questions about the practicality and legitimacy of representative democracy, which centres law making in the legislature, in a world where the centre devolves more than it directs.

In the United States this confusion is largely masked, and the questions it raises are muted. Because of its malleable federalism, its proud tradition of domesticating government by setting its branches to war among themselves, and the validation of US institutions, whatever their actual coherence, by the current successes of the American economy, America revels for now in its disjoint state. Not so the European Union (EU). There the transformation of the regulatory law of the member states into an EU regime— harmonisation is the anodyne but inaccurate term of art—occurs by an obscure process of committee consultation far beyond the supervision of the European Parliament. Excepting a few experts in comitology (who anyway disagree sharply among themselves in claiming some democratic justification for the harmonising consultation), the common view is that this law making itself is an important instance of a larger democratic deficit in the constitution of the EU, and hence a threat to the Union's material successes. Further scrutiny heightens the doubts: Regional policy, again largely beyond the ambit of parliamentary control, transfers vast sums from some areas within the EU to others. At the least the transfers stir up local politics, giving emergent economic and political groups new possibilities to challenge local élites. But the effects can be transformative, or nearly so. In the Republic of Ireland EU regional funds helped finance construction of a national system of local public-private partnerships creating problem-solving, participatory local governments of the kind referred to above, and like those paralleling and competing with the constitutionally provided ones.

No EU member state is more disposed to see in these changes a menace and an opportunity than Great Britain. No other country combines such deep traditions of parliamentary centralism and inveterate localism: whatever forces rend these apart reverberate powerfully here. No other EU member went so far as Great Britain in tearing up the fabric of its modern constitutional order in the 1970s and 80s, trying to distance itself from much of its past while retaining its national identity even as it assimilated to the Union. (The cover of an authoritative book on that period reads simply *The End of Whitehall*. You must turn to the title page to uncover the cautionary addendum: *Death of a Paradigm?* (Campbell and Wilson, 1995)). In search of renewal, moreover, Great Britain, together with the other Whitehall countries—New Zealand, Australia, and Canada—went farther than other countries in applying familiar models of corporate governance based on clear distinctions between conception and execution to the reform of government. It learned, in consequence, more than other countries about the limits of these principal-agent models, and the need, at least, to correct them by forms of governance that take means and ends to be mutually determining.

Beyond all this there is the matter of regional devolution. Great Britain is unique in the EU in managing the (mostly) orderly devolution of quasi-sovereign powers to three historic regions, according them qualities of post- or para-nationality while maintaining the integrity of the existing union. This effort recalls, but surely will do more than simply recreate, the forms of sovereignty and nationality that prevailed in composite states such as Switzerland, Netherlands and the British isles themselves in the period before Westphalian nationalism. Articulation of these new relations imposes on London and Brussels no less than Cardiff, Ulster and Edinburgh the obligation to make democratic, effective sense of the provided resources and institutional apparatus afforded by Great Britain and the EU. The open questions are especially acute in Scotland, where some of the local governance of economic development and schooling already approximates the new problem-solving model. Will the links to be established between the new Scottish Assembly, the ministries of the new Scotland, and local government mirror on a smaller scale the traditional ones? If so, the result may be to create a belated modern nation, but at the cost of disrupting promising innovations. Or will the constitution of those links contribute, on the contrary, to a redefinition of these institutions, and so to a renewal of our understanding of the possibilities of democracy itself? If nothing else Great Britain and Scotland are knowingly at work on democracy.

To think through the emerging relation between national and local government, changing notions of governance, and their implications for democracy in the British-Scottish setting connects a general enquiry with the daring and hard-nosed realism that come when theoretical problems turn practically urgent. Such, in any case, is the ambition of this essay. The argument is compressed, even schematic; so we anticipate the steps here for orientation. Section 2 sets the stage. It briefly reviews the common features and the common limits of the constitutional settlements defining democracy in the advanced countries since mid-century, when not before. It then shows how the Whitehall countries' response to those limits, and especially their use of principal-agent governance as the template for a reformed democracy, created in turn new problems of effective co-ordination and accountability. Section 3 details thoughtful, closely related proposals currently advanced in Great Britain, Scotland, and the US to address these limits in order to respond to the 'wicked problems' of co-ordination: for example, drug abuse, economic development, schooling and others whose solution requires local provision of differentiated, complex bundles of services. The manifest shortcomings of these proposals suggest that the principal-agent model, however modified, can transpose the familiar problems of democracy but not resolve them.

The rest of the chapter develops an alternative. Section 4 argues that modern firms operate on pragmatist, not principal-agent principles. Instead of trying to resolve ambiguity by creating clear goals (the province of the principal) and clear roles for achieving them (the responsibilities of the agents), this firm accepts that ends and means are mutually defining. Hence initial choices of each must be corrected, and corrected again, in the very effort to realise the projects they embody. We illustrate the differences between conventional and pragmatist firms by comparing their respective methods of design and the relations they establish between customers and suppliers. Section 5 shows how the application of the pragmatist model in public administration leads to a new, participatory and experimentalist form of democracy. The role of the administrative centre in this experimentalist democracy is not to set rules and police compliance. Rather, with local units, it defines broad projects, and sets provisional general standards. In addition it provides infrastructure by which local units can achieve their own goals, and pools measurements of performance to allow refinement of the general standards as well as the particular local strategies in the light of results. The resulting organisation is neither a formal bureaucracy nor an informal network, yet it combines the capacities for super-local learning characteristic of the former with the access to local knowledge characteristic of the latter. We illustrate this experimentalist democracy at work by looking in detail at governance reform in the Chicago public schools. Finally, returning to the discussion of the reform of reform underway in Great Britain, Scotland, and the US, we raise questions about the implications of this example for rethinking the role of parliament, ministries, and local communities in a democracy, and wonder whether some Scottish institutions, such as the Local Enterprise Councils (LECs), are already operating on pragmatist lines.

The administrative state, delegation, and the aftermath: the short story of Whitehall from beginning to end

The problems agitating representative democracy today are rooted in an antinomy that has bedevilled self government since the end of the nineteenth century: Formally, democracy requires that all citizens be treated alike, regardless of differences in their life circumstances. But practically effective co-ordination under modern conditions requires attention to just these differences. Reconciling these demands has required institutional innovations as well as changes in the understanding, if not the explicit constitutional design of representative democracy.

The great institutional innovation, and the one that forms the context for the problems under discussion here, is of course the administrative state: the rules and institutions that together regulate economic exchange, and provide services and security to citizens most vulnerable to it. The doctrinal innovation that legitimated the administrative state is the theory of delegation. That theory reaffirms the formal sovereignty of the legislature as the authoritative source of law. But it also recognises that no assembly can itself competently address the complexity of modern society. Hence the legislature is allowed to delegate some of its sovereign authority to other entities, more proximate to civil society and so able to specify rules suited to particular contexts beyond the ken of a central lawmaker. In electing parliament citizens manifest their equality; in delegating authority to administrative bodies parliament takes account of their distinctiveness.

Delegation of legislative authority took two main forms. In the Whitehall system, parliament entrusted civil servants with responsibility for translating general laws into precise rules in distinct policy areas, and co-ordinating activities across areas. Expertise, exercised collegially and informed by dedication to the public good, enabled officials to do both. In the neo-corporatist states of continental Europe—Germany, Italy, the Nordic countries—authority was delegated not to the civil service, but to the affected interests in civil society themselves: trade unions, employers' associations, and the like. These organisations were presumed to represent the natural and mutually complementary constituents of industrial society—labour and capital first and foremost. Because the groups depended on each other, and society depended on their co-operation, they could be entrusted to make law in the name of democracy by negotiating among themselves.

Most countries are in fact, of course, a combination of the two. Trade unions have a place in the British polity as surely as civil servants have a place in the German one. But nowhere is the mixture more evident than in the US. The constitutional battles of the New Deal were fought precisely to delegate congressional authority to expert agencies, on the one hand, and to interest associations, such as trade unions and employers' associations, on the other, who were to resolve differences through collective bargaining.

In the long term these forms of delegation produced neither accountability nor effective co-ordination. The reasons are clear in retrospect. The jurisdictions of interest groups do not naturally conform to the boundaries of the problems they need to solve: not, unless by sheer luck, at first, when problems and groups are initially defined, and surely not when problems begin to change (perhaps in response to the groups' own actions). This is true if only because interest groups have interests of their own, which grow out of, and reinforce initial institutional boundaries. This sedimentation makes adjustment to new circumstances increasingly difficult. The less adapted the organisation of interest groups is to its environment, the more partial and self-interested the interest-group representation. Exactly the same can be said of bureaucracies, their jurisdictions, and the self-interest of bureaucrats. Combining delegation to interest groups, as neo-corporatism does, with delegation to the civil service in the fashion of Whitehall compounds error by obstinacy. Or so at any rate has been the increasingly vehement sentiment in almost all the advanced countries since the late 1960s.

The first measures to issue from the growing concern about the accountability and efficacy of the administrative state were in the way of palliatives and correctives. The US was among the first to react. It lacked both the tradition of the tutelary state and the tradition of government by estates of the realm upon which Whitehall and neo-corporatism could build. In addition it was well armed against any possible aggrandisement of government by the separation of powers. Federal judges tried to pry open the collusive iron triangles of interest groups, expert agencies regulating their behaviour and congressional committees with oversight responsibility for the regulatory agency. Courts also created regimes for the vindication of rights by groups (minorities, prison inmates, women in the work force) whose interests are not well protected either by interest groups or administrative agencies. On occasion the judges simply acted as regulatory bodies themselves, as, for example, in the break-up AT&T (long the equivalent of a European PTT). Congress tried to limit the authority delegated to regulatory agencies by writing detailed legislation (the Clean Air and Water Acts, for example) that substantially reduced the scope for agency discretion. The president tried both to limit congressional interference in the agencies to protect the executive branch, then tried to limit the agencies discretion to reassert the presidency, and so on.

While the branches of government squabbled over accountability, moreover, each level of government—federal, state, municipal—was devolving responsibility for formulating or implementing policy to a lower one, or to NGOs, in recognition of the impossibility of asserting effective control on its own. Periodically this devolution was interrupted by hapless efforts at bureaucratic re-centralisation (imposition of strict rules on NGOs; 'recategorisation' into distinct accounts of funds initially dedicated to separate programmes and then pooled into block grants) to limit the exercise of discretion made possible by decentralisation. The Reagan Administration's overt attack on the New Deal State was thus in many ways as much continuity as change, and debates about its significance remain accordingly murky.

The new public management and its limits

In the Whitehall countries reactions to the problems of administrative delegation came later rather than sooner, but were all the more vehement and thoroughgoing for the delay. The tardiness had to do with the absence of dis-entrenching mechanisms such as the US courts and the separation of powers. Without them interest groups and bureaucracies could fortify their positions. Political traditions valuing social consensus and deference to an administrative élite gave a patina of legitimacy to the bulwarks of the state. The vehemence of the reaction was a response to the backlog of unsolved problems. But it was also a consequence of the first-past-the-post electoral systems and unitary governments of countries like New Zealand and Great Britain. Such systems produced big winners: narrow parliamentary majorities had a free hand to implement radical programmes.

The driving idea of the New Public Management (NPM), taken directly and openly from US economics of the 1980s, was to re-establish the control of the democratic principal—the sovereign people acting through elections—over its agents in government by reducing insofar as possible the ambiguities of delegation. Just as shareholders were to wrest control over the corporation from managers, perhaps in collusion with the work force, so the citizens were to retake control of their state from public officials and interest groups.

This assertion of 'straight-line' accountability required a profound transformation in the organisation and scope of government. Conception was to be separated from execution: If self interested agents can effectively set tasks for themselves as they collaborate in the setting of goals, then they recommend goals that provide themselves with rewarding tasks, regardless of whether those goals are in the interest of the public or not. Instead, politically appointed ministers, supported by expert staffs and hired consultants, were to determine strategy, and civil service managers were to execute it. By the same logic the scope of responsibility of individual ministries, and the programmes within them, was reduced. Asked to pursue multiple goals simultaneously, agents will naturally have to make tradeoffs among them, and will favour trades that serve their interests first, and the public interest accidentally if at all. The narrower the scope of the ministerial portfolio or individual programme, the less the danger that self interest can use competing purposes as a lever for its own ends. These changes led to a decentralisation of authority within administrative units, and an increased emphasis on measuring, and increasing, the satisfaction of the citizens (now recast as customers) who were the beneficiaries of particular services. The clearer the goals, and the less the chances for conflict among them, the smaller the need for middle managers to break complex tasks into simpler ones, adjudicate differences of opinion about the priority of competing programmes, or rate the performance of subordinates in the face of further ambiguities. Instead, given the narrow, flatter structure of administration, front-line managers with a clear understanding of their purpose would determine how best to achieve it. Customer satisfaction would be the measure of their success.

All these changes, went hand in hand with an emphasis on global performance measures: (improvements in) crime rates, numbers of unemployed persons placed in jobs, test scores (of the competence of students at various grade levels and their teachers), and so on. Performance of tasks sufficiently simplified to admit of straight-line accountability could be captured by such metrics; conversely, the definition of the performance metrics helped encourage the necessary simplification of tasks. Instead of trusting co-ordination of public policy to unreliable, because self interested, negotiation among interests or collegial consultation among civil servants, management of public affairs could be by results.

A consequence—for some reformers the very purpose—of these reforms was a reduction in the scope of government itself. The clearer the purposes of government, and the more measurable the results of its actions, of course, the easier it is to translate the tasks of public administration into contracts, and to hold contractual partners to account if they fail to meet their obligations. This made it easier for government, first, to contract with private parties, instead of its internal units, for the provision of service: what mattered to the public as citizens and consumers, after all, was the contractual terms and the respect accorded them. Straight-line accountability thus made the monopoly of public administration on service provision contestable in theory. (Making it contestable in fact took an endless series of battles that are already becoming hard to recall now that they have been mostly won.) Second, contractability and contestability made it easier wholly to privatise some government functions such as the provision of water or electric power. This transfer of formal ownership turned the analogy between private and public governance advanced by the principal-agent reforms into an identity.

The successes of the NPM in establishing the contestability of public administration and devolving authority are indisputable and largely taken for granted by the vast middle of the modern democratic polities. At the most general level, leaving particular victories over inertia and self dealing aside, it has shown that the public can prevail against the interests and experts. We made the state; learning from our mistakes we can remake it. This realisation distresses on the one side advocates of the traditional administrative state, who often treated modern government as a kind of natural organism evolved in the primordial broth of contemporary society and destined to flourish with it. But it also, perhaps paradoxically, discomforts those partisans of NPM for whom the advance of privatisation and contestability were vindications of the truly natural form of co-operation—the market—against unnatural co-operation by means of politics and the state. It is easy to understand their baffled outrage at the ability of governments like those of President Clinton and Prime Minister Blair to absorb key lessons of the NPM—and go on with governing.

But measured by its own standard—as a movement to restore accountability and effectiveness to government—the results of the principal-agent movement are equivocal at best. Government in the Whitehall countries, Great Britain in particular, is arguably less accountable, and on balance, no more effective than before, for two reasons connected to the principal-agent underpinnings of the reform movement itself.

First, it has proved impossible to separate strategy from implementation, or more generally, conception from execution. Those who carried out orders learned not only how to refine the execution of tasks, but also which tasks might be worth pursuing. Nor was it just public or private-sector service providers who acquired knowledge relevant to goal setting in this way. Citizen users of the services provided also turned out to have knowledge relevant to choosing public purpose. Put another way, the principal/agent distinction was untenable in practice. At the limit, citizens proved to be in some measure the co-producers of services as well as consumers of them and, ultimately, their principal authors.

The upshot, as Rhodes (1997) shows in *Understanding Governance*, is that in Great Britain government agencies—responsible in the NPM scheme of things for the operational implementation of strategy—in fact develop a near monopoly of expertise in their policy area, notwithstanding efforts to outfit the politically responsible minister with capacities for strategic surveillance. Policy therefore emerges from innumerable small decisions, such that 'the agency tail will wag the departmental dog'. To increase the confusion, the department, emboldened by official encouragement to assert its directive powers, often uses its oversight responsibility to meddle in the details of agency decision-making. If results disappoint, the minister can play on the ambiguities in the distinction between policy (her responsibility) and management (the domain of the operating agency) to avoid accountability. Civil servants are no longer in charge; but no one else is, either. Rhodes for one concludes that 'British government has undergone a significant decrease in political accountability (pp.102-3).'

Second, narrowing programmes in the interest of accountability had the unintended consequence of making it difficult to co-ordinate the narrower entities. While a certain local clarity was achieved, at least within the limits just described, its price was an increase in general confusion. Given specific tasks, and encouraged by new incentive systems to focus exclusively on them, and contract with others to provide collateral services, what was to induce the agencies to co-operate among themselves to solve problems requiring their joint action?

As Rhodes observes the resulting problems are most conspicuous at the level of local government. There are few efforts at government reform as vigorous and protracted as that aimed at local government by successive British governments. From 1979 to the early 1990s, central government acted to control expenditure, limit taxing capacity, alter management, increase accountability, and redefine the legislative base: in short to attain 'straight-line' accountability by applying all the devices of NPM to the public, private and voluntary sectors. But, Rhodes found, in the wake of the reforms,

> *'services are ... delivered through a combination of local government, special purpose bodies, the voluntary sector and the private sector. Service delivery depends, therefore, on linking organisations. Policy implementation becomes more difficult because policy has to be negotiated with more and more organisations. Organisational interdependence is ubiquitous and the government faces the increasingly difficult task of steering several distinct organisations.' (p.100)*

Both of these problems—the impossibility of maintaining the principal/agent distinction and the need for broad co-ordination to correct the effects of narrow steering—are manifest in the sudden salience of what the British call 'cross-cutting' or 'wicked problems': problems like the reform of schools or the provision of treatment to substance abusers that both draw on the local knowledge of service providers and service users *and* require co-ordination of service provision across a wide range of formal jurisdictions. These two problems have prompted a set of thoughtful proposals that aim to make use of the new plasticity of government created by NPM while attending to the movement's shortcomings. We discuss these next.

Whitehall Redux? Reforming the reforms

The current British Government, through the Cabinet Office and other departments, has been among the most relentless critics of the shortcomings of the old administrative state, even as corrected by NPM, and among the most determined proponents of reforms to address the wicked problems—thought to be particularly acute with regard to social exclusion, small business development and environmental protection. In a series of innovative papers, it develops proposals for policy co-ordination - *Wiring it Up: Whitehall's Management of Cross-Cutting Issues* (Cabinet Office, 2000a) - new relations between the centre and the local - *Reaching Out: the Role of Central Government at Regional and Local Government* (Cabinet Office, 2000b) - and the principles of good policy making and implementation - *Professional Policy Making for the Twenty First Century* (Cabinet Office, 1999).

The starting point for all these reports is the conviction that the functional organisation of government departments—the idea, coeval with the administrative state, that there can be some natural correspondence between the jurisdiction of problem-solving bureaucracies and the boundaries of core social problems—limits the possibility of addressing cross-cutting policy problems. These limits are exacerbated by practices permitted but not entailed by these bureaucratic structures. These include, for example, a failure 'to look at things from the perspective of the consumer', failure to work with local government, being 'over-prescriptive in specifying the means as well as the ends', an increased focus on core business as a result of delegation, and perverse incentives.

In response the reports suggest variants of what might be called a commando centre: a crack team of civil servants at the very centre of government who use the powers of the bureaucracy to foster cross cutting behaviours, and so transcend the structural limits, without actually transforming the structures. The executive summary from the report *'Wiring it Up: Whitehall's Management of Cross-Cutting Issues'* conveys the strategy:

  – stronger leadership from Ministers and senior civil servants to create a culture which values cross-cutting policies and services, with systems of rewards and recognition that reinforce desired outcomes;

  – improving policy formulation and implementation to take better account of cross-cutting problems and issues, by giving more emphasis to the interests and views of those outside central Government who use and deliver services;

  – equipping civil servants with the skills and capacity needed to address cross-cutting problems and issues;

  – using budgets flexibly to promote cross-cutting working, including using more cross-cutting budgets and pooling of resources;

  – using audit and external scrutiny to reinforce cross-cutting working and encourage sensible risk-taking; and

- using the centre (No. 10, the Cabinet Office and the Treasury) to lead the drive to more effective cross-cutting approaches wherever they are needed. The centre has a critical role to play in creating a strategic framework in which cross-cutting working can thrive, supporting departments and promoting cross-cutting action whilst intervening directly only as a last resort.

The central message of the report is that simply removing barriers to cross-cutting working is not enough.... A number of alternative approaches are described in the report...Creating the right environment in which these solutions can work is critical, and the signals which Ministers give civil servants about the priority they wish to be given to cross-cutting approaches is the key to it all.

The reports give a lucid account of the balance that a successful commando centre will have to maintain between intensification and relaxation of control, without suggesting how in practice this balance is to be achieved. Thus the Cabinet Office's *Wiring it Up* paper insists that 'conflicting priorities will be sorted out at a strategic policy level and not allowed to undermine efficient and effective service delivery' (section, 5.1). But it also insists on 'the need for the centre to recognise its limitations and...to look to service deliverers and end-users to signal where there are existing (or potential) failures to work cross-departmentally (section 11.4). The same report emphasises the value of 'a clear over-arching framework of objectives and targets for each policy which can readily be translated into meaningful targets and objectives at lower levels of government' (section 5.1). Yet it stresses as well that a sophisticated approach to local measures and targets is needed so that they 'are not necessarily cascaded from those at national level but define what is needed at local level to deliver the national objective' (section 7.22).

In a closely related paper for the Scottish Council Foundation, *Holistic Government: Options for a Devolved Scotland*, Leicester and Mackay (1998) argue that creation of a new parliament and executive provides an opportunity to incorporate, from the start, the lessons of recent years. Drawing on the debates under discussion here, they too argue for selective use of many different types of civil-service structure—each suited to some tasks but suffering from distinctive limits as well—to promote effective, inclusive and democratic governance. But they emphasise participation and partnership at least as much as an eclectic reform of the civil service. In particular they argue that the new Scottish government must be designed to employ a range of processes or 'operating codes' to make use of reformed structures singly and together. Besides the familiar forms of parliamentary debate, market contract and hierarchical administration these include managing networks, diplomacy, partnership, problem solving, deliberation and provisional consensus, direct democracy and participation, anticipatory government through scenario planning, preventative government through both participation and new forms of measurement, and flexible government through combining insiders and outsiders. (See also Perri 6, 1997, on which much of this is based.)

Many, if not all, the tensions we identify in these reform proposals will be familiar to their authors. They advance their proposals because they assume— often without stating they do—that it is both necessary and impossible to combine the advantages of largely informal, local knowledge passed in networks with the panoramic capacities of formal bureaucracy. The commando centre promises the necessary panorama. But creating a new bureaucratic élite with the flexibility to define cross-cutting projects invites a new centralisation: a Whitehall redux, cut off from local knowledge and therefore co-ordinating in the dark. Devolution to local networks might seem the countermeasure. But this is to put enormous faith in the self-co-ordination abilities of society itself. It is to assume, as Perri 6 puts it that 'the best that can be hoped for is a constant and shifting process of negotiations, bargaining games and mutual adjustment across networks of organisations, without overarching objectives' (Perri 6, 1997, p. 70). (Notice that the National Performance Review—the reinvention of government agency created by Vice-President Al Gore, operating in a setting where the federal government never had the powers of even a chastened Whitehall, comes close to accepting this conclusion. Its current goal is to build 'communities of practice' in which innovative local and state officials network with each other to create cross-cutting programmes.) Given these irreconcilable conflicts between the two types of organisation, and hence the need for tradeoffs, some combination of commando centres and networked locales looks reasonably attractive under current conditions.

At a sufficiently high level of abstraction this assumption is incontrovertible: only an omniscient being can have full knowledge of wholes and parts. But the assumption assumes away crucial, current innovations in the nature of organisation itself, which, blurring the distinction between bureaucratic formality and networked informality, allow for co-ordination in the changes of parts and wholes unattainable by conventional means. These breakthroughs, pioneered, but no longer limited or even best exemplified by modern Japanese firms, are now commonplace in diverse industries including automobiles, computers, semiconductors, athletic shoes and garments. We introduce the new model firm here to demonstrate the availability of an alternative to the principal-agent model, which holds the promise of relaxing the constraints that the principal-agent model treats as inherent in relations between centre and locales.

The pragmatist firm and democratic experimentalism

The setting for the new model firm is the pervasive ambiguity of purpose and capacities we have just been describing. The principal-agent model takes for granted that principals know what they want, and the chief task of organisational design is to prevent opportunism by self-interested agents. The new model firm, and the form of public administration associated with it, assumes on the contrary that the chief problem for organisations is determining what they and their collaborators, internal and external, should do, and how. Firms operating on principal-agent lines try, as we saw, to clarify goals to prevent agents from using ambiguities in the determination of ends to hijack the organisation. New model firms assume, like the scientists and citizens depicted in American pragmatism, that it is impossible, on the contrary, to eliminate such ambiguity. Instead, these pragmatist firms build organisations that allow for the clarification of ambiguous ends through the exploration of means, and vice versa: They deliberately perturb their beliefs by testing them in use, and unsettle what they learn from this by using it in new ways.

But note that in their emphasis on the search for means and ends pragmatist firms do not presume collaborators to be selfless and without guile. The presumption is rather that the same mechanisms that allow for the collaborative exploration of means and ends also permit assessment of the reliability of collaborators. A comparison of the design practices and customer-supplier relations in the two types of firms illustrates the distinctive features of pragmatist organisation, and in particular the novel role of the organisational centre.

In the standard firm initial product designs aim to be integral and definitive. Products are conceived from the first as integral wholes: Their major parts are customised to work only with other parts of the same make or model. This entails as well a striving for definitiveness from the outset in order to avoid inadvertent incompatibilities among the key components: Given the mutual specialisation of parts, the discovery late in the product-development cycle that, say, the car engine is unsuited to the proposed transmission means a costly, time-consuming reconfiguration not only of these, but also of the chassis, electric system and so on. Centralisation of design and timidity of design choices are by-products. The attraction of drawing on expertise outside the central design team is offset by fears that subordinates, even if well intentioned, might introduce innovations ultimately incompatible with other parts of the tightly connected design. With centralisation goes timidity. Fear of possible incompatibilities also leads to the (re-) use of already proven components, at the cost of innovation. In practice, of course, the standard firm is not as centralised or timid as this schematic suggests. Rather, it knows the cycles of decentralisation and recentralisation, networking and commando centralism familiar from the discussion above.

Design proposals in the pragmatist firm are modular and provisional. The product is conceived from the first as a system of sub-systems or modules, each defined by and compatible with the others so long as it meets a set of performance criteria. The first outline of the eventual design is elaborated by benchmarking: a central team reviews the characteristics of the best competing products, evaluates the possibility that potential innovations will move from research lab to market during the current design cycle, and then proposes a design reflecting feasible improvements and market-ready innovations. The design team then identifies module makers with the relevant expertise and asks them to evaluate and improve the module in their domain on the basis of their own benchmarking review of possibilities. As the parts are re-elaborated the centre adjusts the overall design so that changes in one module remain compatible with the performance specifications of the other. Reciprocating changes in parts and whole continue (within time constraints imposed by the market) until a stable solution emerges.

This design process corresponds to an open or federated form of organisation, rather than a closed one; it invites, indeed depends on the open consideration of alternatives rather than discouraging it. It would be pointless to call attention to new possibilities in the outside world through benchmarking only to dismiss them if their pursuit requires collaboration with outsiders. In effect, then, the organisation has to be configured so that it can be substantially re-configured in every product cycle. Indeed such openness to 'outside' points of view turns out to be an indispensable conditions of the pragmatist organisation's success: By using each of many different design proposals as a foil for understanding the strengths and weaknesses of the competing ones, the pragmatist organisation can forgo much of the minute, initial analysis of design implications that standard firms require to ferret out hidden defects. This is why pragmatist organisations can manage the counterintuitive trick of considering a greater number of design variants than standard firms while shortening the design cycle and reducing design errors in the bargain.

These differences are reflected in turn in differences in the kinds of components standard and pragmatist firms buy from other companies, and the conditions under which they buy them: their customer-supplier relations. At the limit, because product designs are integral and parts, specialised for each, are suited to only one make or model, the standard firms buys little of consequence from outside suppliers. It is the only customer for its crucial components, and the only producer able to make them. This is vertical integration. But even firms that are vertically integrated in this general way are not completely self-sufficient. They buy commodities—parts or materials whose relevant characteristics can be fully catalogued—in the open market; they buy products less fully specified than commodities, but not so enmeshed in the particulars of the design as a whole as those made internally from outside suppliers via long-term or relational contracts: agreements recognising that ambiguities in contractual specifications will lead to conflicts, and therefore provide a mechanism, such as arbitration, for resolving them. (By fully specifying all the obligations of service providers in contracts, the NPM aimed at undercutting the need for vertical integration in the provision of services, thereby stripping the legitimacy from monopoly providers, especially government. Contractualisation also made it harder for interest groups and civil servants to play on their expertise to enter into self-serving relational contracts with the government.)

In the pragmatist firm, in contrast, there is at the limit no difference between an inside and an outside supplier. Indeed it is unclear whether the firm need have any in-house production capacity at all. Any entity that can engage in co-design, and then produce modules that meet the agreed performance standard is a candidate supplier. Given the importance of keeping abreast of outside developments through benchmarking, and the risk that internal units can become mired in habit, external suppliers, themselves able to learn from a wide range of customers, may even be advantaged in competition with internal units that can learn only from one.

Similarly, because the parties can not say in advance what they intend to do together they can not regulate their relations by means of either spot contracts, used to exchange commodities, or relational contracts, which suppose clarity about essentials while providing for the resolution of marginal disagreements. They have recourse instead to what are artlessly called new supplier agreements: slim documents by which they obligate themselves to provide the information necessary to advance the collaboration (by fixing, for instance, one timetable for proposing design solutions, and another for responding to the proposals of other collaborators). As this same information provides a detailed look at the performance and promise of the other parties, it serves a crucial governance function as well: Given the agreed flow of information, each collaborator can periodically assess the capacities and reliabilities of those on whom it depends. (More generally, because this method of collaboration gives early warning of possible breakdowns in co-operation, outsiders can enter the system by undertaking relatively demanding tasks, and then working their way up through the tiers of subcontractors as they demonstrate greater proficiency.)

On one hand, therefore, the pragmatist firm is more decentralised than the standard firm and its boundaries more contestable. The design centre of the pragmatist firm lacks the conclusive authority of its standard counterpart. Conversely, specialised collaborators, above all those outside the formal boundaries of the firm, have powers of initiative in the pragmatist model that are denied them in the standard setting.

But on another, deeper level this contrast is misleading. It suggests that the power of decision making must be held either by the centre or by the specialised locales. So the gains of one are always the loss of the other. But what we observe in the innovations of the pragmatist organisation is something else again: The roles of centre and periphery are being re-defined in ways that moot the question of the distribution of power between them, at least as measured by the yardsticks of the standard model. In the pragmatist organisation the centre proposes broad projects, facilitates reconciliation of alternative solutions, and monitors performance along the way. The locales propose solutions and adjust them, with the help of the centre, in the light of proposals by other collaborators. As projects change, so too does the circle of collaborators. This is an organisation that, from the traditional point of view is neither centralised nor decentralised, and lacks clear boundaries without being diffuse or boundless. Strange as it seems by conventional measures, this organisation is, to judge by the epochal changes underway in the economy, more competitive than standard forms. Next we look at how pragmatist organisations are emerging in public administration as potential answers to the wicked problems of co-ordination.

Democratic experimentalism and the new centre in public administration

As pragmatist institutions are at home with ambiguity and complexity, the world of public problem solving is as much their habitat as the world of production and exchange. Indeed, they are particularly suited to addressing the wicked problems, whose solutions change in time, and must be differentiated to suit varied contexts, and therefore require organisations that somehow combine apparently irreconcilable features of formal bureaucracies and informal networks. They do this in the public sector as in the private one by establishing a novel kind of formal relation between centre and locales that provide transparency and possibilities for systematic learning unavailable in informal networks, without creating the fixity that limits the capacity of bureaucracies to adapt.

To show in some detail how this new centre works, and to indicate the very general conditions under which it can arise, we present the case of school reform in Chicago.

We focus on school reform because it presents in sharp relief a series of developments, culminating in governance innovation, observed in the US in areas as diverse as environmental regulation, the treatment of substance abusers, provision of child-protective and other services to at-risk families, as well as reform of the police and many other aspects of the criminal-justice system. After decades of skirmishing, inveterate antagonists (in the case of education: school administrators, teachers and parents) exhaust confidence in their respective strategies and relax doctrinal commitments (more resources for the public schools as against privatisation), not least because the partial successes of each side cast doubt on the validity of its larger programme (more money for schools does not by itself lead to improved performance by pupils; pilot programmes to privatise schools show how hard it is to write effective performance contracts to discipline providers). Facing urgent problems (crumbling schools and disastrous drop-out rates) the actors agree to explore new solutions, without agreeing to put aside differences in values that originally divided them (whether government is in principle good or bad). As they institutionalise their experimental efforts they stumble on arrangements that permit the piecemeal re-elaboration of complex wholes through the reconsideration of their parts: Local actors (individual schools and the parents, teachers and students that constitute them) are given substantial liberty to set goals for improvement and the means for accomplishing it. In return they must propose measures for assessing their progress and provide rich information on their own performance. The centre (the municipal or state school department) pools the information provided by local actors and ranks them according to (periodically revised) performance measures that give substance to standards of excellence and definitions of inadequacy. In the best cases the centre provides assistance to those that are not improving as quickly as their likes. At all events it eventually sanctions those whose continuing failure seems incorrigible. The system increases local innovation by allowing those on the spot to test, within broad limits, their assumptions of what works best. At the same time it makes the exercise of local discretion sufficiently transparent to assure public accountability, allowing each locale to learn from the experiences of the others, and the polity as a whole to draw lessons from the experience of all. Thus is created a framework for establishing what is currently feasible, how those who fall short can work to achieve it, and how those doing well can do better still. These arrangements allow the parties to get a grip, in a way to be specified in a moment, on problems whose complexity once seemed to put them beyond the reach of public action. They create new possibilities for citizens to steer public institutions that affect their vital interests by involving them in forms of problem solving that unsettle encrusted beliefs. Because this architecture, like that of the pragmatist firm, takes its own starting points as arbitrary, and corrects its assumptions in the light of the results that they produce, we call it experimentalist.

We focus on the Chicago reforms in particular for three reasons. The first is simply their scope and complexity. The Chicago school system is big enough, including the 560 elementary (K-8) and high (9-12) schools in the city limits, so that key aspects of the new relations between local schools and superintending centre established in Chicago could plausibly be a model for large-scale change. Second, the progress of reform in Chicago shows that it is possible to advance by deliberately disruptive half measures or bootstrapping: taking a step that both loosens the grip of the old system and prompts an exploration of alternatives, from which emerges a next step that does the same. The protagonists had good reasons for their actions every step of the way, yet came to understand the architecture of the new system they were building and how it avoided the apparently inevitable choice between bureaucratic centralisation and market-mimicking decentralisation only when construction was far advanced. Thus we do not have to learn exactly the right lessons from Chicago (or anywhere else) to address wicked problems as they did. Finally, the reforms are exemplary in their results so far. They demonstrate that large school systems can be made manageable in the sense that particular schools can say what they intend to do by way of reforms, and then actually do what they intend (or be held to account if they do not).

Chicago was one of the last of the large American cities to adopt the Progressive programme of removing the public schools from what was presumed to be (and often was) the despoiling grasp of elected officials, and entrusting it to professionals accountable to their own best, scientific understanding of their responsibilities, and of hierarchical organisations as uniquely efficient and—because of their formalism—incorruptible. But starting in 1947 a central office set budgets and made purchasing and personnel decisions for all the schools. In time selection of textbooks and the scheduling of the school day were centralised as well.

Even as the system was becoming more rule bound and hence less responsive to changes in its environment, the rise of the Civil Rights movement and insistence on school desegregation placed new demands upon it. A study commissioned by the school board in 1963 found that the new administration ignored the needs for local diversity. Central regulations, moreover, blocked local adjustment: Teachers could not even schedule discussions of possible changes in their home schools without headquarters' permission. The only sequel to the report was more reports confirming a worsening situation. By the mid-1980s citizens were so frustrated that advocacy of school decentralisation had become a social movement including business interests, local groupings focused on problems in particular schools, and broad groups, such as Designs for Change, that elaborated decentralisation programmes and built networks of supporters through discussion of the ideas.

The first, deeply disruptive break with the old system came in the period from 1987 through 1996, and produced a thorough, but still largely conventional, form of decentralisation. The immediate impetus to change was a teachers' strike—the ninth in the preceding nineteen school years—which came to symbolise the paralysing system's self-absorption. The conflict seemed to require engagement by wider circles, whose projects were in any case merging. The result was an alliance between Designs for Change and reformers in the business community in favour of state legislation providing for site-based governance.

Under the legislation each school in the Chicago system was to be governed by an elected local school council (LSC) composed, for elementary schools, of six parents, two teachers, two community members, and the principal. High school LSCs were to add a twelfth, student, member. The LSCs were given the power to hire and fire the principal, prepare the budget, and develop comprehensive three-year school improvement plans. As part of the compromise with business interests, proponents of decentralisation accepted system-wide monitoring of results by a central office created for the purpose. Early results were mixed: Some school councils made wise use of their powers, others did not. There were cases of corruption. The reality of decentralisation brought to mind the virtues of centralised administration.

The next and decisive development of reform was the passage in 1995 of further legislation clarifying the relation between local and central governance institutions and making manifest the novel division of labour emerging between them. The new law simultaneously increased the powers and capacities of local school councils to pursue their own course of action, and the powers of the central office to intervene in case the results of local decisions are unsatisfactory. For example, to increase local autonomy and capacity, monies previously passed from the central office to the schools for use for specific purposes—such as the construction of playgrounds—would now be available to them as block grants to be spent as changing local circumstances suggested. Authority over building engineers and janitors passed from the central office to the LSCs. Determination of class size and the schedule of the academic year were excluded as subjects of central bargaining between the Chicago public schools and the teachers union, and thus left to local negotiation. The law required additional training (funded by the central office) in the preparation of school budgets and improvement plans, as well as the selection of principals. To increase local accountability the law authorised the central authority to intensify scrutiny of poorly performing schools and place the poorest performers—those where fewer than fifteen percent of the students tested met national standards—on probation or remediation lists. Listed schools would be inspected by an 'intervention team' that advised the LSC and school staff on instructional, administrative and governance improvements.

In practice the L/Cs are autonomous enough to undertake fundamental reorganisation of local schools, while the central intervention teams have the remedial capacities to establish accountability, but an in a way that reduces the dangers of reversion to centralised control either at the school level or above. Thus, in their three-year school improvement plans the L/Cs can propose specialised programmes in, say, dance or business, innovative methods for teaching disciplines such as mathematics, or new, project-based, collaborative pedagogies broadly applicable to nearly the whole curriculum. In the same plans the LSCs can also obtain financing for construction that facilitates curricular reforms, or makes the school more hospitable. An ambitious LSC can reorient the school and its methods to put learning at the service of a social project and vice versa: In one case a school was rededicated as an academy teaching an Afro-centric curriculum by drill methods (Direct Instruction) thought by the principal and the LSC (but only a small minority of education experts) to be especially beneficial for disadvantaged students.

For their part, officials in the new centre exercise their authority to complement, not challenge, the local autonomy. Even when a school is failing so badly that dissolution is immanent, the new centre issues no directives for reconstruction. Instead, the chief purpose of the intervention teams is to help the LSC prepare a 'remediation' plan for removing the blockages to local discussion and decision-making that prevented improvement by normal means. Only if these turnaround plans fail is the school finally 'reconstituted,' and teachers and the principal required to reapply for jobs. This means that the intervention consists far more in analysing with the local participants the causes of their past difficulties than proposing, let alone imposing, concrete measures for reorganisation. Accountability in the form of remediation plans does not, in other words, plant the seeds of recentralisation.

First indications are that the new institutional machinery works. A crude measure of the interest and participation of local parents in school reform is that elections to LSCs are orderly and attract competent candidates in sufficient numbers. Although it might be expected that only wealthy communities have the wherewithal to profit from the new institutions, poor communities have made as good use of local control as better off ones. Studies that rank LSCs by the effectiveness of their use of school improvement plans find the best performers as likely to be located in poor catchment areas as middle class or rich ones. Test scores are rising, but not, so far, in a pattern that can be connected to the effects of decentralisation.

The one incontestable achievement so far is that, as noted at the outset, local schools are manageable again. Reform plans are made and enacted. This is not, to be sure, a sufficient condition for effective reform: Enacting a bad plan does not improve a school or a school system, except insofar as it warns others away from a dead end. But manageability is a necessary condition of reform: Unless plans can be made and implemented, any success is a matter of chance—the result of stumbling upon something that works—and efforts to learn from it will be haphazard as well. In making the schools manageable, therefore Chicago decentralisation creates a foundation on which further efforts to tackle the wicked problem of education can be built.

A more complete account would have to be at once more expansive and more cautious: More expansive because it would have to show how states such as Texas, Kentucky, and Florida are developing elaborate institutions for assessing performance of schools and pupils. Instead of setting minimum acceptable levels for the performance of teachers and pupils, as was commonplace in the 1980s, the new systems set standards for the improvement of schools, and reset these periodically in the light of actual experience. Instead of focusing exclusively on global outcome measures (math scores, graduation rates), the new systems provide more fine-grained measures of learning (ability to formulate a mathematical problem, ability to choose and manipulate the appropriate formalism). These operational or guiding standards are more like the measures of inventory turns or error rates that pragmatist firms use to improve their performance than measures like stock price or growth rate that investors use to judge overall performance. They allow teachers and students to see where problems arise, and correct them before they ramify. Finally, instead of sanctioning poor performers, the new systems provide resources in the form of programmes in professional development for teachers and, infrastructure for the exchange of experience, and funds for planning local school improvement. In short these states, and many others following their example, are becoming new, experimentalist centres, thus complementing and re-enforcing the governance reforms illustrated in the Chicago experience.

But the fuller account would have to be more cautious as well, underscoring the ways that old antagonisms—between, say public-school advocates and privatisers—can be fought out in new settings: By making standard tests very demanding, failure a bar to promotion and graduation, and refusing aid to students or schools that do badly, opponents of public education aim to precipitate an immediate crisis of the schools, with profit to the privatisation movement from the resulting frustration. But while old conflicts can still be revived, doing so takes an ever less likely alignment of the political stars. That itself is a crude measure of how much has already changed.

Parliament, ministries: democratic experimentalist possibilities for the future?

What are the implications of the introduction of experimentalist institutions on the general framework of representative democracy: legislature, courts, ministries? What is the relevance, if any, of democratic experimentalism for the institutions of the new Scottish democracy in particular? An answer to the first question exceeds the bounds of this essay. An answer to the second is beyond our competence. Nonetheless, by way of conclusion and introduction to discussion, we suggest a practical vantage point from which to consider the general implications of pragmatist institutions for democracy, and ask whether certain Scottish developments may have anticipated the transformations we are considering.

The vantage point that connects large, but still localised changes in democratic institutions to the possibility of a change in democracy itself is the new, framing centre. In the education case we just examined this was the new central office of the Chicago school system, or its counterpart at the state level in Kentucky or Texas. But it could have been a ministry of health or an environmental protection agency as well. Its purpose, we saw, was to create a framework for experimentation by defining broad problems, setting provisional standards, pooling measurements of local performance, aiding poor performers to correct their problems, and revising standards and overall goals according to results. A convenient way to see the implications of such centres for the democratic solution to the wicked problems is to work down from this centre to local units, and up to higher level ones.

Working down we see that it is the local units that do the problem solving. It is they, not the central office, that experiments with cross-cutting solutions, combining various packages of services, delivered by different means, as circumstances suggest. Seen in isolation these units look much like the informal networks or intergovernmental institutions mentioned above, crossing boundaries to solve problems with little attention paid to the transgressions. But they do not operate in isolation. They are accountable to the centre, and to their local constituents, who participate in formulating its plans, and judge it both against those goals and in comparison to the performance to the performance of other locales in like circumstances. This is not straight-line accountability in the principal-agent sense, nor the accountability that comes form the US separation of powers. But as the Chicago example shows it is both a real discipline and a real aide to systemic learning.

Working up from the centre to its authorising body—a legislature, typically—we arrive quickly at a conclusion about the essential features of the latter. If the purpose of the centre is to frame experimentation, then the purpose of the legislation is, as it were, to frame the frame: to create a broad space within which the ministry can itself facilitate the search for and evaluation of solutions. Does this mean that the history of the administrative state has come full circle and that the legislature is being asked to delegate unlimited authority to administrative agencies all over again? No, because the agency is not being asked to fill in the details of rules in the name of the assembly. It is rather the citizens who are doing that, under conditions of transparency that allow review by the public as a whole, the administrative agency, and those affected by the programme in question. The shift is very broadly speaking away from representative and towards participatory democracy. That is 'delegation' of a sort, but not self evidently an affront to sovereign power of a people to make law for itself. The construction of parallel governments—one local government of elected officials, another, dedicated perhaps to economic development—composed of participant citizen problem-solvers—makes discussion of such questions anything but theoretical.

This brings us finally to Scotland here and now, and a final question. At a great remove it seems that Scottish Enterprise, the LECs it groups, as well as parts of the educational system already operate in part—but only in part—on experimentalist lines. Pragmatists, we said, are committed to exploring ambiguity by putting ideas to use. From that vantage, the best way for us no less than for you to sort out what we have been saying is to see whether you could use make us of it, or already are. Can you? Are you?

SECTION THREE

DEVOLVED POLICY STRATEGIES AND INSTRUMENTS

—

CHAPTER 4

POLICIES FOR ENTREPRENEURSHIP

What explains differences in levels of entrepreneurship activity?

There are considerable national and sub-national differences in levels of entrepreneurship activity within the OECD, and it is useful to understand what influences these differences in order to design effective policies to promote entrepreneurship.

One useful source of information at the national level is the Global Entrepreneurship Monitor (GEM) report (Reynolds et al, 2000). This report combined surveys, national data sets and expert interviews in 21 countries to examine the factors associated with differing levels of entrepreneurship and to make recommendations on how policy can better stimulate entrepreneurship. The report shows up significant variations in levels of entrepreneurship activity amongst the 21 countries examined. For example, in the United States 1-in-10 adults was attempting to start a new business at the time of survey compared for example with 1-in-12 in Australia, 1-in-25 in Germany and 1-in-33 in Spain but only 1-in-100 in Ireland and Japan.

There is also evidence of marked variations in rates of entrepreneurship between regions within countries. Here a key source is Reynolds et al (1994), which reports on regional variations in new firm birth rates in five European countries and the United States. Using data mainly from the 1980s, this evidence shows that in the European countries the most fertile regions had annual new firm birth rates between 4 and 7 times higher than the least fertile (with the magnitude of differences partly reflecting the number and size of the regions in each country). Specifically, new firm formation rates were 2.7 times higher in the most fertile region than in the least fertile region in Germany, 4.0 times higher in Ireland and Italy, 6.0 times higher in the UK and 6.5 times higher in Sweden. In the United States between 1986 and 1988 the best-performing region had a new firm formation rate that was 48 times higher than the worst performer.

What explains these geographical differences in entrepreneurship rates? Both Reynolds et al (2000) and OECD (1998a) provide answers to this question. First, the Reynolds et al (2000) report highlights the following critical factors:

– *Finance*. National experts considered problems with finance to be one of the principal factors hindering entrepreneurship in their country and the relationship between finance and levels of entrepreneurial activity was confirmed in the data. The availability of early-stage finance, either from informal sources such as private individuals or formal sources such as venture capital funds, is greater among countries that have higher levels of entrepreneurial activity.

– *Education*. Education plays a vital role in entrepreneurship. The report identified that if the level of participation in post-secondary education were the only factor used to predict entrepreneurial activity, it would account for 40% of the difference between GEM countries. Providing individuals with quality entrepreneurship education was one of the top priorities identified by national experts.

– *Fundamentals*. The GEM report also argued that policies geared towards boosting entrepreneurial activity should not be confined to the entrepreneurship sector per se but should also extend to the macro-economic fundamentals of a country like markets, competition and regulations. In particular, the most entrepreneurially active countries had a greater ease of doing business with the government, more flexible labour markets and lower levels of non-wage labour costs.

– *Social legitimacy*. The perceived social legitimacy of entrepreneurship was also argued to make a difference. Thus it was found that measures such as (a) the extent to which fear of failure acts as a deterrent to starting a new firm and (b) respect for those starting new firms were associated with differences in levels of entrepreneurial activity.

These conclusions are in line with those of the OECD put forward in the publication 'Fostering Entrepreneurship' (OECD, 1998a). This study recommends that governments work on the following three key factors in order to foster entrepreneurship:

- *Conducive framework conditions.* Achieving proper framework conditions - the institutional arrangements within which economic activity takes place - should be the foundation of policy. Healthy entrepreneurship requires the creation of a stable macroeconomic environment and structural policies to produce well-functioning markets. Thus it is argued that governments need to create competitive product markets, efficient capital markets (including venture capital), flexible labour markets, simplify the administrative burden of government and reduce the cost of firm closure and bankruptcy.

- *Supportive cultural attitudes.* Although cultural attitudes are formed through complex processes that are not clearly understood, cultural factors do appear to affect entrepreneurship. In particular, cultural factors appear to affect the willingness to co-operate with others, which can facilitate entrepreneurship. It is argued that the role of education in creating positive attitudes towards entrepreneurship merits further attention.

- *Well-designed government programmes.* Government programmes, if well-designed, can also promote entrepreneurship. Many OECD countries have a wide range of programmes designed to assist business, although not all of these have the fostering of entrepreneurship as their primary objective. In some cases programmes are targeted on different types of businesses, for example, small businesses, high tech enterprises, start-ups and so on. Other programmes are targeted on specific aspects of business such as finance, innovation, development of business skills and so on.

Although both Reynolds et al (2000) and OECD (1998a) focused largely on fostering entrepreneurship at national level, clearly many of these factors are also relevant at city and regional level and amenable to influence by local policies.

Comprehensive entrepreneurship programmes

OECD (1998a) identifies a wide range of specifically local policies and programmes that can be introduced to stimulate entrepreneurship in cities and regions. The instruments identified include finance (Mutual Guarantee Associations, loan guarantees, venture capital, business angels), advice and information services (including one-stop shops), business incubators and science parks, promotion of networks and local enterprise clusters, and skills and training programmes for entrepreneurs. A number of them have been the subject of specific publications by the OECD LEED Programme, on micro-financing (OECD, 1998b), local enterprise clusters (OECD, 1996b), and business incubators (OECD, 1999e). In addition, there are many local programmes designed for specific target groups such as youth (OECD, 2001c), women (OECD, 1990b, 2001e) and ethnic minorities.

A recent OECD review of programmes for youth entrepreneurship (OECD, 2001c) reveals the wide range of actors and initiatives involved, covering regional and local government programmes, private sector programmes, non-profit sector programmes and partnership programmes and covering various types of initiatives. Figure 1 below, taken from that publication, shows the broad range of players and programmes involved. What is problematic then is not a lack of available instruments but the fact that local programmes have tended to develop in an unco-ordinated manner. As a result often there are not clear linkages between the different programmes that could help an entrepreneur and there is no strategic overview of where there are gaps in provision or duplications. One of the conclusions of recent OECD work on the local dimension of entrepreneurship is therefore that cities and regions should examine how they can pull existing and new initiatives together into a more coherent strategy for entrepreneurship. These strategies should address not only traditional instruments, such as access to finance, but should also consider whether other policies and programmes at regional level can improve the framework conditions and cultural attitudes that also influence entrepreneurship levels.

Figure 1.   Programmes to Promote Youth Entrepreneurship: A Schematic Presentation

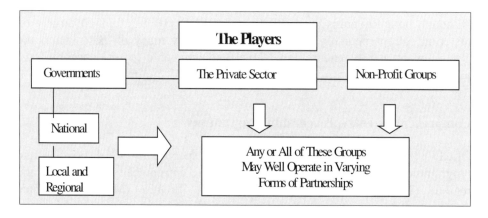

Figure 1.   (continued)

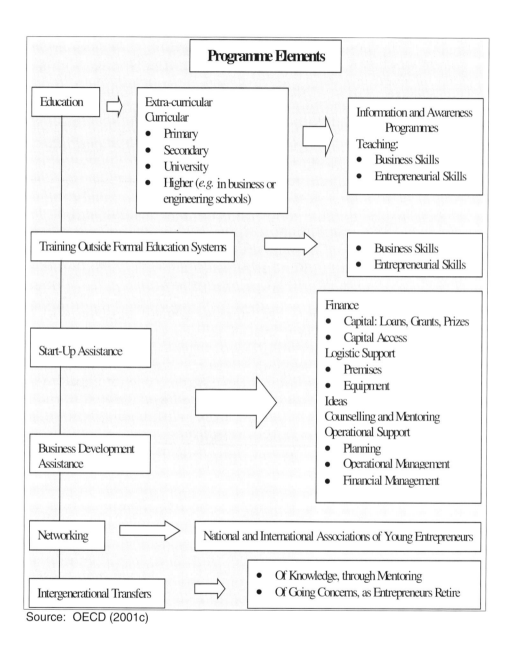

Programme Elements

Education ⇒ Extra-curricular
Curricular
- Primary
- Secondary
- University
- Higher (*e.g.* in business or engineering schools)

⇒ Information and Awareness Programmes
Teaching:
- Business Skills
- Entrepreneurial Skills

Training Outside Formal Education Systems ⇒
- Business Skills
- Entrepreneurial Skills

Start-Up Assistance

Business Development Assistance

⇒ Finance
- Capital: Loans, Grants, Prizes
- Capital Access
Logistic Support
- Premises
- Equipment
Ideas
Counselling and Mentoring
Operational Support
- Planning
- Operational Management
- Financial Management

Networking ⇒ National and International Associations of Young Entrepreneurs

Intergenerational Transfers ⇒
- Of Knowledge, through Mentoring
- Of Going Concerns, as Entrepreneurs Retire

Source: OECD (2001c)

Wales, in the United Kingdom, has recently developed a comprehensive strategy for entrepreneurship known as the Entrepreneurship Action Plan for Wales. In the past, Wales has not been characterised by high rates of entrepreneurship activity, in large part reflecting its traditional dependence on major heavy industries (coal and steel) and its more recent focus on inward investment attraction as a tool for economic restructuring. However, whilst the attraction of inward investment has created many jobs, especially in the parts of the country with good communications and proximity to major population centres, there is now a concern to ensure that attraction of high quality inward investment is balanced by the stimulation of local entrepreneurship. Thus one of the first resolutions of the new National Assembly for Wales, established in 1999, concerned entrepreneurship:

'The Assembly notes that a successful future for the Welsh economy depends on a strong culture of entrepreneurship and agrees that the relevant Assembly policies should reflect the importance of successful entrepreneurship and the need to increase the level of business start-ups in Wales and the rate of survival, innovation and growth rates among small and medium sized firms in Wales.'
Resolution of the national Assembly for Wales, 13 October 1999

The Welsh Development Agency has therefore recently developed a wide-ranging strategy to address all the factors that are important in stimulating entrepreneurship at a regional level. The Entrepreneurship Action Plan for Wales has three main strands, as shown in Figure 2. The first strand is focused on developing an enterprise culture in Wales. The second strand is focused on creating more start-up businesses and more businesses with growth potential. The third strand is focused on increasing the number and proportion of indigenous businesses that grow to their full potential.

Figure 2. Structure of the Entrepreneurship Action Plan for Wales

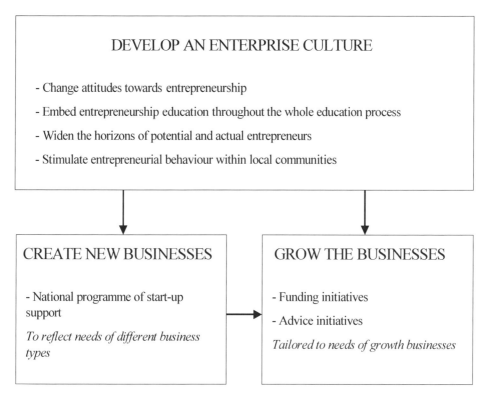

Source: Welsh Development Agency, 2000

Box 5 describes the actions that the Welsh Development Agency has proposed for each of the three strands. Clearly the entrepreneurship strategy is an initiative that is only likely to have its full impact in the long-term and initial targets have therefore been set for the end of 2006.

Box 5. The Entrepreneurship Action Plan for Wales

The following main actions have been proposed for the three strands of the Entrepreneurship Action Plan for Wales:

Strand 1: Develop an Enterprise Culture

i) Change attitudes in Wales towards entrepreneurship

Welsh *role models* to profile Welsh success stories, including people, businesses and products, utilising all aspects of the media, including TV and newspapers.

Creation of high profile *national awards* for enterprise across all sectors and levels and where possible enhance and build on existing events. The objective will be to make these of interest to a wide sector of the population and to increase media coverage.

Development of an *enterprise roadshow* which will travel throughout Wales, providing resources and activities for community groups, educational establishments and family group events.

A National Business Plan *competition* with awards for different sectors. Local competitions (or 'warm-up' competitions with smaller prizes to prepare entrants for the next stage) with entry of finalists into a high profile national competition.

ii) Embed entrepreneurship education

Establish an *Enterprise College* aimed at 18-25 year olds, providing them with an opportunity to obtain an on-line degree in entrepreneurship.

Work alongside the ACCAC (Qualifications Curriculum and Assessment Authority for Wales) to ensure that entrepreneurship is embedded into the *National Curriculum.*

Encourage schools, further education colleges and universities to develop a *strategy for entrepreneurship*.

Encourage schools, further education colleges and universities to incorporate entrepreneurship as a valid and equal *career option* in the career advice provided.

Box 5 (continued)

Encourage young people to understand and experience business through *practical experience* such as Young Enterprise Wales.

Work experience programmes with start-up businesses to help students explore the process of evaluating new ventures and making recommendations for future action.

Small business *summer schools* aimed at providing opportunities for groups of school, FE, HE students and staff and community members to participate in small business education and training programmes offered during short term concentrated periods.

Development of *entrepreneurship teaching materials* for incorporation into existing subjects such as mathematics, languages, art and science to develop entrepreneurial skills and attitudes.

Building on *work shadowing* schemes that would place an individual from any sector into an entrepreneurial environment within or outside their own sector.

Specific programmes of enterprise to be developed for *further education and higher education* students.

Entrepreneurial programmes for *teachers* which encourage and support the development of entrepreneurial skills and experience for teachers, lecturers and advisers involved in the educational process at all levels, from primary to higher education.

iii) Widen horizons

Development of an *internet site* aimed at Welsh entrepreneurs stimulating awareness of entrepreneurship and acting as an ideas bank for those wishing to start a business.

Encouraging *public sector entrepreneurship* as a strategic priority with the development of entrepreneurial initiatives within their programmes of support and development.

Box 5 (continued)

Networking with international entrepreneurs by helping potential and existing Welsh entrepreneurs to link into specialised international networks of entrepreneurs such as the North America-Wales Chambers of Commerce.

Opportunity awareness programmes, such as exchange programmes for individuals and groups to experience and learn from other environments which can stimulate their own entrepreneurial activity.

Entrepreneurship experience programmes tailored to the particular needs of individuals to make direct contact with entrepreneurial behaviour.

Entrepreneurship clubs (E-Clubs), both real and on-line, providing individuals with opportunities for acquisition of knowledge and exchange of ideas.

iv) Entrepreneurial behaviour within communities

A comprehensive *review* of existing initiatives, identifying examples of good practice.

Encouragement of enterprise in the community, by extending the Business in the Community large firm approach, by using existing or retired small business entrepreneurs to develop new community projects in partnership with local people.

Extension of *placement programmes* to the community sector so that those students with the necessary skills can assist development of local community projects and learn from this approach.

Community entrepreneurship action plans for villages and towns in Wales.

Strand 2: Create new businesses

New business *start-up programmes* that reflect best practice.

Specific support programmes for *under-represented groups* such as women-owned enterprises, youth businesses, third-age entrepreneurs, ethnic minorities, Welsh speakers and the economically inactive.

Box 5 (continued)

Encouragement for the establishment of new high technology businesses, especially through *spin-off activities* from the HE/FE sector in Wales via nationally co-ordinated (but locally delivered) support programmes such as Wales Spinout programme.

A *'Return to Wales' entrepreneurial programme* to attract entrepreneurs back to Wales to start new businesses.

A *business birth rate strategy for women* to provide a framework for formulating actions to encourage more women to start businesses.

Unlocking the potential of entrepreneurs, in particular the early retired, by establishing a *talent bank* to help develop new businesses.

Co-ordinating and creating excellent 'full-service' *incubators* to help support the development of start-ups through their first years.

Community hatcheries geared specifically to the needs of community enterprises with full support on site.

Entrepreneurial Zones to provide training opportunities, resources and support for individuals to establish enterprises.

Credit Unions to offer low-cost financial services to their members on low incomes and excluded from mainstream financial support.

Strand 3: Grow small businesses

An *Enterprise Development Fund for Wales* to provide a comprehensive range of funds to support the growth of SMEs, such as the Wales Innovation Fund, Wales Small Loan Fund and Xenos Business Angel Network.

A co-ordinated series of *financial support* packages to assist Welsh SMEs in access the finance they require to start up and expand, such as the Mentor Wales and Wales Spinout programmes.

Box 5 (continued)

An *on-line (internet based) business information resource* building on existing initiatives to provide direct access to business information. The resources could include the development of a database of linked databases to facilitate access in particular by small businesses and those advising them to information on government programmes, industry advisory and assistance services, networks and mentoring arrangements, employment services, education and training services.

A *peer-mentoring* scheme, which will provide experienced mentors for companies/entrepreneurs.

Corporate Venturing delivering resources to businesses to allow individuals to be seconded from the usual activities to develop potential spin-out and growth business activities in partnership with the employer.

Networks for entrepreneurship to encourage and support the development of actual and virtual networks and clusters for minority groups such as women entrepreneurs, graduate, family, community and other sector businesses.

Source: Welsh Development Agency, 2000

The entrepreneurship strategy of the state of North Carolina outlined in Box 6 also provide an interesting model for other areas in terms of how it has promoted all-round technology-based economic development that has enabled it to profit from globalisation. Not all cities and regions have the necessary infrastructures and resources to pursue this type of development but it has proved successful in certain areas, particularly where they have good universities and residential attractiveness. Targeted inward investment often forms part of the approach, together with efforts to stimulate new firm formation.

Box 6. Entrepreneurship Policies in North Carolina

North Carolina is a very manufacturing-intensive state ranking about 8th in the USA in terms of total manufacturing value-added and with one of the three highest percentages of state workforces in manufacturing. The story of its economy since 1960 is one of remarkable transformation from one of the poorest states (ranking approximately 4th from bottom on per capita incomes) to one of the better-performing states in the USA in terms of business vitality and a mid-performer in terms of measures like employment, earnings, equity and quality of life (see Schweke, 2000).

In the 1960s state policymakers made a conscious decision to develop the North Carolina economy through promoting technology and training. There were three main strands to this strategy:

1. A major investment was made in a series of technical training institutes, with the policy that no individual in the state would live more than 30 miles from one of these institutes. There are now 58 around the state.

2. Investment was increased for developing the technology research faculties of the state's universities. This helped the attraction of technology-based inward investment and technology transfer more generally. New technology-based inward investment projects have been attracted from companies such as Cisco Systems and Lussen Technologies that strongly emphasise collaboration with the research faculties of the state's universities.

3. Significant investments were made in the research triangle park. This science park was first envisaged in 1959 although it was not until the late 1960s that it attracted its first significant investment and the 1980s before it really took off. Now there are about 40,000 people employed on the research triangle park with tenants including IBM and Glaxo. As well as creating jobs in the research triangle itself the park has become a real driver for nearby rural areas because of its stimulus to the attraction of manufacturing facilities and because of technology links between firms in the rural areas and firms on the park.

Recently, further initiatives to strengthen the state's manufacturing economy include cluster-building policies and policies to encourage collaborations between universities and private companies for the establishment of new spin-off enterprises.

Box 6 (continued)

Overall, the policies based on technology and training have been successful in increasing incomes in the state by transforming the economy from dependency on agriculture and low skilled, low technology manufacturing to a base of high-skilled, high-technology investment.

However, notwithstanding these successes, there is now a more urgent concern to create jobs and increase incomes for those individuals and areas that have been left behind as the state as a whole has developed. In particular, rural parts of the state, which account for approximately 25% of its population, continue to lag. These areas have suffered from the problem of job-destroying growth in traditional manufacturing staples such as textiles and tobacco, caused by increased capital intensity in production. Policymakers in North Carolina are therefore asking themselves how they can attract investment or create and grow existing enterprises in the lagging areas and how they can provide the kind of training that will enable displaced individuals to get new jobs.

Cluster approaches as an organising framework

Many cities and regions in OECD countries have adopted policies and programmes to encourage the growth and strengthening of local enterprise clusters. These cluster approaches can be very useful as a tool for co-ordinating and tailoring the wide range of local policies for entrepreneurship around the needs of existing or emerging sector strengths. The cluster approach has the following strengths:

- It is an inclusive approach to economic development. Cluster interventions cover all parts of a cluster, rather than targeting single companies, and all the players in the system contribute to the definition of the policy objectives.

- It provides the focus for partnership between different cluster players (including customers, suppliers and competitors and supporting institutions such as the utilities, research institutes and education) and encourages collective learning and collective efficiencies.

- Cluster interventions generate externalities for the economy (i.e. benefits that do not accrue to any individual firm), addressing one of the classic areas of market failure in economic development.

- Cluster approaches are aimed at long-term objectives and building on endogenous capabilities.

- Overall, the cluster approach is focused on creating the right local environment for entrepreneurship and economic development rather than subsidising particular firms or initiatives.

It can also be argued that the practice of cluster policy is closely linked to devolution, because it aims to adapt public interventions to the needs of particular locally-concentrated clusters of industry and these needs are best understood and addressed by organisations based locally, and cannot be satisfactorily addressed by policies designed and implemented at the national level. Clustering can also be seen as part of the local response to globalisation, because the local networking that goes on in clusters helps small firms in particular to compete on an equal footing with large firms in an increasingly dynamic and local economy (OECD, 2000a).

At the same time, however, it is generally recognised that it would be a mistake to try and frame policies around clusters if there is not a genuine local strength in that sector. Furthermore, other enterprises that are not within clusters should not be ignored.

The characteristics of clusters

Clusters are local networks of firms in related industries, where there are strong interrelations and agglomeration economies. They can be found in most cities and regions in OECD countries. Although they are by no means an entirely new economic phenomenon (economist Alfred Marshall (1919) identified the importance of clusters such as the textiles cluster around Manchester and the metalworking cluster of Sheffield in England in the 19th century), there is nonetheless a rapidly growing interest by governments in this phenomenon, which has not been sufficiently recognised in recent years. It is striking how high the proportion of economic activities clustered locally actually is. In the United States, for example, in the mid-1990s, 380 local clusters were estimated to be producing approximately 60% of the country's output (Rosenfeld, 1996). Clusters also appear to enhance the economic performance of the enterprises within them. In Italy, it has been shown that being located in a cluster increases the profitability of firms on average by between 2 and 4 per cent (Fabiani et al, 2000).

One of the critical attributes of clusters is that they create agglomeration economies, with firms clustered together in the same industry gaining from specialised labour pools, business services, sources of finance and so on. However, clusters are not just local concentrations of industry, but places where there are real interactions between local firms and between firms and institutions. Within clusters, firms often co-operate with each other, for example in selling and transporting output. They also co-operate with a wide range of other local players such as universities, trade associations, chambers of commerce and local public administrations. This mutual support and co-ordination is often summed up in the ideas of 'social capital' and 'trust', which reduce the transaction costs of dealing with suppliers and collaborators. Even where firms have not worked together before they have information on each other and informal ties that nurture trust. Moreover, these links also help ideas and information to flow more easily within clusters, stimulating the innovation that is critical to competition in an increasingly complex and rapidly moving economy.

Another critical attribute of clusters is that they tend to be very flexible production systems, and this gives them an advantage in responding to the more rapid evolution of globalising markets and technologies. In the globalising economy, networks of small and highly specialised firms can efficiently exploit rapidly changing market niches and compete successfully against large firms, which can no longer rely on scale alone to dominate markets. In theoretical terms, clusters appear to be at the vanguard of the shift referred to in Chapter 2 from traditional 'Fordist' mass production (dominated by standardised goods and services, standardised production methods, low skilled labour and price competition) to a system of 'Flexible Specialisation' (dominated by production of a wide and changing range of customised products and services using flexible, general purpose machinery and skilled adaptable workers).

Policy intervention and clusters

The cluster development strategies that are now being adopted in OECD Member countries frequently target small and medium sized enterprises and use a variety of means to foster business networks and promote collaborative behaviour. Common features of programmes include the encouragement of networking for learning or supplier chain development, provision of market and technical information to the firms in the cluster, provision of certain cluster-specific infrastructure, skills development and training, support for various business services and attraction of foreign investment to fill gaps in the cluster, support for new firm start-ups, finance and support for exports.

In developing a cluster, several of these policy instruments often need to be used together. It is because of this that cluster strategy can be seen as providing a framework for integrating all the main economic development policy instruments available to regional and city governments in a holistic strategy that is tailored to the needs of the area. This strategy has to be developed in a process of collaboration between all the relevant players in the cluster, from the public sector, firms and institutions. Indeed this very process of dialogue can help improve policymaking by identifying gaps where public intervention may be needed.

Much of the recent debate about enterprise clusters has suffered from a tendency to overgeneralise the notion of clusters and to view what are often quite different experiences in the same terms. In reality, clusters can be argued to be of many different types (Markusen, 1996), varying for example in terms of sector, scope and size, history and the resulting patterns of linkages, infrastructure, institutions and so on. The Italian industrial districts are often seen as models for cluster development elsewhere. But, as Balestri and Cavalieri detail in the following chapter, the Italian districts are in certain ways a special case of clustering. They tend to be very small firm based, small in size, contained within small population areas and focused on a range of artisanal production. Therefore they may not necessarily be the best models for areas with larger firm or high-technology oriented production (such as the clusters in Baden-Wurttemberg, Stuttgart or North Rhine Westphalia in Germany).

In particular, there are aspects of the Italian experience of industrial districts that probably cannot be transferred because of their special history, tradition and culture, which is embodied in the strong social embeddedness of the Italian districts. Moreover, whilst Balestri and Cavalieri note that a range of local policy tools have been used to support clusters in the Italian context, including territorial marketing, extension services, policy on industrial real estate, credit guarantee schemes and so on, most central public policy towards industry in Italy has not been targeted towards the industrial districts. This is partly because the industrial districts are often located in areas which are wealthy and therefore do not merit regional policy support and because the districts comprise large numbers of small firms that have not been the traditional recipients of industrial policy support in Italy.

Policies may nonetheless be able to replicate some of the critical features of Italian industrial districts elsewhere. For example, the labour market is one of the central features of the Italian industrial districts, with large skilled labour pools emerging as the result of market processes. In Italy, training has mainly been carried out on the job, sponsored by employers. But in other regions it may be possible to replicate this process with publicly-sponsored training.

Clearly, any public intervention has to be based on an appreciation that clustering is essentially a market process. But public intervention may nonetheless be able to assist in the clustering process if it is focused on tackling market failures and facilitating dynamic adjustments. This can involve the supply of public goods for the sector (such as training courses or technology infrastructure) and the encouragement of networking and positive externalities between firms and organisations within the cluster. In the latter respect, the public sector has a key advantage in that it is generally regarded as an 'honest broker' that is able to create structures and rules to bring players together in a way that will overcome some of their fears about collaborating with others (including competitors).

In developing strategies for clusters, policies need to react to the emerging opportunities and challenges of globalisation. This includes the need to react to increased international competition, the need to respond to increased foreign direct investment in clusters, the need to innovate and the need to respond to cluster decline where it occurs. These challenges are discussed in turn below.

Reacting to increased international competition

Firms today must compete internationally to secure domestic and foreign markets. Even where they sell a very specific niche product, local firms can lose their markets to those in other locations which innovate more rapidly or have lower costs or other advantages. The quality of the city and region territory, and the infrastructure, services, networks and competencies built up in clusters, are critical in helping firms to respond to the challenges of international competition.

The implications of increased competition from the newly-industrialising countries and other sources has been recognised in the well-known industrial districts in the north of Italy, where there is clearly a strong recognition that traditional models now have to change. One element of the response is a focus on territorial marketing. The chapter by Balestri and Cavalieri in this book emphasises the export orientation of firms in the Italian industrial districts and note the fact that a considerable share of these exports comprise products embodying a territorial image, often with a high design content. There is an intangible value here that helps the districts to compete internationally. A number of the Italian districts have sought to capitalise on this by putting into place territorial marketing campaigns that build the image of their cluster with target consumers and investors, based on its specific competencies and specialisations. For example, Carpi is very well known for its specialisation in knitwear, which is very important for marketing by its constituent firms, but is necessarily the result of collective activity. The local development agency in Carpi has therefore implemented a territorial marketing campaign on behalf of local firms in this sector. It can be argued that this helps them compete in some ways with larger enterprises and multinationals that invest huge resources in advertising and communication.

A second, related, aspect of the response of the Italian districts is a move up-market, into higher quality and niche markets in order to resist competition from lower-cost producers in newly-industrialising countries. A new approach to training is seen as a key condition for successful achievement of the shift. Whilst traditionally, training within the Italian industrial districts has been dominated by learning-by-doing, the new competition requires new skills to be developed in languages, computer sciences and so on, requiring a higher degree of education than in the past. A change in the culture of training therefore appears to be occurring in the Italian clusters, with an increased emphasis on the more codified further and higher education systems familiar in other countries such as Scotland and Germany.

A variety of other policy initiatives can be taken to help firms within clusters to respond to increased international competition. For example, policy may seek to exploit the links between firms in clusters to establish joint initiatives for developing exports and international strategic alliances. Thus entrepreneurs from the footwear cluster of the Marches, Italy, have recently undertaken a joint mission to Mexican footwear clusters in Leon and Guadalajara to arrange joint ventures, sales and distribution agreements and technology licensing projects. A series of further examples of collaborative initiatives that help firms in clusters to respond to the challenge of competition are given in OECD/DATAR (2001), such as the Vincenza export consortia in Italy and the pooling of sales forces in the Adour Basin, France, which both receive support from the public sector.

Reacting to increased foreign direct investment in clusters

Clusters are also increasingly exposed to the challenges and opportunities of foreign direct investment. There has been a notable increase in investment by foreign firms in the local productive systems of northern Italy, for example, and this has aroused local fears that multinationals will simply appropriate markets and shift technologies and knowledge overseas. But foreign investment can flow in two directions, and at the same time as foreign firms set up and acquire operations in clusters, firms from clusters may invest, license or subcontract overseas. This again arouses concerns, particularly where internationalisation is motivated by a desire to reduce costs by outsourcing from cheap locations. Does the gradual internationalisation of local productive systems mean that the internal dynamic of clusters will gradually dissipate? This may happen when the foreign investment represents a significant part of the cluster, but equally openness to inward and outward foreign investment can enable clusters to keep ahead in technology, finance and markets. Further research is required to understand better the role of foreign direct investment in clusters.

The challenge of innovation

In the modern economy, the key driver of economic development is innovation. Competitiveness is based on the growth of productivity, on rapid adjustment to the changing needs of consumers and on the continuous adoption of product and process innovations. In many ways, local productive systems already represent beneficial environments for innovation. For example, it is often argued that a network of small firms is much more capable of making quick adjustments to changes in competition and markets than single large plants. Their fertility as incubators for spin-offs and start-ups is also often remarked upon. And despite the fact that information and communications technologies now enable the rapid transfer of information over large distances, the interpersonal face-to-face interactions and the local mobility of labour within clusters improves the circulation of the commercial, financial and technological knowledge that stimulates innovation.

Local productive systems must nonetheless continually innovate and adjust. They must remain territorial environments that are conducive to innovation. To do so, they need to advance in at least three key areas:

> – *Adjustment.* Local productive systems must secure long-term structural adjustment by keeping abreast of leading technologies and by shifting into new and growing markets. Clearly this is critical for any firm or industry. But the fact that specific local productive systems are associated with specific territories adds a further obligation to innovate, because if the local productive system fails to adjust to changing technologies and market demand the territorial economy will lose its principal motor.

- *Information and communications technologies (ICT).* Clusters also need to make use of advances in information and communications technologies, such as electronic mail, computer conferencing, electronic databases, the internet and intranets. ICT is increasingly important in all areas of business, including recruitment, ordering, market research and process control. It is important that firms within local productive systems are not just connected-up, but also really using ICT to its full capacity.

- *The knowledge economy.* A high proportion of new job creation in coming years is likely to be in knowledge-intensive industries and competition in all sectors will increasingly be based on the exploitation of skills and knowledge. Territories with a highly-skilled workforce, a good technology base and inter-firm networks are therefore more likely to be competitive and successful. In the context of the new 'learning economy', local productive systems must develop skilled, adaptable and entrepreneurial workforces, and networks and infrastructures capable of generating and exploiting knowledge.

Supporting declining clusters

Analysts usually associate clusters with growth and dynamism, but there are also situations where clusters are in crisis or decline. There are many examples of once thriving clusters that have now all but disappeared because they failed to adapt to change, but others, like Silicon Valley, have successfully made the transition to new products, new processes and new forms of organisation.

One example of a cluster in crisis is the town of Mazamet in the south of France which, until 20-30 years ago, was one of the main places in the world for treating sheep skins. In the 19th Century Mazamet was at the centre of a large international trade in skins, with imports from Australia, Argentina and so on, and a large amount of financial speculation. Even 30 years ago it remained one of the main banking centres in France, with many experts in dealing in foreign currencies. But now the cluster has nearly completely decayed with only a handful of enterprises remaining and the town is suffering a major crisis. By contrast, the Italian district of Prato, a textiles area specialising in wool processing, has been much more successful in adjusting to change. The history of Prato for 100 years or so has been based on reclaiming wool from rags. But in the 1960s and 1970s the major fashion designers moved from haute couture into the mass market and there was a sharp decline in demand for the fabrics produced in Prato with reclaimed wool. In contrast to Mazamet, however, the processors in Prato were quite successful in adapting production from reclaimed wool to the production of curtains, linens and silk, something which they attribute to the skills and adaptability of the Prato workers. We need to understand more fully the reason why some clusters decay whilst others find a new direction, and to see whether it may be possible for public policy to assist clusters to adjust to shocks and reverse decline, for example by initiatives to forecast changes in demand and technology on behalf of local firms or to support innovation by such firms.

Box 7, outlines the Scottish Enterprise cluster approach, which is a good model for other areas. The approach starts with an effort to understand the needs and specificities of particular clusters and to develop an appropriate strategy through collaboration with local players. A range of policy tools are then used to address these needs, concentrating on where public policy can make a difference. Critically, Scottish Enterprise has not sought to create entirely new clusters of firms. Instead it has worked with clusters which demonstrate strong existing capacity, a willingness from industry players to work together and with the public sector and where there is the potential for policy to make a difference.

Box 7. The Scottish Clusters Approach

Economic development context

Scotland has a population of approximately 5 million people, with a Gross Domestic Product (GDP) per head just below the European Union average. One of the cradles of the industrial revolution, Scotland has undergone major economic restructuring in recent years involving a shift from heavy engineering to light manufacturing and services. It has an extremely open economy, with significant levels of inward foreign investment and a high level of exporting. Some of its strengths are a very strong science sector research base, a large university graduate population and a strong export base (notably, Scotland produces nearly 40% of Europe's personal computers).

Box 7 (continued)

A new Scottish parliament was created on 1 July 1999, with a range of important economic development powers and policy instruments at its disposition. The parliament oversees two key economic development agencies, Scottish Enterprise (covering the bulk of the country's population) and Highlands and Islands Enterprise (covering the more remote areas). Both agencies operate networks of Local Enterprise Companies that help tailor policies to local conditions. Key policy priorities are increasing the level of commercialisation from universities and government research laboratories, increasing the business start-up rate, increasing business investment in research and innovation, increased lifelong learning by Scottish people and achieving greater social inclusion.

Description of the clusters approach

Scotland has several existing and emerging enterprise clusters, characterised by strong linkages and networks between firms, the presence of specialised supporting institutions and infrastructure and well-developed sector labour markets. Both Scottish Enterprise and Highlands and Islands Enterprise have both been involved in activities to support these clusters and to ensure that they remain sustainable, self-reinforcing systems that foster innovation, new firm formation and economic growth.

Various policy instruments are used to develop the clusters, including policies for inward investment, skills development, commercialisation, finance, trade development and start-ups. Which of these are needed and how they are applied depends on the cluster. Significant research and consultation is therefore put into determining how each cluster functions and identifying problems to overcome or opportunities to exploit. This work is not undertaken by the public sector alone, but rather is developed in partnership with all the industry stakeholders. In this way real industry concerns can be identified and private sector initiatives can be triggered as well as public interventions.

Box 7 (continued)

Scottish Enterprise was one of the first economic development agencies to consider the potential of the clusters approach, with research undertaken in 1993 to identify Scotland's clusters and to assess which could benefit from specifically targeted support. Clusters were identified as priorities for action where they had significant prospects for the future, significant Scottish capability or potential to build on, a willingness or demand from public and private sector partners to get involved and where Scottish Enterprise could add something as an economic development agency. Highlands and Islands Enterprise has also contributed to assessing Scotland's key industries and contributed to specific parts of the Scottish cluster strategies.

The clusters that have been the subject of initiatives to date are biotechnology, food and drink, semiconductors, oil and gas, opto-electronics, creative industries, tourism and forest industries. The activities undertaken have involved:

- Identifying the organisations and relationships that make up the cluster.

- Assessing the future trends within these industries.

- Creating deeper and broader links between organisations and stakeholders in the cluster.

- Filling 'strategic gaps' in the cluster to help development.

- Focusing on developing the skills and infrastructure that are needed by all organisations in the cluster to help it grow.

- For each cluster, an action planning exercise has been undertaken with the industry to identify what actions to deliver over a four to five year period. This planning process underpins the creation of partnerships, networks and links and helps generate industry buy-in. In the case of the creative industries cluster, for example, members of the industry itself acted as the consultancy team for the action plan and undertook a large part of the benchmarking and scenario planning for the industry.

- The first action plans were approved in summer 1999 and differ significantly according to the clusters involved. For example:

Box 7 (continued)

- In biotechnology, the main efforts have been on commercialising the academic research base. Grants have been provided for commercialisation, university spin-outs, international marketing campaigns, a training consortium developed between colleges and a Biotech Scotland website.

- In food and drink, the emphasis has been on increasing the value added from raw materials produced in Scotland. This has been encouraged through provision of market intelligence to the sector, supporting structures for sales collaboration and shared logistics by small producers, supporting marketing seminars and 'Meet the Buyer' events and putting in place a cross-industry training programme. An industry website has also been created.

In semiconductors, the objective has been to move Scotland's manufacturing up the value-chain and add more research and development activities. Project Alba has been launched, creating a new campus for Scottish semiconductor design, research and development with participation from local universities and companies and three centres of excellence have been created in local universities. Funding has been supplied to assist certain key product development activities, vocational courses developed for the sector, inward investment marketing initiatives redesigned and the international profile of the sector raised through the media.

The Scottish clusters approach is still at a relatively early stage of development and full results will take time to emerge. Nonetheless, the early reaction from the industry community has been enthusiastic and there has been visible progress in developing common vision, increasing collaboration, increasing international profile and increasing innovation within the supported clusters. An early lesson seems to be that in developing a cluster approach, it is important to avoid building overly rigid walls around clusters and to be flexible enough to respond to ongoing changes taking place in an industry.

Conditions for successful policy intervention in clusters

In June 2000, the OECD organised a major, high level conference in Bologna, Italy, on policies to support entrepreneurship and the development of small and medium-sized enterprises (SMEs). One of the conclusions of this conference was that in a number of countries clusters and networking can stimulate innovative and competitive SMEs (OECD, 2001f). At the end of the conference, the participating ministers and representatives of governments adopted a charter recommending the implementation of a number of public and private sector policy actions to support SMEs. These recommendations covered actions for clusters, innovation, electronic commerce and transition economies. Ministers agreed the three following recommendations for clusters:

- Partnerships involving private actors, non-governmental organisations and different levels and sectors of public administration in local cluster and networking development strategies should be facilitated.

- The private sector should lead cluster initiatives, with the public sector playing a catalytic role according to national and local priorities (e.g., *inter alia*, facilitating private investment with public incentives, facilitating seed funding and monitoring the results of network initiatives).

- Public and private sector bodies should foster the growth of clusters (existing and embryonic) by: improving their access to accommodation and efficient communications and transport infrastructures; facilitating local specialisation in university/industry linkages; disseminating targeted information, including on locational advantages and investment attractiveness; promoting suppliers' networks, technical support services, learning circles and other collaborative undertakings.

In developing actions in these areas, it is important to be careful to avoid certain pitfalls and to follow certain best practices. It is possible to identify at least five conditions for the successful development of public policies for clustering, as outlined below.

Firstly, public authorities should be careful to identify and work only with clusters where they have genuine strengths. Analysis of the economic development strategies now being developed by regions and cities across the OECD shows that in the countries where cluster notions are popular, nearly all cities and regions see themselves as possessing a number of clusters. Yet in reality the number of strong clusters in each country is very limited. The danger is that cluster policies may therefore be unsuccessful in some areas because they target the wrong sectors with the wrong type of policy. Cluster strategies should be based on the industries in which regions and cities have genuine relative strengths nationally or internationally rather than on some list of industries in which the region or city would like to develop strengths.

Secondly, public authorities should avoid trying to compete in a zero-sum game. Analysis of city and region economic development strategies also reveals that in many cases the same industries are being selected by many different areas as their policy targets, particularly where this concerns high technology sectors. In this situation regions and city authorities may be tempted to cite the need to compete with other areas in order to justify expenditures that would not otherwise be accepted. Again the key is to work only with industries where the region or city has a genuine strength. If policy is developed in the context of the real competitive strengths of each city and region, with cities and regions specialising where they have advantage, then competition between cluster policies should be minimised.

Thirdly, public authorities should avoid developing excessive dependencies on particular specialisations. This is a message that will have a particular resonance for cities and regions that have experienced recent structural shocks as firms in previous manufacturing specialisations have shed jobs together. This is not to say that cities and regions should avoid developing specialisations in certain fields. The presence of such specialisations offers external economies that are important in global competition. What it does mean is that cities and regions should not create excessive specialisations, for example where the economy is dependent on only one cluster. Cities and regions could create the basis for structural problems in the future if that sector is affected by shocks such as changing market demand or technologies. At the same time as developing clusters, therefore, policymakers should take steps to maintain a business environment that is generally propitious for all firms. They should support more than one cluster if they have the scope to. And they should seek to ensure that all their clusters remain innovative in their products and processes in order to increase their resilience to possible future shocks.

Fourthly, public authorities should recognise that clusters are not simply a set of local networks, but also need connections with other regions or countries. Frequently, firms in clusters can benefit from national and international strategic alliances, for example for research, training and marketing, as much as from local alliances. Thus local and external networking should not be seen as contradictory, but as complementary.

Fifthly, successful policy also needs the participation of a wide range of stakeholders. Clusters are underpinned by complex partnerships and networks of local firms, universities, chambers of commerce and so on. Strategy for the cluster cannot therefore be imposed from above. The initiatives and inputs of all the stakeholders are required and local industry should be encouraged to co-operate on its own projects.

Summary

There are considerable spatial differences in levels of entrepreneurship activity within the OECD, both at national and sub-national levels. Key factors that help explain these differences include the state of framework conditions or fundamentals, such as a stable macroeconomy and well-functioning markets, cultural attitudes, the perceived level of social legitimacy of entrepreneurship and the extent and quality of government programmes, for example for entrepreneurship education and access to early-stage finance. It is likely that there are strong interconnections between factors in each of these areas, which tend to reinforce each other.

Devolved governments clearly have much to contribute in creating good supporting conditions at local level. Indeed a wide range of programmes does exist at local level. They involve a range of public, private and non-profit actors operating at various scales and a wide range of instruments such as finance programmes, advice and information services, business incubators and science parks, network and cluster programmes and skills and training programmes for entrepreneurs. The problem identified in this chapter, however, is that these local programmes have tended to develop independently rather than in a holistic manner.

It has therefore been argued that a more comprehensive approach is needed to local entrepreneurship policies that recognises the wide-ranging nature of the influences on entrepreneurship (including culture and framework conditions as well as government programmes for direct support of start-ups) that recognises that different influences reinforce one another and that seeks to build a healthy overall environment for entrepreneurship.

The Welsh Development Agency's Entrepreneurship Action Plan for Wales is one example of how cities and regions can pull together a wide range of existing and new initiatives into a more coherent strategy for entrepreneurship. The Welsh strategy has three interconnected strands, i) develop an enterprise culture, ii) create new businesses, and iii) grow the businesses, and an integrated set of actions in each strand.

The use of cluster approaches can also be a useful way of co-ordinating and tailoring local policies for entrepreneurship around the needs of existing or emerging clusters, when there are genuine local cluster strengths. The Scottish clusters approach is an interesting model in this respect. In developing cluster actions, policymakers need to react to globalisation processes, including increased international competition, the need to respond to increased foreign direct investment in clusters, the need to innovate and the need to respond to cluster decline where it occurs. The key to this is to encourage flexible and dynamic cluster systems. Policymakers should also bear in mind certain potential pitfalls and follow certain best practices. In particular, they should work only with clusters where they have genuine strengths, avoid trying to compete in a zero-sum game, avoid excessive dependence on particular specialisations, recognise that clusters are not simply a set of local networks but also need connections with other regions and countries and recognise that successful policy also needs the participation of a wide range of stakeholders.

In the next chapter, Balestri and Cavalieri examine the classic case of the Italian clusters, focusing on the internationalisation of these clusters in response to globalisation.

CHAPTER 5

PROMOTING THE INTERNATIONALISATION OF CLUSTERS: LESSONS FROM ITALY

by

Andrea Balestri, Prato Union of Industry, Italy and
Alessandro Cavalieri, Regional Institute for the Economic Planning of Tuscany, Italy

Introduction

Broadly speaking, industrial clusters are geographic concentrations of firms (often SMEs) whose competitiveness is reinforced by the web of interrelations and ties which they establish with each other thanks to spatial closeness and complementarities in their activities (Porter, 1990).

World wide, several words are used to refer to these 'meso' organisations (i.e., placed somewhere between the single company -*micro level*- and the sector/country level -*macro*-): *sanchi* (Japan), *distretti industriali* (Italy), *systems productifs locaux* (France), *clusters* (USA, UK). There are also examples of successful development policies deliberately built on the ingredients of clusters: science parks, business incubators, industrial development areas, *poligonos empresariales*.

Although largely neglected in research by mainstream economists, the fundamentals of the competitiveness of clusters were enunciated for the first time by Alfred Marshall between the end of the 19th and the beginning of the 20th century, and were recently highlighted by Paul Krugman and Michel Porter in the U.S., and by Giacomo Becattini in Italy. These authors indicate that the power of clusters to enhance the competitiveness of the individual businesses that make them up derives from three factors:

-   The first factor has to do with the economies of agglomeration. The concentration in one area of a number of activities specialised in the same sector tends to foster the development of a fluid, extensive local labour market where enterprises can draw the skills they need and the residents can find the most satisfactory employment. Another advantage of agglomeration is the facilitated access to infrastructures and sector-specific services: professional training, trade associations, forwarding agents, installation and repair of equipment, up-stream input providers, trade agents, water treatment plants, trade fairs.

-   The second factor is the result of the accumulation over time of know how, personal relations, intangible factors such as the layers of experiences in manufacturing, trading, financing business projects; but also the image of the region due to the direct association of a place name with a specific activity. Intangible factors like these were the pillars of the 'industrial atmosphere', a metaphor used by Marshall to describe English industrial districts in his time.

-   Last, but not least, the competitiveness of clusters is explained also by elements of 'social psychology'. The 'adrenaline' released by internal competitive pressure (large numbers of businesses openly competing with one another) tends to stimulate innovation (Porter, 1990). The 'lubricant' produced by trust and social capital based on mutual knowledge and familiarity makes relationships smoother and reduces internal transaction costs (Arrow, 1974, Putnam, 1993). Finally, the 'glue' provided by the sense of local identity stimulates the business community, administrators, unions and trade associations to face together the challenges of the cluster (Becattini, 1989).

Since the 70s there has been a growing interest in clusters, and many international agencies (including the World Bank, the United Nations Industrial Development Organisation, the International Labour Organisation and the European Union), governments and regions have developed programmes and actions to reinforce existing clusters or foster emerging ones. For some time, however, there has been a nagging doubt in the minds of many observers; they are beginning to wonder if the interaction among enterprises and the bonds of closeness that are the basis for the competitiveness of clusters may be threatened by the process of globalisation. The international integration of economic, social, cultural and governing systems is not new. What is new, however, is the extraordinary acceleration that this process has undergone in the last few years.

Globalisation affects development policies, changes key elements in market competition, upsets the economic and social structure of individual countries and changes the international division of labour. The increasing scattering of manufacturing chains across many countries may also undermine (and to some extent it has already done so) the local character, the bonds of neighbourhood and the special atmosphere of the clusters.

It has been shown that the effects of globalisation on the economic and social structures of different countries and clusters are not unequivocal (Berger & Dore, 1996). On the one hand, it appears that there is an irrevocable trend toward uniformity as the outcome of market integration, the spread of new technologies and best practices, mobility of production factors and the convergence of models of consumption. But there are also those who maintain that the true picture is much more complex and that there are counterbalancing trends that operate both on the production side (i.e. business organisation does not necessarily converge towards the 'one best way') and on the demand side (the desire for novelty, originality and differentiation as an absolute value).

If we look back along this track, we can see that clusters (and particularly Italian industrial districts) were thought of as concrete examples of post-Fordism, that is the production systems that have been establishing themselves since the crisis of mass production (Piore & Sabel, 1984, Rullani, 1995). In just a few years, with a rapidity that is reminiscent of what happened in geopolitical terms in the wake of the fall of the Berlin Wall, many economic and cultural barriers have collapsed but, unlike what orthodox economics led us to expect, the winds of globalisation, instead of flattening one and all to the same configuration, have emphasised the specific qualities of various countries and, on a smaller scale, various regions.

From this mismatch between reality and theory there begins to emerge the idea that, even in a global marketplace, regional economic systems with different characteristics can coexist, each of these systems tied to its own specific historic developments, institutions, governance and even images of various regions.

This undermines the foundations of the interpretation that in a global marketplace, every country or region resembles a company which competes against all other nations or regions. Asymmetries of information, organisational factors, paths of development, differences in social infrastructure and so on contribute to the segmentation of the global marketplace; the specific features of each region or cluster are crystallised into images that, in turn, are transformed into further differentiating factors that tend to reinforce segmentation.

The rapidity of the process of globalisation has significant implications in terms of policy. Aside from the fact that the trend toward uniformity may or may not prevail over the desire for variety, or that there will be a re-awakening of the need to get back to the roots of the local cultures, it is interesting to note that in any case we are heading towards a situation of limitation in the range of classical instruments for the centralised action of national governments.

The introduction of the Euro, for example, has substantially altered the keyboard of policy instruments for the members of the European Union: in particular, standard instruments have lost much of their margin for the classical policy manoeuvres that depended on public spending and adjustment of interest rates. There is no longer much room for local or national trade policies. The only opening left for effective intervention is the creation of a context that can reflect the variety and specific capacities that are the resources of many local systems; this also means exerting a pressure upon the cultural specificity of different regions in order to blend advanced technology and globalisation trends with the specific attitudes of each region, a strategy that is possible only through a bottom up approach.

The progressive shift in policy from macro intervention (fiscal, monetary and trade policies and policies involving factors or sectors) towards intervention on a local scale implies a high degree of sensitivity in gearing actions to the specific characteristics of local enterprises. This is further complicated by an array of forces generated by the opposition of globalisation and local development and the need to 'invent' new policies to strengthen the competitiveness of clusters.

After having sketched out the globalisation scenario, this chapter aims to examine the role of clusters with particular attention to the Italian experience as well as the policy options for clusters and industrial districts. More specifically, part 2 attempts to uncover the main challenges facing clusters vis-à-vis globalisation, while part 3 draws useful lesson from the variegate Italian experience. Conclusions and policy implications are finally presented in part 4.

Clusters and industrial districts in the globalisation scenario

Clusters' dilemma

As pointed out above, the impact of globalisation and, more specifically, the internationalisation of production is widely recognised as one of the main challenges for the smooth development of clusters and industrial districts (Amin and Robins, 1991).

The debate on this issue is particularly vivid in 'mature' and developed economies such as Italy, where industrial districts account for more than 40% of manufacturing exports and similar shares of employment and value added.

The main questions that have been addressed in this debate are the following:

- Is the existence of manufacturing clusters in developed countries necessarily contradictory with the main globalisation trends and with the emergence of newly industrialising countries?

- What are the potential difficulties implied by globalisation for local clusters? And is there already any evidence about it?

- Should local clusters evolve into something different in order to develop and prosper in the globalisation era? In other words, should they become more open and 'global' or, on the contrary, strengthen their competitiveness along their localised and embedded development path?

- With a particular reference to mature economies and to the 'Old Europe' context, what are the feasible policy options for fostering local clusters and industrial districts? Which are the most effective and promising policy measures in practice, given the current globalisation scenario?

Clusters and local/global conflict

Though globalisation does not necessarily mean the destruction of local variation and the supremacy of 'one best way', it may still create problems for the development of manufacturing clusters, especially if these latter are located in mature economies, with relatively high labour and environmental costs.

Some intrinsic characteristics of clusters appear to be somewhat in conflict with globalisation, in particular:

- Local self-containment and direct control over the value-added chain is one of the most characteristic features of many clusters and particularly of Italian industrial clusters. However, global trends in production exert a heavy pressure towards a world-wide scattering of industrial activities. The relocation of parts of the productive cycle outside the clusters (a process often caused by an unfavourable gap in factor costs) may cause a sharp decrease in their competitive advantage, due to weakening of the agglomeration economies that are essential for the feeding of the clusters themselves.

- In many clusters, and particularly in industrial districts, a large part of know-how and technological capability (Bellandi, 1992; Rullani, 1995) is 'non-codified'. Typically, the local know-how is often the product of day-by-day practical problem-solving and face-to-face relations rather than the result of formal R&D activity, so that it can be seen as a 'public good' and spread among the numerous small enterprises. However, the competition induced by globalisation implies an increasing role for codified know-how and technology, which is the only type of know-how that can be easily transferred and communicated outside the local cluster and the local industrial context. Industrial clusters may thus face problems in communicating and replicating their technology with unfamiliar industrial contexts in other parts of the world.

- Social and cultural values are very important in many clusters. They probably account for a significant part of the success of industrial districts by allowing for a more co-operative atmosphere. Globalisation may indeed contaminate and influence negatively social and cultural values at local level, thereby making the local business environment less co-operative and more opportunistic.

- Though economies of scale are becoming less and less important from a strict technological perspective, the predominance of very small firms in many clusters is a potential bottleneck to the exploration of experimental and new technological processes. Global enterprise networks, a key element in these processes, often require management capabilities that are often beyond the possibilities of very small enterprises.

– The growing importance of communication, image and advertising represents a leading trend in contemporary competition. Consumers are increasingly targeted by advertising so that they are less inclined to judge fairly the quality differences in the products whose value is getting determined by subjective and subtle factors rather than by objective and material characteristics. Typically, big enterprises and multinationals invest huge resources on advertising and communication, while small enterprises in clusters and clusters themselves are largely excluded from this kind of competitive struggle, given the scale and the nature of investment required. The competitive advantage of clusters is in fact mainly based on rather 'objective' and material characteristics of the product such as quality, typicality and variety. These product characteristics are still appreciated by consumers but there is a risk of marginalisation of industrial districts which so far have been quite passive in this new scenario.

Evolutionary trends and internationalisation of production in clusters

It is not easy to assess the extent to which current and recent evolutionary trends in clusters and industrial districts do represent a response to global pressures or to endogenous and 'cluster life cycle' forces. Nonetheless, it appears that recent changes in clusters can be interpreted as a sort of adaptation to global pressures (Tiberi Vipraio, 1997):

– Strong evidence from Italy as well from other E.U. countries points to a growing 'tertiarisation' (Sforzi, 1999) and increasing role of services (i.e. design, marketing, and commercialisation, etc.), as opposed to manufacturing activity in its stricter sense. In some cases tertiarisation cannot actually be disentangled from the effects of economic decline or de-industrialisation. Overall, despite the variety of situations, this evolution appears to be quite generalised in the European and Italian context. In some cases one can interpret this transition as 'efficiency-enhancing'. Manufacturing clusters become more specialised in highly skilled products and production phases. In doing this, they relocate lower value added manufacturing activities outside the cluster, a process compensated by the development of skilled and advanced related services. In other cases, however, the outward relocation of manufacturing activities actually corresponds to a process of de-industrialisation in which there is not a compensating development of skilled service activities.

- During the 60s and the 70s, in various sectors and in a number of regions the development of clusters was characterised by an impressive and parallel bottom-up growth of entrepreneurship. In many clusters capital and other entry barriers were more easily overcome and new enterprises were built by former employees who themselves became entrepreneurs. This entrepreneurial blossoming was not only the essence of the economic success of clusters but it also allowed for a 'merit-based' social mobility. However, in most cases this growth engine seems clogged. Entry barriers are now higher, while the current Darwinian selection of enterprises favours a process of industrial concentration and the emergence of larger sized enterprises (Anastasia and Corò, 1996; Ferrucci and Varaldo, 1993). These larger enterprises take a strong lead within the cluster and their competitiveness, as opposite to small firms, is stronger than before, probably due to the changes in the global scenario.

- All in all, it is not easy to identify a clear cause-effect relationship, but the spread of various forms of productive internationalisation (Foreign Direct Investment - FDI - outflows, international sub-contracting, outsourcing, etc.) seems to be a complementary phenomenon with respect to the above-cited tertiarisation and industrial concentration. The evidence in this respect is quite clear (Conti and Menghinello, 1997; Grandinetti, 1993; Mistri, 1993). The overseas manufacturing activities of local firms, while often efficiency-raising and profitable, weaken the local self-containment of the value chain (Cavalieri, 1995). Though it would be wrong to simply equate the overall process of productive internationalisation with delocalisation (Scarso, 1998), these two phenomena are clearly related, especially if foreign manufacturing activities are carried out in low-labour-cost areas.

- The role of TNCs (Trans National Companies) appears to be increasingly interrelated with local clusters and probably many entrepreneurs have this phenomenon in mind when they talk or think of globalisation. So far it appears that TNCs (i.e. large international companies and not just small firms which control some foreign activities) do enjoy a favourable position with respect to several cluster companies. These large companies, rather than being proper local investors, control strategic activities at the top and the bottom of the local value chain (i.e. technology, commercialisation, marketing, etc.) (Corò and Micelli, 1998). Nonetheless, some authors (Becattini and Rullani, 1993) argue that TNCs could also play an important role through FDI and mergers and acquisitions of local and leading firms in the core activities of the clusters. This possibility, though not yet corroborated by strong evidence, appears to be a further - and perhaps a future - way of 'injecting doses of globalisation' into the local industrial context.

Towards global clusters?

Policy-makers and observers do bear in mind the above described scenario when they think of strategies and interventions for local clusters. In countries like Italy, where the knowledge itself of industrial districts is embedded in people and in institutions, there is a wide recognition that a stereotyped description of local clusters following the industrial district model has proved to be useful in the past but its policy implications could be very misleading if applied literally nowadays, that is, without taking account of the current context. Thus, there is a general agreement among policy-makers and scholars that industrial districts should still develop endogenously along their 'embedded' path. This path, however, has to be compatible and sustainable in the global scenario. In other words, clusters and industrial districts should find a balance in the 'local-global' mix (Bramanti and Maggioni, 1997) by looking for a valorisation, in the world market, of their inherited assets, often intangible, and of their competitive advantage. In practice, however, the achievement of an optimal 'local-global' mix means for most clusters a stronger effort towards 'global', rather than the other way round.

The move towards the 'global' implies the valorisation of the economic, historic and social assets of the clusters, rather than being undersold in a global market often dominated by adverse game rules and by unbalanced power relations.

Working on 'intangibles'

This move does not exclude the fostering of internationalisation initiatives for cluster firms (by means of real services for local enterprises, consortia, building SME support institutions, etc.), provided that this does not imply a self-imploding de-localisation and a consequent degradation of strategic local resources such as human capital with the weakening of local ties and firm relationships. Equally positive can be the implementation of territorial marketing policies and the local promotion of FDI inflows, as long as this does not compromise the endogenous base of local development and does not imply a loss of decision power on the part of local communities.

Overall, the move towards the 'global' should be fully understood in all its depth (Mistri 1998) and consequences. This means helping local enterprises overcome their cultural and size-related bottlenecks by improving their codified know-how and their communication with unfamiliar contexts, the spread and diffusion of information technologies, and the use of e-commerce and enhancing communication with all corners of the world.

In this global and virtual era, it seems very important to enhance more immaterial investment and image promotion, thereby making the production of local clusters more 'visible' in the global market, i.e. emphasise the product origin with its characteristics including its productive and social context. The fashion-specialised Italian clusters may be a case in point. Consumers when they purchase a product marked '*Made in Italy*,' are often also consuming a depiction of Italy, or perhaps we should say, of the 'Italian way of life' and the 'saper vivere italiano.' The link between these goods and their 'Italianness,' runs even deeper. They reflect more than a way of life; they are the product of an unusual path of industrial development, which takes its power from a set of institutions, a social fabric, various forms of organisation, and an entrepreneurial culture that history has accumulated in Italy's industrial districts.

It must be not be forgotten that products and modes of production are interrelated, and industrial districts are a great example of embedded, socially, culturally and environmentally sustainable development. Their products can incorporate not only the local way of living but also the local way of producing: human capital ability, historic and artistic content, a beauty-inspired mental approach, high labour and environmental standards, no child labour exploitation, etc... Consumers should be aware of it.

Though the gap in the financial and economic resources devoted to advertising between multinationals and small enterprises in industrial clusters is bound to remain huge, it appears important to promote and to strengthen the visibility and the image of the industrial clusters whose products are in most cases recognisable in their origin and deeply rooted in the local milieu. Given also the persisting local self-containment, specialisation and concentration of the value chain in industrial clusters, the link between the products and their geographical origin is still very strong, so that the promotion of a territory and of its image is strictly interconnected with the promotion of its products. Awareness concerning the product origin should be thus increased in the common knowledge of consumers.

Evidence from Italian experiences

Industrial districts are the Italian 'variation on the theme' of cluster competitiveness[1]. Their outstanding growth during the last forty years fed the widest and probably most rich case history in the field of clusters and local networks of SMEs. The notoriety of industrial districts, which spread far beyond national circles, and the successes of *'Made in Italy'* in a set of consumer products which economic theories assign to countries with lower factor costs, strengthen the idea of a plurality of cluster paths. This success also shows that there is not just one box of tools for supporting local development.

From this point of view, the Italian experience offers useful indications about the rationale and the key variables to be considered for districts and cluster policies. Before tackling these issues, though, it is opportune to look at the specific ingredients of the Italian 'recipe'.

The elements that make the history of industrial districts a chapter apart and well defined in the book of cluster competitiveness are:

- the number of districts and their specific weight in the Italian economy;

- their performance, particularly in international markets;

- the peculiar 'organisational architecture' of districts;

- the contribution of intangible factors in fertilising the economic environment of the districts.

Industrial districts in Italian economy

Over the last few years, various maps of the Italian districts and their products have been drawn up; according to Istat (the Italian Institute of Statistics) there are about 200 industrial districts which account for 25% of the Italian population. Moreover, the definition of districts used by Istat is a rather strict one; it does not include clusters such as the 'fashion system' in Milan (a well known international success; however, unlike the 'true' districts, not covering the whole area of Milan), the tourist 'riviera' in Rimini (even if it holds very

---

[1] *"The case of Italy, where such clusters are quite common, helped spawn a literature on industrial districts. Industrial districts are a special case of clusters"*, Porter (1998a)

high indexes of specialisation, it is not a 'manufacturing' region) and many cases of development based on networks of SMEs such as the 'packaging valley' that extends between Bologna and Reggio Emilia, an area where several manufacturing activities and services coexist.

Nevertheless, despite the strict definition, Istat figures are enough to appreciate the importance of this phenomenon. The 200 industrial districts represent 32% of the Italian workforce and 45% of manufacturing employment; over 40% of Italian exports are made by the enterprises from the districts' regions. No other country has a comparable number of districts and in no other country is their contribution to GDP, employment, trade so high (and to economic theories, too!).

Social and economic performance

Further to the mere quantitative dimension, the role of the districts in the Italian economy has also been very important in social relations. As pointed out by Fabio Sforzi (1999), *'from 1981 to 1991, when large firms were cutting jobs, the districts were creating them. In the 1990s as well – from 1991 to 1996- the districts have employed growing numbers of manufacturing workers. If we set 1991 at 100, the manufacturing employment rate in 1996 was 105'.*

These figures may be biased by the weakness of giant firms in Italy. Out of industrialised countries, Italy has the largest share of very small and small enterprises; in the manufacturing sector, 82.9% have less than 9 employees (Table 1). The share (1995/96) of employment in micro and small companies (i.e. up to 49 employees) is 52.5% in Italy compared to 25.8% in France, 22.8% in United Kingdom and 21.7% in Germany.

Table 1. Italy. Analysis of manufacturing firms according to their size (1996)

	Number	%	Employees	%
Micro firms (1-9 employees)	456,832	82.9	1,183,301	24.2
Small firms (10-49 employees)	82,984	15.1	1,510,909	30.9
Medium firms (50-249 employees)	10,014	1.8	953,486	19.5
Large firms (> 250 employees)	1,444	0.3	1,241,997	25.4
Total	551,274	100.0	4,889,693	100.0

Source: Istat, Censimento 1996

In practice, we observe a 'fragile' productive system with few possibilities to compete in international markets according to standard economic theories. In Italy perhaps there are too many microenterprises and today their competitiveness is seriously threatened by the winds of globalisation. However, in evaluating the Italian industrial structure, one should not underestimate the impetus of territorial factors in enhancing competitiveness: small enterprises, taken alone, do not seem able to pick up the challenge of globalisation but this is not necessarily true for clusters of SMEs.

The same halo of prejudices applies to the specialisation in 'mature' textile, footwear, leather and other traditional products in which Italy does not enjoy tangible comparative advantage as defined by economics textbooks.

These and other interpretations are overthrown by the international performance of the SMEs in industrial districts; actually, the figures show that Italian exports in textiles and apparel, footwear, home furnishings, furniture and eye frames are very high. This should stimulate a reflection on how to interpret the globalisation process (Table 2).

Table 2. Italy's share (%) of 'G7' exports (1996)

Total exports	9
Footwear	66
Leather	55
Tiles	54
Gold jewellery	54
Men's clothing	38
Furniture	37
Women's clothing	34
Lighting fixtures	32

Source: Balestri & Ricchetti (1999)

A number of studies have focused on the backwardness (and hence the vulnerability) of Italian exports, emphasising the absence of high tech, modern products. In extreme examples, this view portrays Italy as a country hovering somewhere between underdevelopment and modernity (the 'tower of Pisa emblem'). The main limitation of this interpretation lies in the fact that, by considering only simple factor cost differences or standard measures of technological innovation, one cannot understand the long lasting success of Italian exports.

Efforts to explain the performance of Italian exports in analytical terms have thrown up enlightening evidence about the role of industrial districts. Marco Fortis (Fortis, 1998) recently drew persuasive new boundaries for *Made in Italy* focusing on the platform of 'person-fashion-furnishings-home-Mediterranean diet', a set of goods produced by the SMEs of industrial districts. The above platform includes a series of goods that are anything but obvious, that share a common denominator and that have a huge content in design, taste and culture. These are the products that, with their exports, sustain the Italian commercial surplus which ranks third in the world (IMD, 1998).

The performance of the districts in the post-war period manifests its imprint also in social life. Italian districts boast dynamic companies, rooted in the territory and projected toward international markets; limited unemployment rates; high levels of participation of the female population in economic activities; per capita incomes above the national average (and often above European averages); and top positions in the Italian ranking of quality of life.

Profile of Italian industrial districts

These preliminary remarks about the role of industrial districts in Italian recent economic history have already brought out some features that identify the Italian districts inside the general phenomenon of clusters. Other recurrent elements in their profile are:

- *Their size:* The districts are located in small regions (with no more than 300,000-400,000 people) with a 'thick overlapping' between every day life and economic processes.

- *The presence of one identifying sector, generally a very narrow one:* Silk products of Como, marble of Carrara, women's hosiery of Castelgoffredo, leather of Santa Croce and Arzignano, woollens of Prato and Biella, sofas of Altamura-Santeramo in Colle, silverware and household furnishings of Omegna and Lumezzane, jewellery of Valenza Po and Arezzo, footwear of Fermo, Verona and the Valle del Brenta, hiking boots of Montebelluna, eye-frames of Belluno. As is the case for Italy as a whole, single districts, too, have their own mercantile image, known mainly by 'traders' (and, to a lesser degree, by final consumers, an element which paves the way to public investment in clusters policy).

— *The projection towards foreign markets:* Despite their size, small enterprises in the districts are not afraid to push their products supported by the efforts of thousands of entrepreneurs and the association between the manufacturing specialisation of clusters and their mercantile image spread world wide. In many cases, the market share of the districts within world exports ranges from 30 to 50 percent; nearly 40 percent of the world's ceramics exports come from Sassuolo and a few neighbouring towns; one-quarter of the world's exports of silk products come from a few small towns on the shores of Lake Como; the provinces of Biella and Prato account for nearly a quarter of the world's exports of woollens.

— *Their organisation:* The districts count a large number of networks of SMEs that make up a close connective tissue of business. The organisation of production is based on a complex and careful division of labour among groups of small and mid-sized companies that benefit reciprocally from the concentration of activities belonging to the same manufacturing chain. Their way of operating is reminiscent of the last moments of concerts when, without any preliminary agreement, the burst of applause, little by little, changes into a finely timed clapping.

Intangibles and the fertilisation of districts

Italian districts are fairly well organised micro-worlds. They are the regions that have best preserved the heritage of art, nature, culture, folklore, and fine cuisine inherited from the Renaissance. In many districts post-war development took off in the footsteps of pre-existing handicraft traditions in the production of fabrics, objects in metal, shoes, furniture and suits. Still today, the international image of the 'Bel Paese' is reinforced by the achievements of the 'Third Italy', a group of regions made up primarily of small towns that have succeeded in grafting the values of modern industry onto the branch of fine craft skills, in blending new technology and creativity. From this point of view, the districts are a giant reservoir of manufacturing activities organised around good taste and a gift for creativity.

Within the districts there is a general sense of trust in doing business with local agents since behaviours between them are based on mutual knowledge and familiarity; this makes relations easier and smoother.

The districts' competitiveness, furthermore, is not independent of the sense of belonging to local communities by local administrators, unions, industrialists' associations; everyone feels involved in a collective gamble. Museums of traditional professions are frequently opened because the people belonging to the district are the descendants of the best Italian craftsmen and because of their passion for beauty.

In this particular climate, made up of diffuse entrepreneurial activities, unspoken rules governing economic activity and a widespread spirit of emulation and commitment to venture in the new, Italy's small and mid-sized companies have developed a special skill for rapidly designing and industrialising a great array of new products, while successfully satisfying the consumer's need for personalisation and value. In the way that they operate, Italian districts are reminiscent of a huge fair within which businessmen can quickly gather a great quantity of information, compare features and bet on the prices of their products.

There are many factors of added value associated with the organisation of production in districts; most of them have to do with intangible elements such as design, style and image but they also extend to managerial and organisational practices.

Studies on the companies in the districts have revealed a set of elements which make up an original 'business style' shaped over time. The elements of this style are:

- Mental habit to compete in a tough competitive arena where tens of companies of the same district compete openly with each other for market share.

- Solid technical control over manufacturing processes. The SMEs in the districts generally do not have internal operating manuals; nevertheless Italy is a leading country in the production of machinery for textiles, leather, furniture, valves, faucets, plastic injection. The average efficiency of small firms in the districts does not lag behind that of competitors.

- Companies are family-run, organisations are lean and empowerment is widespread.

- 'Collective market research'. Entrepreneurs in the districts lead small firms but are dynamic and travel frequently around the world. Direct contact with key clients makes for the gathering of detailed, first hand information on market trends. All information collected by competing entrepreneurs is sorted and translated into production programmes by the districts' 'cement mixer'. From this point of view there is no institute which could rival the eagerness and commitment of entrepreneurs.

With this reconstruction we have traced a general picture of the industrial districts to throw light on their powerful engines of competitiveness and the mechanisms that make it easier for them to adapt. However, this is not the whole story. In the Italian industrial districts there are problems made evident by falls in competitiveness and social disarray. Moreover, they are forced 'to grab the bull of globalisation by the horns', a process which in many cases might be painful. This is likely to be the case if proper actions are not promoted. This new chapter in their history is still open. Meanwhile the analysis of the Italian districts offers empirical evidence to reflect on and from which to derive normative indications on the most appropriate politics to promote local development. The formulas of the districts are not necessarily the best or the only ones possible; nevertheless, they present governments with objectives that are generally desirable in terms of economic performance and social balance.

Policies for industrial clusters and districts

Districts vs. clusters policy

Clusters differ in sectors, scope, size and density of relationships among their firms and therefore there are several policy options under the label of clustering. The recipe of the Italian industrial districts, however fascinating, is not easily repeatable; thinking about the unusual combination of historical, social and economic elements in their take-off, it is a difficult path of development and full of risks. Nevertheless, forty years ago many districts (from the most spectacular in the North East to the emerging ones in South Italy) were regions devoted to agriculture whose residents were forced to emigrate to other regions to find a job.

From today's perspective there are, indeed, many elements that can be borrowed from the history of industrial districts and their ongoing internationalisation; however they do not offer a ready to launch pattern for policy, but rather a set of analogical principles and practices useful both for enhancing existing clusters and for creating new ones.

140

We synthesise below some key lessons from the showcase of this particular class of clusters.

The mould of Italian districts

A first order of considerations that springs from the showcase of Italian industrial districts concerns the main objectives of policy makers. Broadly speaking we can sort policy options of local development promotion into two major directions:

1. Attract external or foreign resources (capital, managerial skills etc.);

2. Mobilise - investing in local resources.

Part of the two pathways flows in parallel (creating favourable economic contexts, training, infrastructures, industrial zones etc.). Partly, however, their roads (and therefore the tools to be used) clearly diverge.

In the first case, for example, the tools most used are tax breaks, aid schemes to reduce labour costs, and investment in university and research centres facilities (i.e. general clustering policies). In the latter case services to entrepreneurs and involvement of local actors in drawing and implementing policies are prevalent.

The experience of the Italian districts is interesting above all for the policies aimed at building on the potential for development already present in a region. This choice is not strictly necessary and in fact generally there are more cases of policies that look to attract external resources.

Among the strengths of these programmes of endogenous development it is worth underlining:

– the protection or revitalisation of the heritage of know how and existing skills present in a region;

– discouragement of the abandonment of country side and small towns and, in general, reduction of the demographic pressure on large urban centres by offering people the chance to find a job in areas, for example, which do not possess the necessary characteristics for the installation of university, centres for advanced research and other engines of locally based development.

These 'district-like' policies, promote the stability of the location choices of enterprises (an element that is not always found in the case of multinationals). Furthermore, they do not assemble all the fruits of intervention in a few areas.

Devolution, governance and institutional frameworks

The effectiveness of a policy aimed at reproducing the development of districts also depends closely on the institutional framework. In all districts the need and the opportunity for support are different and these can be faced effectively only by operating as near as possible to the grassroots.

Even if there are not valid rules in every case, the functions and control of local policy must be attributed to local organisations. The interventions that have given the best results have sprung from the establishment of targets and joint programmes between organisations of different categories; trade unions, banking and local authorities (a process called 'concertazione'). Devolution in favour of local actors is to be welcomed insofar as it promotes this.

District and cluster pre-requisites

The Italian experience also helps us to appraise and to select regions with the proper pre-requisites and potential resources to launch new district programmes.

The analysis of elements such as the population characteristics of the region, handicraft traditions, the existence of batches of know how in one or more activities, or the presence of artisan production, often furnishes indications that are useful for establishing whether for a given region it is preferable to aim for a district-like policy or rather to think about other types of clusters. Trust and social capital, although intriguing ingredients of the working of these systems, are not pre-requisites of the development of districts, they are an outcome of it.

The tools

The flowering literature on Italian districts has helped inform the development of the policy tools that have been used most frequently:

  – *Professional training.* In the history of the districts the technical institutes always occupy foreground roles as forges of technicians and, in many cases, also of entrepreneurs.

– *Industrial areas and buildings.* The entrepreneurial resource, with the continuous start up of new firms, is one of the main drivers of the districts. When the enterprises are born they need limited space, but in time, if the entrepreneurs are successful, the demand for space for production and office facilities increases. In practice the enterprises often require increasing space and it is very important that their demand is matched quickly. The provision of specific areas for new industrial buildings was, for example, one of the instruments used most frequently by the Emilia Romagna region.

– *Small credits and guarantees.* Since the 1960's, Italy has launched programmes of guarantees in favour of SMEs to encourage investment in machinery. The scale of public aid was modest in terms of actual transfers of resources but the result has been particularly effective.

– *Consortia.* In Italy over 300 consortia are operated, made up of thousands of SMEs. Their activity is concentrated in promotion and is connected with sector fairs. This has given a strong impulse to the commercial strategies of the enterprises in the districts.

– *Service centres for enterprises.* In many districts specialised agencies were created that assist SMEs in various ways, such as laboratories for the analysis of products, training, certification of quality, technological transfer and information. Their sphere of action does not go beyond certain thresholds because their services are fundamentally accessible to all members and the centres cannot invade the commercially-sensitive ground of individual firms' strategies.

– *'Intermediary agents'.* The role played by trade associations, trade unions, consortiums, district agencies and local authorities (i.e.: 'local élites') is extremely important. The capability of any district to get organised, to enhance local identity, to undertake tasks to achieve set objectives and to develop the appropriate resources is mainly down to local intermediary agents.

– *Image.* For many districts it is relatively easy to earn a reputation with direct customers. However, it is more problematic to achieve visibility with the final consumers. When this happens (as for Swiss clocks, Japanese electronic equipment and Italian fashion) all the enterprises draw great benefits from it. The image of the district, nevertheless, is a public good and therefore the related investments must be encouraged.

A light and comprehensive policy approach

It should be clear, by now, that a strong policy therapy does not emerge from all these fragments. According to Becattini, a policy for districts has to be light (not invasive)[2] and comprehensive, i.e. to embrace all the ingredients of district life: economic, geographic, historical, social and cultural.

For several reasons, the lesson from Italy for the development of districts is full of gaps. In Italy, in fact, there are no judicial or governmental bodies that deal specifically with the industrial districts institutionally. In a few regions local development agencies have been created, but this only happened once the districts had already proven themselves and their activity is often limited to collective projects in the field of promotion, training and disseminating economic and technical information about the sector.

Furthermore, the programmes of industrial policy adopted in Italy (as in many other countries) have concentrated on high-tech sectors, on the chemical and car industries, on large companies, on the creation of new businesses and new jobs in disadvantaged areas. In most cases, industrial districts do not possess the pre-requisites to benefit from these policies: they are specialised in traditional sectors (for example, the fashion business, household products); they are made up of networks of SMEs; they have low unemployment rates and are not based in regions that have problems with development or de-industrialisation. The industrial districts are often described as successful systems which do not require resources or specific intervention and they have not come together to claim public intervention in their favour (although the *Italian Club of Industrial Districts* was set at the end of 1995).

It should not be surprising, therefore, to find that the industrial districts occupy exactly the opposite position on the Government's political agenda to that granted them in research documents and debates. The experience of the

---

[2]   *"to play the card of industrial districts is not a marginal operation because it implies following on from the whole economic policy approach; at the same time it is a light operation because it should favour, accelerate or slow down decisions that the agents are close to making by themselves; its space of operation lies in the actions essential to the development of the district but that are perceived as too risky by the operators'* (Becattini,1998, pg. 11)

industrial districts shows that the flexibility of small businesses and their capacity for innovation is closely tied to their territory and their interactions within it. However, even European Union programmes, which dedicate plenty of space to small and medium-sized enterprises, have not grasped the spatial dimension of competitiveness and the importance of relations between groups of businesses located in the same area.

This does not mean that there was no policy for districts in Italy. The lack of initiatives on the part of central government has been partly compensated by the action of local economic organisations and bodies which have supported the development of districts with the few options at their disposal. For example, the regional authorities have funded 'service centres' (public and private partnership companies specialising in keeping the districts' manufacturing systems up to date); local government authorities have provided industrial sites or constructed water purification plants; the trade unions have organised industrial relations in non-confrontational ways; enterprise associations and Chambers of Commerce have taken care of professional training and developing collective services (trade fairs, transport, etc.). These are some examples from a fairly varied survey of minor initiatives promoted in the Italian districts using funds allocated by Community, national and regional laws. Nonetheless, overall, public support has never played a primary role in the development of the districts.

All these considerations, anyway, apply to the past, a period during which the development of the districts has been extraordinary. One should not underestimate, in fact, that in today's more globalised world there are problems, and sometimes serious problems, present in many industrial districts.

CHAPTER 6

HUMAN CAPITAL POLICIES

Human capital, the knowledge economy and competitiveness

The OECD Growth Project, which examined how policies can enhance long-term growth prospects in the emerging economic environment, highlighted five main areas for action: getting the fundamentals right, seizing the benefits of information and communications technologies, harnessing the potential of innovation and technology diffusion, fostering new firm creation and entrepreneurship and enhancing and exploiting human capital. The previous two chapters have explored the role that city and region governments and development agencies can play in fostering firm creation and entrepreneurship. This chapter and the next explore the role of cities and regions in enhancing and exploiting human capital.

Recent work provides robust evidence that human capital is an important determinant of economic growth and competitiveness and that it has been one of the key factors behind the growth processes of past decades in all OECD countries (OECD, 2001d; Bassanini and Scarpetta, 2001). This operates partly through the link between skills and competencies and labour productivity and reflects in addition the increase in demand for 'knowledge-intensive' employment (scientists, engineers and technicians). For the OECD as a whole, it is estimated that each extra year of full-time education is associated with an increase in output per capita of about 6 per cent. Moreover, human capital is also associated with a wide range of non-economic benefits, including improvements in health, a greater sense of well-being and a narrowing of the digital and knowledge divides. However, because companies and individuals tend to under-invest in training, public intervention is often needed and city and region governments and development agencies have an important role to play in this.

Recognition of the need to invest in human capital policies is often linked to the idea that OECD countries are becoming knowledge economies as globalisation progresses (OECD, 1996c). The knowledge economy can be defined as an economy in which knowledge becomes an essential factor of production alongside the traditional, more tangible factors. With knowledge as an essential factor of production, the ability of people, and cities and regions, to acquire and develop it becomes critical to their successful integration into the global economy.

Burton-Jones (1999) examines the characteristics of the emerging knowledge economy and some of the main implications. He argues that with the balance of economic activity shifting from manufacturing and the production of physical goods to information handling, knowledge accumulation and knowledge goods, the shift to the knowledge economy is progressively altering the role of the traditional factors of production: labour, materials and capital. Symbolic resources are replacing physical resources, mental exertion is replacing physical exertion and knowledge capital is beginning to challenge money and all other forms of capital.

This shift to the knowledge-based economy demands that traditional relationships between education, learning and work are fundamentally reappraised. Work and learning are becoming increasingly inter-related and interdependent. A coalition is building between education and industry as demand increases from firms for more highly-qualified workers and more broadly-based expertise, whilst the demand for low-skilled labour declines. According to Burton-Jones, the current, largely publicly-funded infrastructure of schools, universities and colleges of further education, which was built to satisfy the needs of an industrial era, is no longer appropriate as we move into a post-industrial era.

The shift to the knowledge economy not only requires governments, firms and individuals to raise skill levels, but it also calls on them to update skills more frequently. As Greffe argues in the next chapter, skills development now needs to be thought of in terms of a process of permanent change. Thus the 'just-in-case' learning associated with the traditional industrial system has given way to 'just-in-time' learning. Just-in-time learning increases the flexibility of enterprises and economies to adjust to changes in demand and technologies and increases the returns on the training undertaken. There is therefore a need to shift our understanding of training away from the idea that it is a one-off exercise undertaken after school and before entering the labour market towards an understanding of training as a process of lifelong learning. Globalisation and the shift to the knowledge economy has made skills demand much less predictable and more rapidly-changing than it was in the traditional post-war economy. Skills also need to be updated and retraining undertaken to enable people to adjust to economic restructuring by moving between occupations and by staying ahead in their current occupations.

The shift to the knowledge economy also changes the types of skills demanded, emphasising skills that will enable companies and organisations to develop their flexibility, innovation and responsiveness. As Greffe highlights, employers are looking just as much for people who can perform well all-round and who have a talent for problem-solving as they are for people who possess specific occupational skills. Thus traditional technical skills have to be complemented by more generic skills, which Greffe terms 'helicopter' skills.

These changes in skills demand require a different conception and delivery of training based on the notion of lifelong learning and the training provided through apprenticeship systems or post-school training is often not sufficient. There is a clear need to encourage enterprises and organisations to increase their training effort and to anticipate training needs. This is particularly a problem for small and micro businesses, which are often reluctant to invest in training. Furthermore, in the globalising economy, characterised by more rapid economic change, people stand a greater risk of losing their jobs at some point in their working lives and facing the need to retrain. Thus the problem equality of opportunities is no longer only an issue of access to initial education and training but is a permanent issue.

What sort of human capital policies?

A number of policy actions need to be undertaken to promote the generation and use of human capital. The OECD Growth Project identified in particular the need to:

- *Invest in high-quality early education and childcare.* These investments are more cost-effective than later interventions to remedy school failure and they help boost participation in the labour market.

- *Raise completion of basic and vocational education and improve the quality of the system.* Dropout rates from secondary education have to be lowered. ICT literacy has become part of basic competencies and has to be improved, notably by recruiting qualified teachers and making pay more competitive.

- *Improve school-to-work transition.* Create or strengthen pathways that combine education with workplace experience. To ensure cost-effectiveness of the system, establish mechanisms of co-financing between employers, trainees and government.

- *Strengthen the links between higher education and the labour market in a cost-effective way.* This can be achieved through developing shorter course cycles with a healthy orientation to job market requirements. Involving firms in the definition of curricula and funding can be valuable, as can strengthening performance-based financial incentives.

- *Provide wider training opportunities.* Increase possibilities for adults and workers to participate in higher education. Innovative instruments, like individual learning accounts and systems of recognition of competencies can enhance incentives to engage in training while helping to control costs. Ensure that firm training is not penalised by tax systems.

- *Reduce obstacles to workplace changes and give workers a greater voice.* Employee involvement and effective labour-management relationships and practices are central to fostering change and raising productivity - governments must allow this to develop. Ensure that working time legislation and employment regulations do not hamper efficient organisational change. Adapt collective bargaining institutions to the new economic environment.

City and region governments and development agencies can make a significant contribution to these measures, for example through early education and childcare programmes, through local active labour market policies that help improve the school-to-work transition, through programmes to strengthen the links between higher education and the labour market and through funding wider training provision.

How should human capital policies be delivered?

Changes in skills needs also imply changes in the way human capital policies are delivered. In order to raise skill levels, increase the frequency of skills updating and teach new skills, learning will have to become a lifelong process and a major activity. Systems of training and skills development will have to adjust to take advantage of technologically-assisted methods of education and distance learning technologies, to involve new training suppliers from the private sector, to reduce old demarcation lines between vocational and academic training and to provide greater access to learning from the workplace and two-way flows of people between work and learning.

One element of the required response is the decentralisation of the design and delivery of skills and training policies from national to local level, with an increased role for actions created and co-ordinated at the city and region level. OECD (1999b) discusses the role of local actors in delivering active labour market policies. Whilst it is argued that local flexibility must be balanced by a central framework, a number of key strengths are attributed to decentralisation of labour market policies:

- Ability to design services that are more adapted to different local circumstances by capitalising on local knowledge.

- Capacity to co-ordinate locally the range of different national, regional and local policies affecting employment in an area.

- Ability to mobilise people, employers and community groups in support of national policy objectives based on the exploitation of common local issues and objectives and the existence of local forums and networks.

- The possibility to experiment with new policy approaches at the local level, helping to fill gaps in the existing policy framework and generate innovative policy ideas that potentially could be transferred or adapted elsewhere.

- The possibility to channel additional resources to areas with a particular need.

There is also clearly some need for a central framework as well, for example in contributing to training budgets and in ensuring the mobility of the labour force at national and international levels.

A number of OECD reports (OECD, 1998c, 1999b, 1999d) describe how Member countries are using decentralisation to redesign their employment and training policies around the concepts of activation, integration and mobilisation. These publications highlight how the public employment service has been reorganised since the early 1990s in many OECD Member countries. Some governments have recently embarked on ambitious reform plans that substantially modify the way competencies are shared between central and regional government. In other countries, steps have been taken to increase the role of consultation between the social partners at different levels and some public employment service activities have been transferred to the private and voluntary sectors. All these measures amount to greater decentralisation of employment and training policies.

151

As documented in OECD (1998c) recent decentralisations have been undertaken in four main ways:

- *Gradual and asymmetrical regionalisation.* In Italy, Canada and Spain, powers for employment policy are being transferred to the regions gradually and responsibilities, at least in Canada, are being transferred in such a way as to meet the needs specific to each territory.

- *Autonomy in budget allocation.* This approach, which is applied in France, gives more powers to the lower levels of decision-making without altering the institutional structures of employment policy.

- *Greater role of the social partners.* In a growing number of countries, government authorities refer to localised groupings of social partners on questions relating to employment and social exclusion. This is the case for example in Ireland (Area-Based Partnerships) and in the Flemish region (sub-regional platforms).

- *Assignment of responsibility to local actors.* Governments have often taken steps to increase the involvement of municipalities regarding active labour market policy. For example, in Germany the federal government subsidises work activities organised by the municipalities for welfare recipients. In the United States, following welfare reform, counties have been assigned tasks in several states (OECD, 1999b). Actors in the private and voluntary sectors are also increasingly being turned to for participation in labour market policy.

The use of local partnerships for the design and delivery of training can be thought of as taking devolution of training policy one step further than the level of city or regional governments and agencies by involving in addition a number of sub-regional partners. As Greffe argues in the next chapter, local partnership is important for training policy for at least three reasons.

1. A number of different agents control relevant assets, resources and knowledge. Some are private, like enterprises or training institutions, others are public and others are from the Third Sector, such as associations, enterprises for social integration and so on. Training policy will be more effective if these are pooled together.

2. Training must be closely linked to employment if it is to be useful. It is therefore important to have future employers involved in the design and delivery of training programmes.

3. People sometimes face other problems that need to be addressed if training is to be effective, such as housing, health, income replacement and so on. Training programmes therefore need to be placed alongside programmes that address these other problems.

Local partnerships therefore promote the mobilisation of local agencies, the involvement of employers and the integration of training with other programmes. They also have another critical role in enhancing policy effectiveness, in that they diffuse information through the network that can be used to help tailor actions to local needs.

In order to exploit the potential of the local partnership approach to training, city and region governments should avoid determining the design and delivery of training programmes in isolation from other local actors. Instead they should build on the resources and local knowledge of a wide range of players in their local area, including the social partners and voluntary organisations, which can also participate usefully, particularly in tackling problems for people with special needs. The public sector sometimes still does not fully recognise the barriers that need to be overcome in order to bring appropriate agencies from the non-profit or Third Sector into public initiatives. Administration needs to be simplified, proper accountability created and information provided to agencies on how to participate. The fact that in some countries, budgets available for training from employer levies are not always spent whilst at the same time non-profit organisations look for funding seems to illustrate the continued presence of difficulties.

Trade unions are a further important local partner for training programmes. Unions can provide an important second chance for workers to enter the education system. Many unions employ education officers to deliver union training programmes which upgrade the skills and qualifications of members. In addition, many workers who are prepared to train through their union would be reluctant to train if the training was proposed by their employer or by traditional education institutions. This is particularly relevant for industrial regions going through major change, where retraining programmes are needed. In the past, adult training programmes have often tended to have the greatest take-up from people who already have higher educational qualifications and this has widened disparities in opportunities.

Box 8 gives the example of the Partners in Training and Technology (PITT) initiative in the Netherlands. This initiative seeks to co-ordinate the large number of partnerships for training that have grown up in recent years in the province of Limburg. PITT has helped to build trust between the different organisations and partnerships involved in training programmes in the province and to increase synergies and fill gaps in provision.

Box 8. Partners in Training and Technology (PITT), Netherlands

Partners in Training and Technology (PITT) was founded in 1998 in order to support regional industry and governmental training and employment bodies in designing and implementing the technical training policies required in the region of Limburg in the south of the Netherlands. PITT enjoys broad-based support from trade unions, employers organisations, local and regional government and the education sector (schools and universities).

Limburg has a population of approximately 1 million people and is located very close to the Netherlands border with Belgium, Luxembourg and Germany. The region has recently been through a period of extensive economic restructuring associated with major shifts in skill requirements. In 1965, all the region's coal mines were closed with the loss of approximately 28,000 jobs. At this time the unemployment rate was approximately 24%. However, unemployment in the region has since fallen steadily, to 19% in 1980, 14% in 1990 and 5% in 1999 and the trend is expected to continue in the immediate future. This success creates certain problems in terms of meeting new labour market skill needs, for example in new sectors such as call centres. In fact, at the end of 1999 there were some 5,000 unfilled vacancies recorded and this is likely to increase as economic growth causes the labour market to tighten further. PITT sees the provision of technical training as critical to filling these vacancies.

PITT promotes training particularly for the 35,000 unemployed people in Limburg, including the 20,000 of them that are classified as disabled or as having particular difficulties with insertion into the labour market. One of the solutions being tried is a regional partnership approach to training and matching vacancies with trained workers. The partnership is not only with other regions in the Netherlands but also with regions in Germany, Luxembourg and Belgium that are part of the Euregion grouping (a cross-border regional partnership supported by the European Commission). There is a special emphasis on language training and infrastructure in order to promote mobility within the cross-border region.

Box 8 (continued)

In Limburg, it was perceived that there were too many different partnerships in operation. One of the central tasks of PITT is therefore to co-ordinate the existing partnerships, to combine them where possible and to increase the extent to which they share infrastructure and resources. One of the most important conditions for this is to build trust between the different partners and promote awareness of shared objectives.

A second key activity of PITT is the MIT programme, which can be translated as 'Make It in Technology'. MIT was founded by industry in 1999 in order to address the major shortage of technical workers that is being experienced in the region. It pursues the following activities:

- An internet-based, free-access system that allows job seekers to monitor employment and training opportunities in Limburg.

- A special programme for training and job matching for handicapped people and people seeking asylum.

- A retraining programme for women to encourage them to enter the labour market.

- A programme called 'Quality Regular Education' to encourage young people to pursue secondary education in technical subjects and to reduce the drop-out rate from such courses.

- A programme called 'I Like Technology', to improve the image of technology jobs with young people aged between 8 and 10 years, involving twice-yearly school visits from a team of approximately ten people.

- Public relations and communication of the programmes and partnership approaches.

The following factors appear to have contributed significantly to the success of the PITT approach. First, it operates in the form of a partnership, with active involvement from the trade unions, employers organisations, local governments and education institutions. Second, it concentrates on providing additional training provision with the support of its partners that fills gaps in the existing public/private training provision. Third, it works on attitudes to technology in schools in order to increase the take-up of technical education. Finally, it has invested in good infrastructure, such as the internet for lifelong learning and software for labour market monitoring, and seeks to share this infrastructure where possible.

In addition to partnership, Greffe in the next chapter points to three further requirements for effective training policies in the emerging knowledge economy. These are training through concrete projects, alternation of training and work and a multidimensional approach to solving the specific problems of marginalised people or communities. As Greffe argues, each of these features of effective modern training policies also favour local organisation of training. Thus, the project approach, which involves matching training to actual business needs or projects, requires the placing of trainees in local enterprises. Alternation, which involves the association of phases of training in workplace surroundings with phases in a more classical education setting, requires working in close collaboration with enterprises at local level. Multidimensionality, which involves comprehensively tackling all the skills and non-skills barriers to labour market participation of excluded people, requires association between various different local actors.

Summary

Human capital is an important determinant of economic growth and competitiveness in the globalising economy, but because companies and individuals tend to under-invest in training, public intervention is often needed.

Recognition of the need to invest in human capital policies is often linked to the idea that we are entering a knowledge economy in which knowledge is becoming an essential factor of production. This means that work and learning are becoming increasingly inter-related as skill levels have to be raised, updated more frequently and new types of skills developed. Our education and training systems have to adjust to these new conditions, based on the notion of lifelong learning. Systems of training and skills development need to adjust to take advantage of technologically-assisted methods of education and distance-learning technologies, to involve new training suppliers from the private sector, to reduce old demarcation lines between vocational and academic training and to provide greater access to learning from the workplace.

As argued in various recent OECD LEED Programme publications, one element of the response involves devolution of the design and delivery of skills and training policies from national to local level, with an increased role for actions created and co-ordinated at the city and regional level. Local partnerships have a key role in this, in promoting the mobilisation of local agencies, the involvement of employers and the integration of training with other programmes and in diffusing information through the network that can be used to help tailor actions to local needs.

In the context of devolution and globalisation, city and region governments should therefore develop measures to adjust existing training systems in order to promote skills enhancement and lifelong learning. In doing so, they should make use of local partnerships, whilst ensuring proper co-ordination between them (as illustrated by the PITT programme in Limburg, the Netherlands). In the next chapter, Greffe sets out the case for devolving key elements of public training policies to local bodies and partnerships and explores in more detail the sorts of training approaches required.

CHAPTER 7

DEVOLUTION OF TRAINING:
A NECESSITY FOR THE KNOWLEDGE ECONOMY

by

Xavier Greffe, Professor at University of Paris I, Pantheon - Sorbonne, Paris,
France

Introduction

Today's economy is a knowledge economy. Now that knowledge and skills
have become determining factors in production, people are better fitted to
partake in this economy if they possess abilities which they can refresh by
means of continuing education.

The acquisition of knowledge is thus a prerequisite for integrating people,
communities and regions into the global economy. The training involved must
respect four requirements:

1. Association of different partners in order to define correctly the
   skills needed and provide or re-provide work when training is
   completed.

2. 'Project culture', to foster creative and problem-solving ability.

3. Continuous intermeshing of practical knowledge and theoretical
   knowledge so as to induce a learning situation.

4. Understanding of living and social conditions so as to take into
   account the barriers preventing marginalised persons from
   acceding to training.

These four requirements are better met when training is decentralised.

Action in favour of decentralised training is thus a lever for full insertion into the knowledge economy. Devolution is a way of improving not only the efficiency of public training policy but also its effectiveness; this is because its goals are redefined when an area's inhabitants are the agents who remould it. However, this is not to deny the importance of more central policies in guaranteeing personal mobility, certifying skills quality or correcting the effects of uneven provision. Rather, training policies in a knowledge economy are most effective when action on behalf of devolution is balanced against the constraints that justify centralisation.

The overall aim of this chapter is to demonstrate the contribution of devolution to successful insertion in the knowledge economy. The following section will briefly describe some recent trends in globalisation and the knowledge economy and their implications for training policies. The third section examines the kinds of skills required by the knowledge economy and the obstacles to acquiring them that are associated with the present state of training systems and policies. The fourth section then discusses the four conditions required for producing these skills and examines how devolution acts as a catalyst for them. This catalytical role of devolved policies comes through partnership, 'project culture', linkage of practical and theoretical training locations and comprehensive awareness of trainees' social and living conditions. The final section reviews the conditions needed for devolved policies to operate well. It is argued that individuals and groups alike must be able to move between industries and regions, which supposes common references and quality control, and that unequal territorial provision must be corrected, an area in which the new technologies can contribute. The result is a new set of blueprints for the governance of training.

Globalisation, knowledge economy, ability to change

We live in a global economy that is also a knowledge economy. By global economy we mean an economy in which each geographical area, wherever it be, forms part of a larger whole which applies its forces, possibilities and constraints without any impediment from such increasingly artificial barriers as regional or national borders.

By knowledge economy we mean an economy in which knowledge has become an essential factor of production alongside the old tangible ones. Because of this, the ability of people, communities or areas to acquire and develop knowledge has become the prerequisite for their successful integration into the global economy and the means for avoiding their being sidelined or shut out.

Defining the main points and nature of the knowledge economy

It is nowadays usual to link the appearance of the knowledge economy with the technology revolution in computerisation and telecommunications. In fact, the latter has spawned a series of revolutions: software, data compression, intelligent interaction between wire and wireless, materials or energy processing, robotics, biotechnology, teleservices, and much more. The very connection between time and space has been altered. The knowledge economy, which has found that it can recover some of its investment in globalisation, is itself a driver of globalisation. It leads whole countries to work on a just-in-time basis. It enables traditional villages to market their products in the global village. Every day, it engenders new strategic alliances.

The new world economy has its own new characteristics:

- Knowledge is daily becoming a more, if not *the*, decisive factor in it.

- It is lightning-fast and has no boundaries.

- The consumer, aided by swiftly available and simple information, plays an ever more determining role.

- Businesses organise towards knowledge activities so as to meet the challenges of adjustment. They must capture information from within and without and synthesise it for use. They are quick to metamorphose in the direction of less verticality and emphasis on hierarchy – a 'flatter' corporate structure is better able to secure and disseminate knowledge.

- Personnel must be self-reliant, good team players, reacting and contributing to the gathering and processing of information. A worker's chief asset is not so much his trade as his ability to adjust.

These features, which affect the goals and mainsprings of training systems, pose a challenge to the way they have hitherto operated.

- Training has stopped being a phase or privilege occurring at a given point in a person's life; it is a permanent element in a person's life cycle.

161

- Since knowledge floods in from everywhere and quickly becomes obsolete, a person must always be in a position to learn to learn. Just-in-case learning has given way to just-in-time learning.

- Technical skills must be bedded in more generic skills, such as the ability to work in a team or to solve problems. The term 'helicopter skill' expresses this need to take a broad view of problems and concentrate immediately on solving those that seem the most important at a given moment (Berryman and Bailey, 1992, p. 14).

- There is a permanent risk of being cast aside. The revolutions referred to generate centrifugal forces whose strength is proportional to the weakness of generic and technical skills. The idea of equal opportunity, which was for a long time restricted to basic formal education, must now be enlarged to include training systems.

The new relation between training devolution and the knowledge economy

Training devolution did not spring into being with the knowledge economy. Some training systems have always been devolved whereas with others it was seldom the case. In the context of the knowledge economy, however, devolution takes on a new light.

Its purpose is no longer simply to increase the efficiency of public training policies by shielding them from the criticism levelled at centralised ones, e.g.:

- lack of precision in diagnosing problems,

- systematic use of top-down organisation, hindering the welling up of innovation,

- dissuasion of adults from re-entering systems ill-adapted to their needs,

- exclusion of target groups whose needs cannot be analysed except at local level,

- curriculum duplication.

Devolution should seek to improve the efficiency of training policies by shortening decision paths and making savings in time and money.

The issue is one of greater effectiveness. Production of new skills presupposes the application of new training principles: partnership approach, 'project culture' and linkage between on-the-job and off-the-job training locations. Devolution, by allowing these principles to be put into practice, helps in the production and spread of those skills which enable people to find their place in a knowledge economy and helps regions to 'stay ahead of the pack'.

Acquisition of skills, prerequisite for integration into the knowledge economy

The skills for change

Under relatively unchanging systems of production, it was fairly simple to know what sorts of credentials or skills had to be acquired. Relatively stable technical standards made it possible to cross-match school leaving and labour market entry. Credentials, which were predetermined by technical parameters, were codified in agreements concluded among the social partners.

In a knowledge economy, where activity and job content change perpetually, it is no longer possible to peg skills to stable and exact reference frames. What must be taken into account are permanent change, the ability to adjust to change and perhaps even the ability to engineer change.

Broadening and deepening the notion of skilling

The concept of 'competency', which embraces the following ideas, has therefore come into general use.

- It is just as important to perform well as it is to possess knowledge or credentials which are quickly outdated by economic progress.

- The ability to perform well is connected with the talents required for problem-solving.

- This ability is enhanced when analysis and solution of present problems are used to predict and solve future problems.

The concept of competency involves a blend of knowledge, know-how and knowing how to survive. Or it could be regarded as a combination of Knowing, Knowing How, Knowing Why, Knowing to Improve and Knowing to Learn.

The fifth of these is probably the most important. When extended to every member of a productive unit, it fosters the aptitude for group learning. Competency springs from three factors: absorption of past experience, practical ability to spot and formulate problems, and imagination.

Competency is thus characterised by three aspects – technical, behavioural, managerial – whereas the classic notion of qualifications set store on the technical side only. Henceforth the technical aspect will be fortified by such generic abilities as self-reliance, and aptitude for team work.

An example of these changes: cultural employment

As an illustration of this amplification and what it implies for training systems, we may consider the developments in cultural employment. For a long while, qualifications for cultural work were summed up in a single requirement, 'artistic talent'. The requirements now are increasingly varied; they stretch from artistic to technical and administrative ability, under the influence of several factors:

- new technologies,

- narrowing distinction between artistic and technical work in sound and picture production,

- development of ancillary activities and markets in which once separated functions are now married together,

- appearance of new specialities.

Here are a few examples:

- New technologies are having a decisive influence on how the music sector operates.

- They enter into composition, whatever the style of music or context. It is now possible, with computers and the right software, to transform one's home into a production studio without any need for performers or orchestras.

- The new technologies are affecting distribution, with the introduction and success of DVDs (Digital Versatile Disks) which improve sound quality, and mini-disks which offer almost endless possibilities for storing music.

- They are influencing broadcasting, allowing radio and television to cater for individual preferences and make full use of interactivity.

- Lastly, via the Internet, they are completely remodelling the landscape.

Talent remains at the heart of the system, but a musician needs to become adept at other functions, since artists are in a team situation with agents, managers, publishers, broadcasters, legal experts, etc. Even where the team is virtual, each of its members needs to understand or exercise the skills of the others, with consequences that differ according to the point of departure.

In the audio-visual field, digital techniques have precipitated changes in jobs and their associated skills. They have done this by underscoring the need to interweave three basic talents: audio-visual design, technical expertise and organisational skills. An example is the media designer whose job it is to devise and electronically fashion audio-visual products. He must be able to:

- discuss production issues and goals with programme directors,

- select, operate and maintain the requisite equipment,

- analyse and check recordings, retrieve material from sound and picture archives, and cope with variations in formats and standards,

- record, analyse and process sound and pictures,

- see to publishing the products on their support medium, edit visuals under the direction of producers and cameramen.

All this means uniting skills from such varied fields as technology, design and organisation.

In book publishing, versatility results from two trends:

1. The shortening of the design-production chain (Computer Assisted Publishing imposes synthesis of editorial and productive functions).

2. The growth of the marketing chain (need to know the public and the variety of distribution channels, to deal with intellectual property rights, to manage multimedia relations).

This move towards skill realignment gives publishers greater control over the marketing system but obliges them, in addition to supervising content, to be competent in management, marketing, finance, and media promotion.

In the eyes of several authors (Schmidt Braul, 1998, p.3), the most striking feature of these changes is the appearance in every sector of a new breed of skill, that of the 'information officer'. He works at the interface between production and the supply and use of information. He is a mediator between systems and users, constantly combining artistic, creative and communication skills. He must be capable of crossing from one form of expression to another, and linking together different cultural situations. Content, design and communication are the pillars upon which varied abilities must build.

Accepting the principle of skills development

Describing the type of skill needed for successful entry into a knowledge economy does not mean that everyone can or should advance at the same pace. Two consequences flow from this.

The first has to do with the identification and acquisition of the desired skills. People's situations are different. Persons who have been absent or excluded from the labour market for a long time cannot always be thrust overnight into a position of independence and technical specialisation. This has to be done by stages, each stage being geared as exactly as possible to a person's background. The customised training project established by the Sunderland New Deal Partnership is a good example (OECD, 1999b, pp. 102-103). It was decided, in an employment area where the Nissan corporation was reporting massive skills requirements which the local long-term unemployed could not satisfy, to create an association, the Automotive Sector Strategic Alliance, whose aim was to help firms to accept job-seekers and diagnose the latter's abilities. This 'gateway' screened persons who already possessed basic skills such as teamwork, numeracy and manual dexterity and directed them into more advanced fields of training. It devised a basic training package for those who did not possess these skills.

The second concerns the certification or accrediting of competencies. Where skill requirements are more or less stable (and people able to satisfy them are inter-changeable), it is fairly easy to establish a certification system applicable to all. Where requirements are fluid and people satisfy them in varying degrees, the certification system has to be adjusted. It is better in that case to let a person obtain certification for all or part of his abilities at his own pace and in proportions that he determines for himself.

Local development, territorial quality and individual skill levels

As R. Florida has pointed out, enterprises must, in order to grow in a global economy, have workers who learn continually, can apply their intelligence to the production process and draw new knowledge from it (Hastings, 1999, p. 29). The result for all the enterprises making up a region will be a collective learning capacity that comprises a 'learning region'. Today this concept refers to the capacity for communication and participation among persons in the same region, both inside their enterprises and among them, their ability to inform each other of their intentions and problems, and their ability to enter into a process of negotiation and co-operation. According to R. Treptov, a learning region is a region capable of extending 'its repertoire for balancing interests and promoting communication' (Treptov, 1999, p. 120).

The development potential of a region depends not only on what happens inside a firm but also on what happens in the business environment (Florida, 1995) and hence in the relations among its defining institutions: the training market, the labour market, the capital market, etc (Morgan, 1997). This supposes the development of competencies that extend beyond the professional sphere to the connections between this sphere and other spheres. According to M.S. Gertler, 'the concept of the learning region has emerged to describe those places that offer an institutional environment that encourages both private and social learning at four different scales: the individual worker, the individual firm, within groups of related firms, and within governmental bodies.' (Gertler, 1999, p. 36)

The types of skills needed for the knowledge economy are becoming increasingly varied. They have social implications, since they improve a region's aptitude for learning and change.

Malfunctioning of local training systems

Do local training systems match up to the challenges posed by these skills? Their performance is uneven, owing to two sorts of difficulty:

1. weaknesses in expressing training demands;

2. shortcoming of training systems.

Weaknesses in local training demands

Skills production depends on needs being correctly expressed. In regions having trouble entering the knowledge economy, enterprises and workers alike sometimes express their demands badly.

Enterprise demands

Enterprise demands need to be analysed in different ways according to size of enterprise: large, small and micro.

Large enterprises occupy a place apart. In general, they organise their own training. They can even, when they are engaged in hiving off or worker recycling strategies, act as 'net providers' of training in a given region. On the other hand, an enterprise delocating in order to launch new activities in a region outside its own is a 'net demander' of training. It addresses its demands to the regional authorities or local training networks; it may even subordinate setting up business to the solution found to meet its training needs.

The problem of small and ultra-small enterprises is different. Training is not their major concern, even if their environment faces them with challenges of adjustment which they cannot meet on their own. Experience has shown that their needs are at best expressed in connection with some other need – technical, financial, commercial – deemed to be more urgent. When they do express needs, a paradoxical situation can arise. The small firm is too short of funds to finance this kind of initiative, but it disdains training provided free of charge. Time also is precious, that of the owner and that of his employees whom he cannot release, even for short periods. Repeated observation shows that the training problem needs to be tackled along with that of other urgent tasks; it has to be demonstrated that it will lead to a return on investment; and it must be treated on a network basis.

In addition to the case of small firms, there is the situation of enterprises located in areas undergoing sweeping industrial redeployment, such as that of Jena in Germany.

After reunification, the number of persons receiving training in enterprises still in activity despite the area's competitiveness crisis dwindled sharply (Christmann, 1999, pp. 95-97). In 1998, learners in the 118 firms in the chemicals sector in Jena, which employed a workforce of 13 600, should have numbered 1 300; in fact, there were only 92 (idem, p. 96). This was especially surprising in view of the fact that alternating training is a key feature of the German economy. Explanations for industry indifference to training in times of crisis are not wanting, but one is plain to see. When facing the strains of competitiveness, these firms increasingly abandon long-term planning and look for the fastest possible forms of adjustment. This correspondingly attenuates their traditional role in training.

Worker demands

It might be expected that someone who loses his job will express a desire for training that will enable him to find another job. A study of redeployment crises in various regions shows that things are not so clear-cut.

Workers who have lost their position can very often pride themselves on a skill, frequently acquired on the job and related to an occupation that forms the basis of a social fabric. In many cases, this occupation has been an emblem of group resistance to any kind of individual or mass redeployment. It is viewed as an inalienable possession, an unsurpassable talent, and even as a shield against disaster. 'Becoming perfect at one's trade is a lock-in; the working man's career is the chronicle of his loss of liberty.' (Rolle, 1997, p. 48)

In consequence, these workers (and even their children) express little desire for training. An offer of training seems ridiculous to them – it sounds the knell of the skills they have acquired; it does not have apparent meaning since it is not provided in the workplace. The incongruity is worsened by the fact that the courses proposed are often lengthy, their accessory costs are high and future job offers are by no means certain. Candidates also run an economic risk in that attendance at training can often be interpreted as refusing job transfers, or lucrative anticipated departure and early retirement schemes. Lastly, undergoing training has an air of returning to school or to places associated with under-achievement, where a person can still risk being exposed to failure or the taunts of his fellows. All these functional, economic and psychological risks reinforce one another. 'The offer of training made to them in this crisis situation seems absurd, since their experience has taught them that training is a long process of learning, concomitant with having an ever more complex job to perform. For them, it cannot take the shape of a brief course divorced from the concrete conditions of production.' (idem, p. 52)

Shortcomings of training systems

The first of these has to do with the training institutions' own time-frame. It is not often the same as that of firms facing competition or that of the crisis conditions in struggling regions. Whereas these regions must be able to adjust with speed, training operations can require long time-spans, all the more so where systems are centralised.

Part of the time needed is that devoted to 'training the trainers'. Trainers working professionally in institutions where they continually perform the same tasks tend to become extremely specialised. This is a particularly delicate point, in that it raises two sorts of problem – a person's ability to change, and the organisation of change. The difficulty experienced by many countries in re-tailoring vocational training stems from these problems. A number of lessons may be drawn from the situation:

- These problems should be handled in the closest possible conjunction with the people concerned, and devolution helps in this respect.

- Trainers should be recruited ad hoc, by drawing on the potential of industry or the resources of distance learning, without relying exclusively on 'institutional' trainers.

- The work and careers of trainers should be more flexibly organised. This is something which depends more on central government action.

The second inadequacy concerns teaching systems which rely more on abstract deductive approaches than on practical inductive methods. The ability to identify and deal with problems requires concrete situations, in which the notion of 'project' provides the connecting thread. Immersion in a 'project situation' has the advantage of being related to real problems, and the participation of the people at grips with them. Theoretical deductive approaches should take a back seat to more empirical inductive procedures, although they may be brought into play later to deepen the lessons learned and transmute them into knowledge, i.e. competencies.

Unfortunately, most training systems remain tethered to the theoretical deductive model. There are many reasons for this, ranging from the wish to give everyone the same background to the heavy costs entailed in changing over to inductive methods. Devolution of training systems, by not only associating local players with problems but also profiting from the availability of concrete situations, makes it easier to introduce the inductive approach.

Training provision – be it human, financial or technical – is also unevenly distributed across regions.

Certain regions are lacking in trainers, for a number of reasons:

–   When trainers do not live in a region, they tour it only briefly, and thus cannot make meaningful contact with trainees.

–   Trainers, 'obliged' to work in certain centres, believe that they will escape as soon as possible, and so do not commit themselves to their work there.

–   Deprived of support and refresher training programmes, they gradually become ineffective.

Another obstacle is insufficient budgeting, by both industry and local bodies. The solution is here again dependent on the kind of difficulties facing the region.

Technical assets – infrastructure, communications facilities, machine tools, etc. – are related to the state of the industrial fabric in a particular region. Where this fabric is badly decayed, the assets often do not exist.

It may be noted lastly that training problems are global in character whereas the solutions provided are often partial. Sending somebody to train in an area where traditional service and family solidarity networks have disintegrated means not only launching educational action but also finding answers to health, child-minding, transport and other problems. Potential solutions to the range of problems sometimes exist but, being handled by decentralised authorities or services, they tend to remain ineffectual.

These observations lead us to a contradiction. Although everything points to the need to acquire skills, actions and efforts come to little, especially in struggling regions. In the light of these frustrations, many people underplay the role of training (OECD, 1999a, pp. 19-21). To the Eurobarometer (Eurostat, 1997, 1998, OECD, 1999a, p. 40) question, 'What would you do if you found yourself unemployed?', only one young person in eight said he would be ready to take up apprenticeship or change jobs – a reflection of mistrust in the power of training to solve problems.

This remark is borne out by two criticisms often levelled at training:

1. by countries which, to avoid possible abuses of welfare schemes, prefer to put work before other forms of reinsertion ('work first'), including training (deemed to be too time-wasting or inefficient).

2. by firms which set more store on 'fundamental virtues' such as punctuality, conscientiousness, etc. than on technical skills which can be acquired only in the workplace.

The criticisms give a good idea of the difficulties encountered by training schemes ill-suited to the persons concerned, badly administered, and ultimately counter-productive. They are addressed more to the way training is conducted than to the principle of training itself. It is clearly of interest therefore to redefine the organisational underpinning of training whose purpose is the acquisition of the skills of change.

Devolution, prior condition for effective training systems

Training systems must, if people are to enter successfully into the knowledge economy, produce 'active knowledge' and 'venturesome knowledge'. People will then become agents of change within their workplace and the region where they live. 'Everyone must be enabled to better understand the technical, social and economic constituents of his environment, and made into an agent of change by becoming able to act on the structures in which he lives and aware of his role as an actor in society.' (Rolle, 1997, p. 58)

It follows that four conditions must be met for training action to be effective:

– The mapping, implementation and evaluation of training must be carried out in partnership, this being the way to define the new competencies and bring together knowledge, experience and resources from various horizons.

– Training must be based on a project approach in order to teach trainees how to sustain or join in a project, that is to say, be self-reliant and innovative.

- Training must, so as to interconnect knowledge, know-how and life skills, conjoin the locations of apprenticeship and of knowledge.

- The conduct of training requires a multi-dimensional approach, since the training problems of socially marginalised or excluded persons are invariably linked to other living-condition problems.

A closer look at these four conditions will show that in each case devolution helps in meeting them.

Partnership

Training needs engender situations in which the information to be gathered (estimation of skills and markets, human resource status in a given region) and the assets to be pooled (finance, training provision, technical facilities, time, training-related services) are under the control of different participants: enterprises, training institutions, trainers, trainees, local authorities. At any given moment and in any given region, partnership provides the means for creating the needed interactions and synergies, which neither a centralised public system nor a market intent on short-term opportunities can easily do. Partnership, far from being a nostrum or a gadget, enables mutually interdependent stakeholders to pool their strengths and find common solutions to the problems which each of them encounters separately.

Partnership has another justification. Often in the past, training was seen as a useful way of passing time, leading eventually to finding work. But it has also been observed that certain forms of training led to nothing more than further stints of training. This resulted in poor use of resources and the demoralisation of trainees – an aberration all the more serious in that it affected socially vulnerable and left-out individuals. The best way to correct it is, as far as possible, to situate training within the perspective of a definite job. This entails setting firms at the heart of the process, even if they do not shoulder all the details.

Putting partnership into practice

Examples of such partnerships abound. Among the first were probably the 'compacts' in the United States. They were contracts between local training authorities, schools and local employers for improving the level of training of school-leavers and their opportunities for updating it (Davenport, 1989). The

173

system's origins go back to experiments tried out in Boston in the early 1980s. The Private Enterprise Council, along with schools and training centres, organised information, evaluation and refresher courses for young people or adults to help them in returning to or finding full-time employment. In 1983, the Governor of Massachusetts decided to react against the confusion and irresponsibility resulting from the gradual accumulation of additional training programmes for young people in difficulty. He invited the business community to participate and introduced a system of joint management for the collective entity so formed. Business corporations sat on the programme's governing board and their executives occupied certain administrative posts.

Several basic principles were overhauled. Training programmes were to be retailored to local development needs and made available to all. The revised system was to contain optional alternatives that could be monitored by means of efficiency indicators. Training system management was to be devolved in liaison with the labour market.

In 1986, the experiment was adopted as a model for the rehabilitation of certain areas of London: the Docks, Tower Hamlets and Hackney. Newly established enterprises could not find the manpower they needed and the pupils of the surrounding schools could not find jobs. A group assembling teachers and employers settled on a number of yardsticks for co-ordinating school-leaving and recruitment by the enterprises. An assessment system was introduced to evaluate absenteeism, punctuality, literacy, numeracy, ability to work at home and specific proficiencies, according to the career-paths chosen. The teachers undertook to work towards satisfying these criteria, while the employers agreed to offer trial employment to the young people who met them.

The record of these early compacts was not invariably good. Apart from the pious intentions expressed, they could be used by each of the parties as a way of discharging its responsibilities upon the other. Yet their implementation proved a powerful incentive to the young, who had a clearer view of how they might obtain employment. Employers gained by the system, since it enabled them to manage their training budgets better. Training centres benefited from business resources, in the shape of information input, added expertise, and equipment loans. The community itself profited, with employers turning their attention to underprivileged groups.

On the minus side, certain employers concentrated their favours on particular training centres and demanded quick returns which could not always be supplied. Size of enterprise was a determining factor. The largest firms seemed more receptive to the idea of adjustment periods and acceptance of problem groups. Lastly, pupils who did not match up to the predetermined yardsticks found themselves practically shut out of the labour market and with very little chance of finding employment.

Today these partnerships have various objectives, ranging from drafting local training policy, estimation of the resources needed for its implementation and planning for youth employment to the placement of adults and long-term unemployed.

As an example of <u>partnerships to determine training needs and local training provision</u> may be quoted the consultative teams established in Sheffield as part of the UK New Deal Partnership programme (OECD, 1999b, p. 70). A Consultative Task Team (CTT) was set up within the Sheffield New Deal Partnership for the purpose of associating potential training partners with the action carried out. One of its two working groups, containing several employers, was devoted to providing employment to people who had been jobless for more than six months. The working group's agenda covered the following:

- − defining the content and form of training provision and how employers could contribute to it;
- − discussing perception of the new initiative in the light of the barriers of poor perception of previous initiatives;
- − seeing how employers could take advantage of hiring persons supported by the programme;
- − undertaking action for producing sustained employment for employees entering the scheme.

Employers in the working group made a number of recommendations, such as the introduction of a 'mentoring' system for youth and a single contact point for employers, and ways of forestalling obstacles liable to prevent employers from subscribing to the initiative.

As to <u>partnerships for achieving adjustment</u>, mention may be made of the Austrian *Cluster-Netz* experiment in Styria. Styria has a big automobile parts industry made up mostly of small and medium-sized enterprises (The Copenhagen Centre, 1999a, pp. 14-15). The problem is that these SMEs cannot find in the education system the human potential needed to manage themselves in ever larger groupings, even though this is vital if they are to escape from sub-contractorship and conquer the markets which will guarantee local employment. Twenty SMEs in the Acstyria industrial cluster therefore founded a training network, the *Cluster-Netz*, with the main local technical training institute, the

Technikum Joanneum. The network diagnoses firms' skills needs, devises a system of continuous training and makes intensive use of a multimedia training centre, relying largely on the Internet.

As an example of a <u>partnership for finding new jobs for the unemployed</u> we may point to the *itinéraires du Limbourg*. In the Limbourg province of Belgium, there were a multitude of overlapping training programmes which turned out to be ineffectual in bringing back jobless people to the labour market (The Copenhagen Centre, 1999a, pp. 16-17). In 1996, several of the protagonists directly concerned – the Flemish employment service (VDAB), private firms, labour unions, the cities and training institutions – decided to found a partnership 'Working Together for Employment'.

The idea is to plan an 'itinerary' for each individual to be re-employed. According to the steps in the itinerary, the individual is 'steered' by a particular protagonist, it being understood that all the protagonists know when and how they should intervene. The partnership begins by pooling information and resources, but assumes specific forms according to the individual's training problems and the speed with which these can be solved. The partnership has not always been easy to implement, especially where the sharing of information is concerned. An effort is therefore being made to go further in that direction pending the creation of a genuine skills observatory.

The establishment of partnerships of this kind runs into a recurring difficulty, namely <u>the participation of private enterprise</u>, without which training can only limp along. Such participation is triply important:

- It contributes to the identification of training needs.

- It enables training initiatives to be undertaken.

- It can lead to the hiring of persons in serious difficulty.

Enterprises do not, however, always have the free time to do this. They do not always express their needs. Some of them are not organised to partake in training. Others can be reluctant to receive problem cases. Attempts to overcome these obstacles can be fruitful if they are addressed to (Brown, Buck and Skinner, 1998; OECD, 1999b, p. 103):

- enterprises with pressing needs,

- small businesses, via their representatives,

- firms with a direct stake in community development.

The role of devolution as regards partnerships

Whatever their value, partnerships will work properly if they are established within a context of devolution:

- Local stakeholders are the ones who possess the necessary information.

- Action must be tailored to the specific nature of local human resources and living conditions.

- Partners must be well informed concerning their separate activities so that problems of trust and co-ordination may be brought to light and corrective measures taken as early as possible.

While the first two of these aspects of devolution's contribution to partnership are familiar, the third requires further explanation.

Partnership, unlike the market and regulations, organises co-ordination among institutions or people on a basis more of mutual trust than external sanctions. It is nevertheless vain to pretend that joint values or cultures 'inherited from the past' – acting as a binding and driving force – will ensure the coherence of the interactions in question. Rather the contrary:

- The players may, like their values or immediate goals, be different in kind.

- Changes in expectations or technology can occur as partnerships develop, raising the question of preserving consensus.

- The operation of partnerships and alterations in their environment have an effect on the benefits and gains derived from attitudes shared in common at a particular moment, and may trigger forces for or against their continuation.

Instead of making the effectiveness of partnerships depend on shared values, it is better to start from a broader interpretation. The partnership situation involves social interactions characterised by input/output costs and personal relations among its members. A certain regularity in attitudes is essential, which implies that each member preserves this regularity and can count on the others preserving it also. To attain this result, the social interactions in partnerships must be so structured that (Greffe, 1999a, pp. 127-135):

- contacts among members are frequent and considered as worth pursuing; each one must therefore act constructively (reputation or co-operation effect) in order to expect like behaviour from the others;

- the cost of information on the action of the others is as low as possible, so that measures for foiling attempts to seize economic rent or windfall effects are taken promptly (retaliation effect);

- interaction is the privilege of the partnership members; otherwise it loses its rationale (proximity effect);

- any disintegration of the partnership before it has achieved its goals is kept to a minimum (segmentation effect).

The partnership will work well to the extent that the co-operation, reprisals and proximity effects are strong and the segmentation effect is weak. In all cases, devolution makes it possible to detect these effects and crystallise them in the desired direction, whereas centralised policies are liable to prevent their being easily foreseen and suitably handled.

'Project culture'

Reasons for project culture

In no matter what technical field, skill value is nowadays bound up with initiative and learning capacity. Acquired knowledge must be looked upon as a lever for change rather than an end in itself. Training should on this account be keyed to the problems needing to be solved. It should educate persons for a project culture, enabling them to acquire theoretical knowledge, practical experience and problem-solving ability.

Inculcating project culture

The way project culture is taught during training will differ according to context. In some cases, it will be taken to its logical conclusion by making business creation its goal. In other cases, its aim will be the development of self-reliance. At the very least, it will seek to bathe the training actors – trainers and trainees alike – in project thinking.

In one configuration, it can aim at <u>hiving off and activity creation</u>, as may be seen from the experiment of the *Centro Sperimentale per lo Sviluppo dell'Electronica* (Schumack and Greffe, 1997, pp. 18-20). The Centre, located in Orbassano on the outskirts of Turin, was created by a consortium of thirteen private enterprises, the Province of Turin and the Commune of Turin. Its purpose was to disseminate the technical knowledge and technology needed for creating new products and activities. The area had inherited a concentration of its processes around the industrial reflexes existing in many sectors. This being so, it was possible to devise and bring into being new products, training schemes and enterprises. The programme's approach is always flexible. The choice is to locate and adapt training schemes in line with needs rather than codify them beforehand and open them to all comers. Three companies were formed from the parent corporation – one for bringing out new products, one for organising exhibitions and producing publications, and a European company to promote the exchanges needed to achieve these objectives. The whole programme today assembles 120 wage-earners.

There has been a diversification of activities into such areas as chemical engineering and multimedia. Developmental work and expertise in hypertexts has led to expanded activities that are both innovative and economically sound. They have enabled the creation of eighty businesses by the persons so trained. Even trainees who do not go into business have no trouble finding work:

- Selection standards for training applications are very stringent.

- The jobs trained for are not limited to traditional software, a field that is becoming heavily congested.

- Teaching is constantly refreshed by inviting back former trainees who have gone through the experience of launching innovative projects. In this way, business management courses do not lose touch with reality.

- Professional ventures are monitored and given the advice and backing they need.

In another case, trainees' capacity for self-reliance is developed so that they bring the benefit of their abilities to the firms in which they will work. We may take the example of the *Institut de créativité industrielle de Saint-Nazaire* (idem, pp. 24-26). In this French employment area long centred on ship-building, the very many small businesses were in a situation of sub-contractorship, churning out the same products for the same order-givers. This prevented research and innovation and made it almost impossible to switch to other products. The local training system was totally geared to this system of production, providing skills that were both narrowly-focussed and unchanging.

Local partners, faced with a crisis in the city's key activity and the need for its established sub-contracting firms to achieve greater independence, set up an Institute for Industrial Creativeness. Its guiding idea was consistently to place its trainees – former technicians, future executives, etc. – in a business enterprise setting, making them identify with its goals and constraints. To this end, three courses were amalgamated in a single whole: training in theory and the tooling needed to develop new products; customised specialist training to cover a full range of technologies; practical work based on selected projects within firms. As a result, firms were provided with human resources whose level of training helped in supplying them with the wanted innovative capacity.

In yet another variation, generalisation of project culture consists in steeping all the training partners, including trainers and training administrators, in this form of culture. Here we may mention the experiment of the Futuroscope College, also in France, which provides training for young people and adults (Uturaud-Gireaudeau, 1997, pp. 28-30). Its integration of enterprise and project culture takes several forms: teaching subjects, learning tools, new technology mirroring. The culture acts as the training institution's source of energy, and enables the targeted site to acquire such values as creativity, communication, association and adaptability.

At the college, enterprise culture is an educational discipline, as may be seen from the courses devoted to the running of an enterprise, the discovery of economic realities, and project management.   Such teaching, for all its usefulness, is often limited by its abstract character. For this reason, project culture includes compulsory workplace learning for all trainees. Enterprise culture is also experienced and acquired through an appropriate use of new technologies, fostering the absorption of some of the values of enterprise culture: creativeness, especially through the use of graphics, word processing, CAD and other software; mobility and flexibility (today's computer tools being shareable and networkable); and complexity management.

For this culture to take hold, the lives and careers of trainees must inhabit a framework enshrining its values. This is why it must be espoused by the training and administrative teams, who must agree to goal-achievement contracts.   The prizing of human resources, the organisation of training institutions as centres for initiative, environmental adaptability and the quest for effectiveness are all contributing factors.

Role of devolution in spreading project culture

The dissemination of project culture is not an abstract exercise. It is through observation of, or immersion in, an occupational milieu that a person becomes capable of distinguishing fields of potential from fields of constraint, of testing success and failure, of developing an ability for memorisation and collective learning. Training centres cannot therefore be content with teaching enterprise culture; they must at the least simulate situations in which it can be tried out, and, even better, place their trainees in these situations. The importance of this is all the greater in that this culture is not necessarily identical from one region to another. The concept of entrepreneurship relates to a region's opportunities and realities, whereas the entrepreneurial spirit is more a matter of knowing how to take risks.

Progress can be made only by working in practical terms and hewing as closely as possible to local realities. It is possible to achieve this goal by taking a decentralised approach from the outset. This is corroborated by the fact that:

-   the steps to familiarity with project culture necessarily involve partnership;

-   the factors that shape project culture in a particular region often depend on organisational, institutional and managerial patterns that are discernible only at the local level.

Alternation

Why alternation?

Competency training requires acceptance of the alternation principle, that is to say, the association of phases of training in workplace surroundings with phases in a classical education situation. Since competency relates to the ability to handle the unexpected and exercise initiative, trainees must learn to cope with constraints and develop their aptitudes for self-reliance, co-operation and initiative. Formal teaching in commonplace surroundings, despite its value, has its limits. Even if trainees are taught to think about the 'enterprise', this is no substitute for a plunge into enterprise thinking. By introducing trainees to business reality, it may be expected that they will develop versatility and flexibility, that they will perceive space differently, that they will be motivated to become creative, and that they will cultivate a taste for efficiency, which is the cardinal virtue in business life.

The point of alternation in this context is not merely to supplement knowledge with know-how; it is to use the synergy between two training situations to foster creativity (Greffe, 1993). It is also a way to remotivate or reacclimatise people who have left the business world or never experienced it.

Further to these reasons may be added the pressure observed in recent years in favour of training programmes directed towards the fastest possible return to working life. The 'Work First' movement expresses this demand. Rather than indefinitely prolong training that does not teach what can be learnt only in the workplace, it is better to subordinate training to job prospects and determine training needs on a case-by-case basis. The principle of 'mutual obligation' introduced in Australia for young unemployed aged 18-24 entails paying unemployment benefits for longer than a 6-month period in exchange for training and activities, which are geared as closely as possible to real working conditions (OECD, 1999b, p. 21).

Practising alternation

While the organisation of alternating training is by no means new (especially in countries like Germany and Austria), it is far from being universal or unvarying – it can be made to accommodate such varied items as briefing on trades, project sponsorship and short-term hiring. It is nevertheless true that it is increasingly being adopted in retraining and redeployment policies.

An interesting case is the training of turners in Marinha Grande (Portugal). The vocational training centres in Marinha Grande, a city whose crystal and glass industry is now being obliged to redeploy into plastics and mouldings, were unpopular and ineffective. The Marinha Grande school, dependent on the Ministry of Education, decided to join forces with the business community, the glass industry federation and the Vocational Training Institute, which alone was entitled to certify vocational proficiency and qualifications. The plan was to train each year a class of a dozen or so young persons or adults who had already had at least nine years of schooling. They were to acquire the trade of turner after six months of classroom training followed by six months spent in the workplace.

Again, there are the Learn-at-Work Centres of Flevoland, a Netherlands training scheme for promoting re-employment. Original solutions are needed to enable long-term unemployed to find their way back to the labour market. In a situation where large numbers of people have, in fact, never entered the labour market and are lacking in certain basic skills, it is important to create 'way-stations' where the re-learning of essential job subjects is combined with training that is an improvement on the existing provision. In the Netherlands province of Flevoland, the city authorities have instituted centres which 'teach employment' (The Copenhagen Centre, 1999a, pp. 66-67). These are public centres organised by the cities (six in all) which operate in collaboration with local firms, training institutes and employment agencies. This partnership goes beyond the usual frameworks, in the sense that it must accept people who in many cases have dependants. It consequently works in association with day-care centres, retirement homes for the elderly, etc.

The Centres operate as protected workplaces, their principle being to ensure the personal development of the workers concerned. As appropriate, workers are directed for fixed periods towards more institutionalised training centres. Over the past four years, 1 300 people have passed through the Centres. The guiding idea has always been to channel people back to the mainstream labour market. The Centres see and judge themselves as intermediate places of transit, not as places for permanent stay.

As a final example, we may cite Glasgow Works, which probably takes the principle of alternation to its limits, making it a key ingredient in its intermediate labour market approach. At the outset and for a pre-assessment and counselling period of 3-4 weeks, a number of requirements, including training, are laid down for the purpose of helping long-term unemployed to return to work doing jobs that are locally useful. During the ensuing year of work, additional training is provided. At the end of this year, beneficiaries facing entry into the labour market proper can receive further specially suited training. The programme's philosophy therefore is that employability increases with work experience and that this is improved by doses of case-by-case training (OECD, 1999b, pp. 77-79).

The role of devolution in alternation

These initiatives reap success or leave problems uncured according to how they are organised. Among the success factors (or failure factors when the assumptions are reversed) may be counted (Greffe, 1995, pp. 119-163):

- networking of data;

- prior negotiation and agreement on targets and ultimate aims;

- personalised action, trainees being regarded never *en masse* but according to their strengths and demands;

- provision of practical solutions to trainees' living problems (dependent families, travel distance, etc.);

- setting training programmes in a context of forward movement;

- the host enterprise's ability to organise itself as a place of training; in firms which practise the division of tasks, a job-ranking system and internal mobility procedures that prevent skill transfer from one post to another, trainees may not benefit;

- financial compensation for enterprises; if they do not receive offsets, they may leave it to other firms to provide the services and pay the costs.

These factors all point to the value of devolution, providing that an appropriate regulatory framework exists. Once this framework has been established, all action requires working in the closest possible touch with the people and realities concerned.

Multi-dimensionality

The rationale of multi-dimensionality: combating exclusion

The problems involved in training marginalised or excluded people are never a simple matter of underskilling. The aspects of the problems extend to the conditions of these peoples' everyday lives. Unless the problems are solved, they risk jeopardising access to training and the good that may accrue from it. The handicaps include health, distance, lack of replacement income, child minding or elderly person responsibilities, and sub-standard housing.

Such barriers to receiving training cannot be ignored. This implies that the problems be addressed comprehensively. The organisation of a training programme demands specification of the standards and conditions of living under which it is feasible.

Making multi-dimensionality work

The establishment of second chance schools – the one in Bilbao (Spain) in particular – illustrates the how and why of a multi-dimensional approach (European Commission, 1999, pp. 16-19). In this employment area, the jobless rate tops 25 per cent and over half the unemployed are aged under 30. In the neighbourhood Bilbao la Vieja, where the training centre is located, social conditions are abject: run-down housing, drugs, prostitution. Most of the unemployed found themselves drawn there as the result of industrialisation which could no longer deliver the number of jobs wanted. Any viable training programme was obliged to take this environment into account, for example, by providing working or learning premises for individual activity – whence the importance of computer or audio-visual workshops. The team charged with carrying out the training project therefore brought in welfare workers and representatives of voluntary organisations right from the start. The latter play a vital role in spreading information and convincing people of the worth of training, an idea which more 'classical' stakeholders have great difficulty in popularising.

Multi-dimensionality requires the observance of certain rules:

- Readiness to train without immediate results; training work should not be conceived of as a simple commercial or outsourcing operation.

- Time set aside for training must take account of other demands on time; they must as far as possible be reconciled.

- Welfare service, association and community development institution staff must be associated with traditional training personnel.

- Transparency in financial management must be guaranteed.

Devolution's role in multi-dimensionality

Such associations of actors make sense only in a local setting, where problems can be grasped in their actual context. The local approach is therefore essential, and supposes that programmes be implemented in decentralised fashion. Emphasis on this principle should not, however, lead to snubbing the local representatives of central government. Their involvement is vital – very often they control substantial resources. They can, when resource planning is conducted from the start within a sectoral framework, commit resources with greater efficiency.

Optimising training policy devolution

Training system devolution meets the challenges of a global economy (OECD, 1999b, p. 41 & p. 114) by:

– enabling information to be obtained from the actors at first hand,

– permitting better co-ordination among the actors,

– uniting their action and resources behind common objectives,

– catalysing innovations that can arise only from the local situation,

– correcting sectoral central government action that is poorly co-ordinated or unco-ordinated at local level.

For all this, devolution is not a cure-all. It raises problems and contains risks:

– It may obscure certain underlying trends which, correctly diagnosed, would facilitate manpower mobility.

– It may overlook the uneven distribution of training provision across the area.

– It does not always produce accountable systems (OECD, 1999b, p. 46).

– It may lead to programme duplication.

– It may introduce deviations from national objectives or make it difficult to achieve them.

A number of precautions need therefore to be taken in order to optimise the hoped-for effects of training devolution: increasing manpower mobility; correcting the uneven distribution of provision; making training systems accountable and getting them to work in synergy. Each is discussed in turn below.

Increasing manpower mobility

The knowledge economy requires a constant redefinition and redistribution of jobs, skills and places of work. Three conditions must be satisfied if people are to profit genuinely from the training they receive:

- identification of skills with the utmost discernment;

- attention to training quality;

- ensuring that persons acquiring skills can obtain recognition for them in workplaces anywhere; this supposes their certification.

Predictive guidance on vocational prospects and the corresponding skills may exceed a given region's information capacities or sphere of competence. The region does not at any one moment display all the choices that may exist later. It may even be feared that some of the criteria around which it builds its training system will become unclear in the future. Forward thinking gains from standing back and taking the broadest possible view of the situation. The central government should therefore make sure that forecasting is carried out and extend it by information campaigns directed at the different regions and parties concerned in training.

The central government has a duty to watch over the quality of training, since devolution has the effect of altering traditional oversight patterns based on superior or even supervisory authority. The objective can be attained by contract schemes under which the central government supports training efforts in exchange for a commitment to meet a number of targets.

A third task for the central government is to help with the development of systems for accrediting knowledge and certifying skills. The commonly used systems of certification overlook the problems specific to each trainee and pay scant heed to each trainee's rate of progress. It is preferable to:

- establish flexible rules for certifying acquisition of training at varying speeds;

- accept partial certification;

- make provision for certification to allow changes in orientation or field of specialisation if the need so arises.

This style of skill certification would not clash with more traditional credentials systems based on broader criteria and providing more general information. It would rather permit them to become more flexible. A person would develop his own abilities and have them certified in line with his situation and ambition instead of being systematically forced to attain grades and win credentials that, by definition, cannot reflect the perpetual changes in the economy and its industrial combinations.

Correcting the uneven distribution of training provision

Training provision is distributed in unequal proportions, with struggling regions probably being the ones that suffer most from quantitative or qualitative deficiencies:

– The industrial fabric does not have the needed potential for diagnosis and equipment.

– Local public funding is insufficient for setting up and maintaining training programmes.

Two ways of remedying the impact of inequalities may be imagined:

– Using new technologies, in the shape of self-teaching computer software or distance learning, to allow the region concerned to benefit from extra-regional resources.

– Having the central government reallocate resources, preferably under contracts designed to ensure the accountability of all the parties concerned.

New media and self-teaching software

The new media contribute appreciably to the modernisation of training systems and are capable of correcting some of their shortcomings (Greffe, 1995). Of the media, the *written word* is the most traditional, but it is not ideal, owing to its almost invariable lack of interactive content. *Sound* has come to occupy an important place in teaching, despite its seeming unsuitability – radio programmes are not interactive, cannot be personalised and are not particularly flexible. *Images* remain among the most attractive teaching vehicles – the most expensive also, since in practice they have become synonymous with television. Television programmes, in comparison with radio, give the impression of being more convivial and easy to follow; yet they suffer from the same basic handicap. They do not offer trainees much opportunity to graduate their progress, personalise their approach or ask for more explanations. Attempts to remedy these problems have been made, as in the Open University, by joining telephone communication with television broadcasts. Video cassette recordings are considered by some as a better way of meeting this problem and introducing a degree of personal control into the process.

Teaching machines or learning kits are nowadays gaining wide acceptance in training, mainly in the technical disciplines (electronics, computer technology, etc.). They would seem to overcome certain basic handicaps, as for example lack of conviviality and interactiveness. But certain programmes are far from living up to their promise; communications fail to materialise in time; and the cost of loading and procurement remains high. The use of *computers* is an extremely sensitive and controversial subject. They may be employed in three different ways: as a tool for rehearsing and acquiring knowledge; as data banks; and as simulators for problem-solving. While there appear to be good reasons for using computers, their conditions of use must make the exercise worthwhile. It can be of help to have a permanent hot-line to counselling centres or tutors. Regular meetings among trainees can provide insights and solutions to problems encountered. The opening of resource centres where material and advice are permanently available is an extremely valid option; there are countries, such as Denmark, which have already established them.

Does *the Internet* enhance this environment to the point of 'revolutionising' training? By providing access to more numerous and more personalised programmes, it enlarges the potential for information and repetition – allowance being made for the cost of downloading the software. The Internet, with its greater interactiveness, notably improves training efficiency in situations where the other media quickly run up against economic or technical limits.

Training centres are in any case paying increasing attention to this aspect of the problem. In the Cologne Second Chance School, all classes make use of computers and every computer has its modem and e-mail (European Commission, 1999, p. 37). The difficulty resides in the under-use of this material and the relative paucity of equipment installed in trainees' homes.

Under these circumstances, self-teaching software is useful on four counts:

1. It contributes to self-training.

2. It makes up for resource shortages that may exist at local level.

3. By introducing flexibility into the pace of learning, it gears teaching technique to the tasks of skills acquisition and certification.

4. By the practice of new technologies, it affords training in new technologies.

Such software is becoming more and more plentiful. It is now possible to find computer programmes (Liautard, 1999, pp. 141-155):

- on self-knowledge; they range from knowledge of self or personal aptitudes (JOB orientation) to awareness of one's preferences, via the recognition of representations;

- on occupations and working life;

- that are teaching tools in the strict sense, or learning programmes;

- that provide models for self-evaluation (such as the evaluation simulators developed with funding from the Commission of the European Union);

- for skills certification, accessible through networks.

The development of this software nevertheless faces a number of hurdles:

- the very high fixed cost of introducing quality products,

- the difficulty of making the diagnoses needed for introducing these products,

- technical problems of compatibility,

- synergy between products and the practice of trainers.

Distance learning

Distance learning, by combining some of the aforementioned media, enables training systems to adapt themselves to discontinuities in space and time (Greffe, 1994, ch. 5), and overcome some of the limitations imposed by inadequate training provision in a given region. Distance learning, which once consisted only in 'correspondence lessons', has evolved under the influence of technological progress. The most recent innovation, the computer, will literally revolutionise distance learning once its costs – mainly those of programme and information transfer – are brought under control. This does not detract from the value of regular gatherings or attendance at resource centres where may be found equipment kits for experimentation, computers, learning software and, of course, tutors or advisers. Resource centres must naturally be well distributed geographically, and opening hours must be sufficiently long to allow attendance despite occupational constraints.

Demand for distance learning keeps growing on account of training requirements and technological capacity. Yet the supply of distance learning schemes falls short of its potential, and they are not always regarded as a vital ingredient in the devolution of training. Although everything, on both demand and supply sides, would seem to plead in favour of its development, this type of education continues to pose three sorts of problem:

1. Demand can be too small to warrant investment whose start-up expenditure is very heavy. This holds for schemes that gamble on technological innovation and place too much faith in economies of scale. These schemes, when they do not attract a large enough clientele, are doomed to either a sudden stop or a drastic reappraisal of their objectives.

2. Programme production costs for narrow target audiences are extremely high, whereas the principal charm of distance learning has for a long time been the notion of expected economies of scale. This argument was finally admitted in the case of the Open University. In a first study by Laidlaw and Layard (1974), the chance of achieving economies of scale was presented as the main attraction of distance learning. In a later study, this point of view changed considerably – as the number of students grows, curricula have to be diversified, entailing heavy new fixed costs (Greffe, 1994, pp. 282-283; Wagner, 1982).

3. Teaching effectiveness is a permanent challenge. Does this type of education really structure and enhance the knowledge of its pupils? H.G. Wells, who had been advisory tutor at one of the oldest of all correspondence schools, the University Correspondence College, gave an account which provides food for thought and is still perfectly relevant. It may be paraphrased as follows: 'We divided the text-book into thirty distinct and equal-sized lessons, then drew up a set of precise questions corresponding to each lesson, so that the test could be carried out properly. The pupil, after studying his thirty lessons, could sit

down and answer the questions in a special exercise-book which he then sent to his tutor. The tutor read, noted and corrected it, all in red ink. There was nothing reprehensible about that. Except that, in all seriousness, we were missing the mark. The single upshot was that only the examination results had any worth; they became the only tangible reality. Faithful to the principle of competition among individuals, all we were doing was selling umbrellas that would never offer protection from the rain, and food which would never provide sustenance.' (Wells, 1934, pp. 342-352)

The root of the problem is that too often distance learning is seen as a social innovation coupled with economic potential, whereas at bottom it is a technical innovation that opens up certain possibilities but does not guarantee their putative results.

Accountability and synergy in training systems

The combination of decentralised initiatives with regulatory national policies, like the association of private and public partners, creates a situation of governance which can be interpreted in two ways (Dunsire, 1993, pp. 21-34):

1. In terms of steering. The central government tends to prevent deviations from the chosen path. This mode of control implies information systems and control variables for modifying players' behaviour.

2. In terms of balance or calibration. The central government takes care to see that the combination of initiatives and acts does not end up producing negative effects. This implies a minimum of information on the play of forces and instruments for rewarding good behaviour and penalising harmful behaviour.

The knowledge economy calls into play both of these interpretations:

1. Its post-industrial character posits trust in knowledge and technology for attaining society's ideals and solving existing conflicts. Its governance is 'scientific', and involves the steering of training and research.

2. Its post-modern character lays accent on the change in values and cultures (control over one's personal environment, protection of

192

the natural heritage, etc.), without pretending that knowledge can solve all conflicts.

The central government, in dealing with training systems, must therefore:

- develop tools which will clarify the problem of objectives, choice of the most efficient functions of production, posterior evaluation, etc.;

- opt for synergy among decentralised initiatives, to be obtained by incentives, impact studies, production analysis of new services, establishment of new forms of negotiation, participation and accreditation.

Conclusion

The devolution of training policies and action is necessary to help in the acquisition of the skills demanded by the knowledge economy, to avoid the exclusion of a number of people in difficulty and to enable regions to 'run with the leaders'.

These results are attainable, since devolution makes it possible to:

- gear action to needs,

- create information and resource synergies,

- mobilise capacity for innovation,

- correct the effects of centralised or sectoral policies.

The results will be attained if four principles are respected:

1. Action in partnership, which ensures the efficiency and effectiveness of training.

2. Dissemination of project culture in training.

3. Organisation of alternating training.

4. A multi-dimensional approach to training situations.

Devolution is not a panacea for all ills. When insensitive to broader issues, poorly directed, or applied to regions with unequal resources, it can generate waste, be inefficient and hamper actor mobility. Centralised training policies are therefore needed to:

- fulfil a forecasting and information function which is not really within the reach of local approaches;

- ensure a minimum of coherence in definitions and itineraries so as to guarantee transparency, which is itself a source of mobility, and so of opportunities, for workers;

- control quality, by avoiding the sort of parochialism that can produce inefficiency and irresponsibility. National policies must thus coherently knit together the instruments for regulation and contractualisation (The Copenhagen Centre, 1999b; Greffe, 1999b).

CHAPTER 8

POLICIES FOR SOCIAL COHESION

Why do city and region governments need policies for social cohesion in a globalising economy?

The current era of globalisation, open markets, international investment flows and competition, is characterised by substantial economic restructuring as well as wealth creation, and this could increase social inequalities and social exclusion unless governments put appropriate policies in place. There has therefore been much recent discussion of 'winners' and 'losers' in the globalisation process, which may involve not just relative losers but also absolute losers. Whilst globalisation has important consequences for all individuals and communities, the problems tend to be relatively concentrated in certain communities dependent on declining industries and groups of people with relatively low skills, who risk being excluded from the growth associated with globalisation. A set of policies are needed to tackle the problems of these communities and people. Whilst policies at national and international levels remain critical in this respect, there are also important measures that can be taken by cities and regions to help integrate social cohesion with economic development.

One of the major forces that has increased social exclusion in the current era of globalisation compared with the post-war boom is the large-scale job loss resulting from 'de-industrialisation', or the decline in manufacturing. Virtually all OECD Member countries have experienced de-industrialisation, particularly during the 1970s and 1980s, partly because of increased competition from and relocation of production to non-OECD countries and partly because of the trend to substitute capital for labour. Because of the increased capital intensity of production, jobs have been lost even where output in manufacturing has remained stable or increased. New jobs have been created as well, of course, some of them in manufacturing itself, but particularly in the service industries. However, this has not been enough to ensure that those groups of people who have been the most adversely affected by job loss have been fully reattached to the labour market. One part of the explanation is that the spaces of new job creation have often been in different places to the spaces of decline whilst there are social and economic barriers to migration to growth areas. Another part of the explanation is that the new jobs have been taken by different groups in the labour market from those losing jobs. There is now a general surplus of low-skilled and semi-skilled labour but growing demand for higher skilled, technical and professional labour in OECD Member countries.

One of the critical aspects of the social cohesion problem in relation to globalisation is that 'a rising tide does not lift all boats'. Despite a long period of economic expansion in OECD Member countries during the 1990s, there is still persistent worklessness and marginalised employment. In Europe and many other parts of the OECD, unemployment and worklessness is very high, despite recent economic growth. In the United States, unemployment and worklessness is lower but there is also a larger marginalised segment of the labour force with poor quality jobs. The individuals who have been the most heavily hit by economic restructuring tend to be those who are the most undereducated and underskilled and who have the least fit with the skills requirements of the New Economy. But importantly, there are also strong spatial aspects to the problem, with worklessness and marginalisation tending to be concentrated in two particular categories of area. The first category comprises the remote rural areas that have experienced loss of jobs in agriculture but are too remote to attract new activity. In these areas, exclusion is often just as much about underactivity and low incomes as unemployment. The second category comprises the distressed urban communities affected by job loss, either on the edge of cities or in inner city areas. Within cities there are additional forces that lead to concentration of unemployment and exclusion in certain areas, to do with zoning of social housing and market forces that lead poorer people to migrate to areas of cheaper housing.

A response is needed to the exclusion and marginalisation being experienced, both on grounds of social justice and in order to overcome limits to economic prosperity and the provision of services. Behind all this there is a need to ensure that the economic development policies that are pursued actually serve people by supporting social well-being as well as growth. Some forms of economic development may actually have a negative effect on a community or on particular groups of people, for example if new, emerging industries are attracted to a distressed area but local people do not have the skills or opportunities to work in these industries. In responding to the adverse consequences of economic restructuring on certain groups of people and communities it is therefore important to pursue policies that promote the interests of the people who live in those areas or communities.

What role can cities and regions play in promoting social cohesion?

Although central government policies for tax, employment and so on are still critical for promoting social cohesion it is also clear that city and region governments and development agencies have an important role to play within their territories by adjusting the way they deliver public services and by designing special programmes for target groups and distressed localities.

City and regional government authorities:

- Have the capacity to develop local partnerships bringing together all the local public and private players to promote active labour market and community development initiatives.

- Can use their outsourcing of public service delivery to help create employment and training opportunities for marginal groups in fields such as personal and social services, education, environmental protection and culture heritage.

- Are themselves important employers, with the capability to directly develop the employment and employability of excluded people.

- Often operate initiatives to regenerate distressed areas, tackle high concentrations of exclusion, improve skills and overcome the digital divide.

The next chapter in this book, by Carlisle and Scharer, explores United States programmes for distressed areas, underlining the important role that state governments play in promoting social cohesion in the United States. During the last two decades, states rather than federal government have developed almost all new programmes for distressed areas and provided the majority of resources for these programmes, notwithstanding significant federal contributions. The devolution from federal to state level of the community development block grant programme in 1982 provided a strong stimulus to state efforts to support distressed areas through investment in economic development, housing, community development, infrastructure and so on. In the mid-1990s, there was a further growth in policies targeted at distressed areas, driven by perceptions of an increasing mismatch between economic growth in rural and urban areas.

The important role that city and region governments and development agencies can play in promoting employment and reducing exclusion from work is also recognised in Europe. There is a profusion of independent local initiatives and local employment actions supported by European cities and regions. The European Commission is also active in supporting innovations, strategy building and transfer of good practice in local employment development across Europe. In particular, the 'Territorial Employment Pacts' programme, the EQUAL Community Initiative and the European Social Fund programmes provide important resources towards meeting these objectives.

The European Commission is now seeking to reinforce the role of city and region actors in delivering the European Employment Strategy. This strategy was first defined in 1997 based on four pillars, (i) improving employability, (ii) developing entrepreneurship, (iii) encouraging adaptability of businesses and their employees and (iv) strengthening equal opportunities for women and men. Initially the strategy was seen as operating at two levels. Firstly, at European Union level, a process has been created to establish common employment guidelines and measure progress. Secondly, at national level, employment guidelines are now translated by each Member State into a National Action Plan for Employment and the results achieved are reported to the European Union as part of the review process. The objective of the Commission is now to add a third level that will mobilise local government authorities and other regional and local actors in supporting the employment strategy.

This effort to add a third level to the strategy has led to a strengthening of the emphasis on local issues in the annual guidelines for Member States' employment policies. Thus employment guideline 11 of the year 2001 calls on Member States to encourage 'local and regional authorities to develop strategies for employment in order to exploit fully the possibilities offered by job creation at local level, and promote partnerships between all institutional and social actors, including the social partners, in the implementation of such strategies at the local level'. To further stimulate strategic local approaches to employment, the European Commission has recently launched the 'Acting Locally for Employment' campaign described in Box 9.

Box 9. The European Commission 'Acting Locally for Employment' Campaign

The European Commission launched a consultation and awareness campaign in April 2000 called 'Acting Locally for Employment'. The campaign aims to add a local strand to the European Employment Strategy that will complement the objectives and measures agreed at European and national levels.

Box 9 (continued)

The campaign involved two main activities during the year 2000:

1. A consultation on how local actors can promote employment at local level and how regional and national actors can establish a supportive and enabling environment for local action. The consultation was underpinned by discussion of the Commission Communication 'Acting Locally for Employment - A Local Dimension for the European Employment Strategy' (COM(2000) final 196, 7 April 2000).

2. Funding of 33 pilot projects to test methods and tools for promoting local actions for employment, under the initiative 'Preparatory Measures for a Local Commitment for Employment'. Thirteen projects involve piloting the preparation of Local Action Plans for Employment by national or international associations of local authorities. These plans aim to demonstrate how to create counterparts at the local level to the National Action Plans for Employment, based on the four pillars of the European Employment Strategy (employability, entrepreneurship, adaptability and equal opportunities). Twenty projects aim to promote transnational co-operation and dissemination of good practice concerning local action for employment. They cover a range of actors, themes and issues, including enterprises, social partners, third system organisations, equal opportunities, urban regeneration, benchmarking, local partnerships and support from national and regional levels to local actors.

The Commission supports further local employment action projects through the innovative actions programme of Article 6 of the European Social Fund (COM(2000) final 894). This includes support for the development and implementation of local employment strategies based on wide partnerships and action research on benchmarking methods and identification and dissemination of good practices.

A follow-up action programme is now underway that aims to develop and extend the use of Local Action Plans and local employment initiatives. It involves preparation of a new Commission Communication providing guidelines to help develop local employment strategies, a second round of Preparatory Measures for a Local Commitment for Employment and further innovative measures under Article 6 of the European Social Fund. The aim is to help local actors to move from individual initiatives to a more strategic approach to employment policy.

What tools can cities and regions use to promote social cohesion?

City and region governments and development agencies have a wide range of tools they can use to support the development of distressed areas within their territory or to address directly the needs of their disadvantaged people whatever their location. Some of the most promising tools are discussed below.

Tax credits and subsidies

In the United States, there has recently been a strong growth in the use of various forms of tax subsidies. These usually take the form of either investment credits or job creation credits. They are often place-based, i.e. directed towards the regeneration of distressed areas with subsidies targeted on redevelopment of inner city areas, poor rural areas or brownfields sites. Similar initiatives, such as Enterprise Zones, have also been used in other OECD countries. The key to the success of such initiatives is that they must be tightly targeted on the problem to be addressed. Subsidies are also often people-based, targeted on individuals with certain kinds of characteristics such as welfare recipients, displaced workers or other disadvantaged people.

Infrastructure provision in distressed areas

One of the most important roles of government is to ensure the provision of the basic public infrastructure required for economic development, such as roads, sewerage and schools. In seeking to ensure provision, governments face the issue that unit costs are often higher and ability to pay lower in distressed areas. In distressed rural areas the population is often sparse, making infrastructure provision more costly. Moreover, in distressed rural and urban areas the tax base is weaker and people are less able to pay direct charges for infrastructure use. Often governments do not provide infrastructure directly but ensure provision through public-private partnerships or a regulatory environment governing investments made by private companies. Whether infrastructure is provided directly or whether provision is organised through partnership agreements or regulations, governments often need to support higher investment costs in distressed areas on social grounds. Increasingly, information highways can be seen as part of this essential public infrastructure. Regulatory mechanisms and investments are therefore needed to ensure that broad-band electronic infrastructure is put into place in distressed areas.

Box 10 describes the policies introduced by the state of North Carolina in the USA for supporting investment in its distressed areas, combining the use of tax credits and incentives for infrastructure provision.

Box 10. North Carolina's Tax Credits and Infrastructure Projects for Distressed Areas

The state of North Carolina first created a special development organisation for its economically-distressed areas in the 1980s in order to target programmes and resources towards distressed parts of the state. For example, development zones have been designated inside inner cities, receiving direct spending, community financing programmes and tax credits. One of the state's more powerful instruments is an innovative system of awarding job creation tax credits to enterprises, relating the size of credits to the degree of economic distress experienced in an area. Each sub-state region has been classed into one of 5 tiers of relative distress for this purpose, such that in the most distressed tiers job creation credits can now be awarded to a value of US$12,500 per job created compared with only US$500 per job created in the least distressed areas.

North Carolina has also recently placed a lot of emphasis on ensuring that its distressed rural areas have adequate infrastructure to support economic development. In particular a US$1billion bond issue was made in 1998 to find resources for developing water and sewerage infrastructure in distressed rural areas. Furthermore, in 2000, legislation was passed to facilitate rural internet access. The legislation created a special authority, the Rural Internet Access Authority, to oversee a three year effort to provide high-speed, affordable broad-band internet access to rural areas. The authority will devise a plan and work with telecommunications providers to manage that plan. The authority received US$30 million from a state-funded non-profit organisation to provide subsidies as needed where a business case cannot be made for private investment alone.

Local active labour market policies

Active labour market policies are a critical part of policies for social cohesion in most countries, and city and region actors have an important role to play in their design, funding and delivery. OECD (1999b) reviews some of the policy instruments that local actors can use (social enterprises and the creation of new work opportunities; in-work financial incentives; the personal adviser or counsellor; new electronic technologies and job matching; local one-stop shops; local employer-based training projects; promotion of the local mobility of labour). It also highlights the important role that local partnerships can play in making policies effective.

In Europe, the regional government of Flanders provides a good example of how a regional government can develop an active employment strategy in order to combat social exclusion. Its initiatives are outlined in Box 11.

Box 11. Flanders: An active employment strategy for social cohesion

The regional government of Flanders in Belgium has developed an explicit active employment strategy to promote social cohesion. The objective is to give everybody the opportunity to enter the labour market and in this way to combat worklessness, which is one of the root causes of exclusion. There are five main measures in the new employment strategy:

1. Monitoring the labour market and co-ordinating programme management. The region's employment and training agency has moved from direct delivery of programmes to a more indirect role of monitoring labour markets and directing partnerships for programme delivery.

2. Resolving the unemployment traps. A number of measures are being taken in order to remove barriers to people entering the labour market. For example, tax reduction on lower wages has been negotiated with the federal government, childcare credits have been created for the unemployed and free public transport has been provided for job seekers.

3. Boosting the social dialogue between employers and trade unions. A legislative framework has been created for social agreements within the region.

4. Increasing the training effort. Employers and trade unions have agreed to increase their share of total mass salaries by up to 1.9% in order to make it possible to invest more in the training.

5. Creating one-stop shops. Flanders has created 32 One-Stop-Shops for Work within cities and rural communities that aim to assist employers and the unemployed with job match.

These five measures are all brought together within the framework of the active welfare state, based on the philosophy that the regional government must intervene to ensure that decent and sustainable jobs are created and made accessible to excluded people.

Problems of social exclusion are often mixed up with issues of immigration, particularly in the larger cities within the OECD where immigrants from foreign countries tend to concentrate. Immigration is an important trend in the globalising economy that is likely to continue and evolve, particularly in terms of changing origin countries. Indeed, in the longer term important levels of immigration may prove necessary in those OECD countries with low birth rates if service provision and economic growth are to be maintained whilst indigenous populations age. In this context, it is a high priority for many cities to find innovative ways of overcoming the exclusion often faced by immigrant populations. The Milan city government has recently developed an innovative project in this respect which could serve as a model to other areas (Box 12). It is also a good example of how initiatives can often be introduced at the city and region level that would prove difficult to introduce nationally. In this case it was possible to negotiate special agreements between the social partners within the city that it would have been difficult to negotiate nationally.

Box 12. The Milan Agreement for Work

Milan is one of Europe's most prosperous cities. The province of Milan accounts for 8% of the companies located in Italy and more than 10% of national GDP. Milan is also a city that, with reference to pure statistical data, has very low unemployment. However, even in Milan unemployment is a reality for a group of 'marginalised' people: in particular non-EU immigrants, people with physical or mental disabilities and older workers who have been made redundant. The city government strongly felt the need to promote the integration of this group of people in the job market and their exit from informal work, which is widespread in Italy. A further objective was to promote the social and cultural integration of recent immigrants.

In February 2000, the Milan municipal administration and the social partners - trade unions and employers associations - signed an agreement to promote the creation of new employment in Milan and to combat the phenomenon of irregular or black economy work. Specifically, the agreement allows employers to extend the use of fixed-term contracts when employing workers belonging to marginal groups. This is balanced by a series of interventions to support the stable insertion of these workers in the job market, from courses in the Italian language to specialised training.

Box 12 (continued)

The main tools of the Milan Agreement for Work are:

- *The use of fixed-term contracts.* The signatories of the agreement have listed a series of situations where employers may legitimately use fixed-term contracts in addition to those specified by the national legislation. Work/training contracts, in-company placements and employment subsidies are also made available for these purposes. Employers seeking to use the fixed-term contracts must present a specific proposal to a Concertation Commission where all signatories to the agreement are represented. The Concertation Commission must approve the project for the fixed-term contracts to be used. When judging a new proposal from an employer to use the fixed-term contract provisions, the Concertation Commission takes into consideration primarily, among the various considerations, the level of investment made in training and the number of past fixed-term contracts that have been converted into contracts of an indefinite duration.

- *A mechanism for co-ordinating employment services.* With the aim of favouring a match between the supply and demand for labour, the public actors (the municipality, police, province and the region of Lombardy) have created a direct mechanism for the rapid and efficient co-ordination of employment services, facilitating for example the practice of regulating non-EU workers and the training interventions necessary to improve the possibilities of stable insertion in the job market.

- *Pressure on municipal service providers.* The Agreement will also have an effect on the provision of labour intensive services to the city by private companies. If these companies are considered to be using too few workers the municipality will require them to increase their employment for the period during which they are working for the city. This is expected to result in better quality services.

At the immediate launch of the programme, the projects proposed were associated with 1000 projected new jobs. Despite being limited to the municipality of Milan, the agreement has created national interest and is regarded as a pilot project for employment that could be duplicated in other metropolitan areas in Italy. Indeed, after an initial experimental phase, it could represent an example of a good practice local action for employment at the European level within the context of the European employment strategy. The Agreement could therefore have a significant impact on jobs in the long-run.

Financing for local development projects

City and region governments and development agencies operate a range of programmes to provide finance for local development projects targeted on distressed areas or excluded people. In the United States, almost all states operate some sort of local development financing programmes. Increasingly, these sorts of programmes are devolved down to sub-state regions rather than operating at state level, so that programmes can be adapted to different kinds of opportunities, environments and populations. The programmes include a variety of direct subsidies to investment and job creation in local enterprises and a range of community development projects.

Unions can also bring financial resources to local development efforts. Recent work on pension strategies by the Trade Union Advisory Council to the OECD, the International Trade Union Confederation and various sector organisations has shown that there is some US$13 trillion invested in pension funds. Very often unions are responsible for investing this money. In many other cases they are amongst the fund trustees or have an important influence over trustee decisions. Clearly, investment decisions must be made to ensure that contributors have a secure and decent income in their retirement. However, within this, there exists the flexibility to make choices between alternative investments with similar projected risks and returns, and in doing so to support investments with local development objectives. There are a number of examples of unions participating in funds with local development objectives. For example, United States unions have been active in setting up pension fund schemes for development in Poland and Quebec unions have been able to direct Solidarity Fund investments towards the development of local industries. OECD (1998b) outlines the case of one of these funds, the Caisse d'Économie des Travailleurs in Quebec. This fund aims to promote Quebec's community economy by using savings collected from its partners, including unions and community movements. It agrees to provide partners with the same services at the same terms as any other financial institution, while guaranteeing that funds deposited will be used according to their concerns for social and community change by groups sponsoring projects to improve social conditions. It invests strongly in social economy businesses in Quebec. To help manage risk, it obtains all necessary guarantees on financed goods, complemented whenever possible by government guarantees.

Supporting the social economy

Supporting the social economy is very much a bottom-up strategy based on exploiting new markets for socially-useful goods and services and tackling social exclusion directly rather than relying on trickle-down from local employment creation. There is a wide range of non-profit organisations in the social economy sector, filling the gap between the public and private sectors in meeting social needs, for example social enterprises, co-operatives, mutuals, credit unions, religious groups and so on. They undertake a wide range of community development and social projects.

The strong potential of the social economy sector to create jobs and provide social services is highlighted in OECD (1999c). This book documents the expansion of social enterprises in many OECD countries, providing socially-useful goods and services that are not satisfactorily delivered by either the state or the market and contributing to hiring disadvantaged groups of workers. It is argued that social enterprises respond to five main challenges:

- New sectors of activity, which are often unprofitable in their start-up phase.

- Highly segmented demand, centred on geographical, ethnic and community units, which is inadequately covered by standardised supply.

- Reduced public budgets, leading to the withdrawal of the state from not-for-profit collective projects.

- Empowerment of private, co-operative and community operators and reassessment of the forms and conditions of public support (temporary rather than permanent, co-financing by operators, self-financing in time).

- Capacity of social economy operators to co-ordinate with the private sector and to form public-private networks.

Cities and regions can encourage the emergence of the social economy by promoting the establishment of social enterprises, helping social enterprises to access development funding, bringing social enterprises into new and existing public-private partnerships and supporting efforts to professionalise the sector.

Box 13 summarises London's strategy for community development and fighting social exclusion, based on the Draft Economic Strategy produced by the London Development Agency. It has been based on an understanding of some of the lessons emerging from the wide range of initiatives and programmes aimed at addressing social exclusion in recent years. These lessons include (London Development Agency, 2000):

- Explicit adoption of an integrated approach, linking economic development and social inclusion initiatives.

- Targeting priority area/neighbourhoods to focus capacity and linkage.

- Active community and voluntary sector partnership, to reach groups traditionally excluded from conventional mainstream programmes.

- The importance of linking special regeneration funding to the more effective deployment of main programme budgets.

- The critical importance of working with employers to ensure recruitment practices do not inadvertently contribute to individual groups' exclusion.

- Promoting innovation and learning.

Box 13. The Community Development and Social Cohesion Strategy in London

London, whilst having many positive World City attributes, is characterised by a deep and growing polarisation. Throughout inner London, and in parts of a number of outer London boroughs as well, concentrations of disadvantage and exclusion are to be found in intensely deprived neighbourhoods. In addition to these spatial concentrations, these patterns of disadvantage fall disproportionately on different sections of the community. For example, unemployment among black and ethnic minorities is substantially higher than for white people. The barriers to employment facing these excluded groups are multiple and complex.

The creation of the post of Mayor of London in 2000 led to the creation of a new institution, the London Development Agency that will work with public, private and voluntary sector partners to help take forward existing programmes and develop new programmes to empower London's communities and support disadvantaged people into work. The following key actions have been proposed:

Box 13 (continued)

♦ Promoting a Mayoral campaign against employment discrimination, on grounds of race, sex, disability, age, sexual orientation or religion, working with all relevant local and regional partners.

♦ Supporting community-based regeneration, including development trusts and other forms of social enterprise.

♦ Working with London's business sector to achieve fair and inclusive recruitment practices, particularly in areas of major employment growth and opportunity.

♦ Championing effective community involvement by developing a London compact on relations between the government and the voluntary and community sector, continuing to support capacity building, examining the possibility of establishing a fund to support Borough initiatives in neighbourhood renewal, continuing to support and promote voluntary sector led regeneration.

♦ Adopting specific targets for raising the proportion in employment in disadvantaged areas.

♦ Supporting intermediate labour market projects and developing new labour market intermediaries.

♦ Developing effective working relationships with the new Local Strategic Partnerships. Developing pilot programmes in conjunction with the Local Strategic Partnerships for linking economic opportunity to community safety/crime reduction programmes.

♦ Ensuring that in the areas targeted under the neighbourhood renewal policy there are effective Neighbourhood Learning Centres with the aim of supporting disadvantaged groups in obtaining the skills necessary to get back into work.

♦ Assisting organisations seeking to overcome key barriers to employment, including improving employment practices, addressing problems with the benefits system, promoting childcare provision, improving the quality of training, and addressing homelessness.

Source: London Development Agency, 2000

High-road or low-road strategies?

In considering social policy responses to globalisation, commentators sometimes refer to a choice between the high road and the low road to development. The high road can be seen as one where governments, including subnational governments, put in place appropriate programmes and provide a tax and regulatory framework that ensures that social goals are met as well as goals for overall economic growth. The low road, on the other hand, can be seen as one where policies focus on removing perceived barriers to the growth of existing enterprises, including high taxes, regulations and wages, often in response to perceived threats from lower cost locations. Some cities and regions have chosen the high road. Their strategies involve developing social capital, upgrading skills, introducing technology, investing in education and emphasising production of high value-added goods and services. Other cities and regions, however, appear to be choosing the low road. They are developing strategies to remove high taxes and social charges and regulations on employment, wages, health and safety and environment, which are seen as burdens on employers.

Low road policies are sometimes justified with reference to the need to remain attractive to business within an environment of strong competition between regions resulting from increased trade and increased mobility of capital and labour. The globalising economy is thus sometimes used as an argument for reducing taxes and charges and removing regulations that impose socially-responsible development on firms. However, it is also important in this debate to recognise that there are close links between social and economic development, such that policies to support social cohesion may also increase investment attractiveness and business competitiveness in an area. Thus OECD (2001d), for example, explores how standards of knowledge and skill, social capital and social cohesion feed back into economic performance. OECD cities and regions that offer a high productivity environment helped by social policies that support social cohesion should be able to retain and attract investment even with relatively high taxes and tight regulations.

In the discussion of economic competitiveness in earlier chapters, it has been argued that with globalisation the quality of local environment is increasingly important to the success of enterprises located in any territory. With access to basic markets and materials levelled out, this local environment helps maintain the high productivity and innovation that enables an area to compete. Factors such as skills and knowledge, social capital and social cohesion are part of the quality of this local environment. Within OECD countries, high-road strategies would therefore seem to be the key to facing increased competition.

Box 14 illustrates how the city of Barcelona has developed a wide range of policies to attract investment to distressed areas and to overcome exclusion amongst distressed populations within the city as part of a comprehensive and holistic economic development strategy for the city. The Barcelona approach can be characterised as a high-road strategy.

Box 14. The Economic Development Initiatives of the City of Barcelona

Context

The city of Barcelona has a population of approximately 1.5 million within a wider metropolitan area of approximately 4.2 million people. Economic and employment development is one of the main priorities of the municipality, which aims to help restructure the city economy away from traditional industry towards new services and advanced products. Since the municipality does not itself have specific prerogatives or own-resources for economic development, its strategy has been to develop initiatives in partnership with other levels of government (the European Union, central government, the autonomous region of Catalonia and local administrations), with the private sector and with other social and economic agencies. During the last 10 years, 300 organisations and institutions have participated in the city's strategic planning process, identifying the central priorities for the strategic plan for Barcelona. In addition, some 50 collaboration agreements have been developed with various social and economic actors in the city, including academic institutions, social agents, business organisations, non-profit associations and local corporations. These partnerships cover various aspects of economic development within the city, including the Barcelona Logistics Centre, the Barcelona Financial Centre, the Environment Forum, the Barcelona Design Centre, the Forum of Towns and Trade and the Barcelona University Centre.

The local development strategy for Barcelona has the following four main strands, which are outlined below:

- Positioning of the territory.

- Employment and transformation of the city.

- Employment and companies.

- Combination of macro and tailor-made interventions.

Box 14 (continued)

Positioning of the territory. One of the central axes of the promotion of economic and employment activity in Barcelona is the positioning of the territory as an attractive and welcoming place for enterprises, both inward investors and enterprises from within the region. A recent study by Healey and Baker suggested that Barcelona occupies the six rank amongst the most attractive cities in Europe for business. However, in order to maintain and consolidate this position the municipality plans to put into place a permanent benchmarking mechanism with competitor towns that will help identify where improvements are needed. An observatory has already been created to survey the opinions of the foreign enterprises that invest in Barcelona. Assessing the strengths and weaknesses of the city's economy requires a continuous effort to generate information and to organise and participate in seminars and expert meetings. All the city administrations and all the important public and private sector actors are involved in this process, through a range of sector development groups.

Employment and transformation of the city. A great number of municipal policies have employment impacts even where employment is not the primary goal. Urban planning in particular has direct employment consequences for the districts of a city, for example when the decision is made to develop a commercial axis or to create a zone of office buildings. The important employment stimulus of urban redevelopment was originally triggered by the major redevelopment carried out for the 1992 Olympic Games in Barcelona, which involved some US$8 billion of investment. Similarly, the communications infrastructure in a city affects the development of its logistics sector, and employment issues have been taken into account in recent proposals for road, rail, airport, port and telecommunications projects. Thus it is forecast that the city's strategy to develop a multi-nodal logistic hub should lead to the creation of 50,000 jobs in transport and distribution by 2004. City environment policies and public services can also support the creation of employment in new sectors of economic activity. For example, the environment sector accounts for more than 25,000 jobs in Barcelona and cultural industries and social services have comparable totals. Tourism is also being developed, and now accounts for 40,000 direct and indirect jobs in the city. The municipality seeks to assess the employment effects of all its main activities so that employment generation can be stimulated as far as possible whilst also meeting other objectives.

Box 14 (continued)

Employment and companies. In the context of economic globalisation and growing competition between companies and territories, Barcelona aims to develop an economy based on services and advanced products that are capable of driving growth and creating high quality employment and in which the city can have a competitive advantage relative to other areas. Such development will require the city to be aware of and capitalise on the new parameters of the information and knowledge society. In particular its enterprises will be have to be more linked and open internationally and its human resources more attuned to the needs of the learning city.

Combination of macro and tailor-made interventions. In supporting the redevelopment of Barcelona, the municipality makes a distinction between macro interventions, concerned with basic support infrastructure to economic activity city-wide, and tailor-made interventions focused on particular problem areas or target social groups. It is considered that action at both levels is required for success. The city's macro interventions include support for the International Fair of Barcelona, the arrival of the high speed train at its port and airport and the redevelopment of 170 hectares of industrial land foreseen by the project 22 @ BCN. At the same time, tailor-made interventions provide individualised guidance to people who are disadvantaged in the labour market and mentoring for new enterprises.

Barcelona Activa - a municipal development agency

Barcelona Activa is a municipal company set up in 1987 as the main local development agency for Barcelona. It is responsible for the design and delivery of the municipality's policies to support entrepreneurship and employment development. Through its entrepreneurship programmes it is active each year in the creation of more than 1000 business start-ups and in support for collaboration and internationalisation of established SMEs. Its employment services serve some 72000 job seekers, principally through guidance and training. The following are some of the innovative products and services of Barcelona Activa:

- *Barcelona Net Activa* (http://www.barcelonanetactiva.com) is a telematic platform of advanced services to entrepreneurs that gives business start-ups access through the internet to a network of companies promoting quality, co-operation, innovation and training. It is the first virtual business incubator in Europe, currently hosting some 70 companies in a virtual community for continuous co-operation.

Box 14 (continued)

- *Infopime* (http://infopime.bcn.es) is a telecommunications service that provides information, liaison and support for SMEs and for the professionals of Barcelona. It offers quick and easy access to economic information concerning the city and provides a basis for digital mapping that can be used as a tool for companies undertaking market research studies. It is also a convenient channel for companies to complete required administrative procedures with the municipality.

- *Barcelona Emprèn* is a venture capital company for investment in small entrepreneurial projects with a very strong innovative character. The municipality has a minority stake in the company, which also has participation from some 15 other large enterprises, insurance companies and financial establishments.

- *22 @ BCN* is a project to rehabilitate 170 hectares of brownfields situated in the heart of Barcelona in an attractive area that is well-suited to the settlement of new high tech/new economy based economic activities. The project is probably one of the most ambitious operations in Europe of its type. It is hoped to create some 75,000 jobs through this action in the district of Poblenou linked to the development of new industries.

- *Barcelona Welcomes Business* is an information support service for businesses, professionals and institutions that want to settle in Barcelona. It offers electronic access to information and numerous databases as well as the possibility to make certain enquiries on-line. Using this service, investors can ensures that they have the contacts and technological and logistic support required to set up an economic activity in Barcelona.

- *The Employment Promotion Service* aims to simplify the path to employment for job seekers and people who wish to improve their position in the labour market. It offers seminars tailored to the occupational profile of participants and the type of jobs for which they are suited, a personalised job search plan and training and experience programmes. There are further programmes for specific target groups e.g. young people, women and the long term unemployed. The service has recently developed a programme to identify job opportunities in emerging new technology and knowledge based sectors and to deliver practical training to help young people with difficulties to access these opportunities. Many of the areas identified are new occupations or professions, for example the programme has baptised one 'infonomiste'. After having participated for one year in this programme all 100 youths on the first round of the training programme found work.

Summary

This chapter has argued that city and region governments need policies for social cohesion in order to counter problems of inequalities and marginalisation associated with the economic restructuring of current globalisation processes. Worklessness, poverty and other forms of exclusion tend to be concentrated in certain communities dependent on declining industries and groups of people with relatively low skills, and there are strong spatial aspects to the problem.

City and region governments and development agencies can promote social cohesion within their territories by adjusting the way they deliver public services and by designing special programmes for target groups and distressed localities. They can bring together local partnerships to promote active labour market and community development initiatives, can use their power as direct and indirect employers to help develop the employment and employability of excluded groups and can operate local initiatives to regenerate distressed areas. The European Commission is active in supporting these sorts of local initiatives to combat social exclusion, for example through its Acting Locally for Employment programme. Some of the most promising tools that city and region authorities can use to promote social cohesion are place-based and people-based tax credits and subsidies for investment and job creation, infrastructure provision in distressed areas, local active labour market policies, financing for local development projects and supporting the social economy.

It is possible to envisage both high-road and low-road strategies to respond to globalisation, with the high road emphasising social as well as economic investment and the low road emphasising the elimination of barriers and costs to economic activity that social investment entails. In a globalising economy, where the quality of the local environment is increasingly important to economic competitiveness, including characteristics such as social capital, skills and cohesion, high-road strategies would seem to be the way forward for OECD cities and regions.

In the next chapter, Carlisle and Scharer review United States programmes to tackle the problem of distressed areas. These programmes are mainly delivered by state and local government. Devolved governments elsewhere could consider similar initiatives to reintegrate excluded areas in their territories.

CHAPTER 9

AN OVERVIEW OF U.S. FEDERAL, STATE AND REGIONAL PROGRAMMES TO PROMOTE ECONOMIC DEVELOPMENT IN DISTRESSED AREAS

by

Rick Carlisle, Managing Partner and Chief Executive Officer of the North Carolina Economic Opportunities Fund and former Secretary of Commerce for North Carolina, USA and
Joanne Scharer, Development Consultant, USA

Introduction

This chapter provides a brief overview of the devolution of federal economic and community development policy to the state level, and the parallel development of state policies that devoted additional state resources to economic and community development. Following a significant build-up of federal policy in the nineteen sixties, the ensuing decades saw the transfer of this responsibility to state governments. In addition to taking on responsibility for federally financed programmes, state governments also initiated their own policies and state-funded programmes. In addition, state governments aggressively applied tax policy to stimulate economic development, particularly in distressed regions.

The first section of this chapter briefly reviews the evolution and devolution of the federal role in economic and community development. The second section then provides an overview of the federal role today and its use of tax policy and programmes for regional development. Section three reviews the rise of state policies and programmes in the seventies and eighties, and section four reviews the state role today in tax policy, development finance, and direct programmes to stimulate economic development. The fifth section then quickly profiles several state programmes in development finance, tax policy, development authorities, regional and local partnerships, and microenterprise development. The final section offers some concluding thoughts.

Obviously, given the breadth of the topic, this paper necessarily provides limited details on any single programme initiative. Rather, it is intended to stimulate ideas for further investigation.

The evolution and devolution of the federal role in economic and community development

The evolution of the federal, state and local roles in economic development has undergone distinct modifications in the United States over the last several decades. While efforts to stimulate the national economy have been a hallmark of the twentieth century, federal initiatives to stimulate regional and local economies that were under-performing the national economy began in earnest in the nineteen sixties. During the 1960s and 1970s, federal administrators began to play a larger role in state and local policy making. Furthermore, as these national programmes were developed, they also played a crucial role in shaping state and local priorities. Some of the changes that occurred during this period include:

- the number of federal grants to state and local governments increased tremendously;

- the amount of funds transferred grew rapidly;

- grant programmes were based increasingly on national purposes, instead of providing funding for unique state and local problems;

- a variety of strings and conditions were attached to the grants;

- direct grants to localities, by-passing state governments, were instituted;

- fairly specific categorical grants, many of which were competitively awarded, proliferated; and

- grant-writing skills increased in importance for states and localities that desired federal funds to pursue their own policy objectives (Jennings et al., 1986, p3).

In addition to the funding increases and new grant programmes instituted during this time, the federal government launched area-development programmes, with an emphasis on infrastructure improvements, to promote economic and social development (Redburn and Buss, 1982, p. ix). One such programme, the Appalachian Regional Commission (ARC), created in 1965 [3], is the only one still in existence today.[4] Around the same time, Congress established the Department of Housing and Urban Development (HUD)[5] as a Cabinet Department by consolidating a number of other older federal agencies. As HUD is the federal agency responsible for national policy and programmes that improve and develop communities, its establishment was an important event for local and regional economic development in the U.S. Another pivotal programme attesting to the evolution of the federal involvement in economic and community development came with the Public Works and Economic Development Act of 1965. Under this Act, Congress created the Economic Development Administration (EDA) to generate jobs, help retain existing jobs, and stimulate industrial and commercial growth in economically distressed areas of the United States (US Department of Commerce, 1999). EDA targeted loans and grants for infrastructure, small business, revolving loan funds, and other economic development initiatives to 'distressed areas', as defined by EDA. By requiring that states form regional districts in order to receive these funds, and requiring in most cases state funds to match federal grants, this federal agency also brought state government into regional development policy.

Another major development in federal economic and community development policy began in the mid nineteen seventies. A major new programmatic initiative, known as the Community Development Block Grant (CDBG) programme, resulted from the consolidation of several different categorical programmes operated by HUD during the 1960s and early 1970s. A number of distinct programmes, with separate application requirements, were consolidated into a single 'block grant' to cities and smaller urban areas. These 'categorical grants', so called because of the distinct categories of assistance (such as Urban Renewal, Sewer and Water Grants, Model Cities, and others) were eliminated, and, in their place, the Community Development Block Grant was created pursuant to the Housing and Community Development Act of 1974 (Jennings et al, 1986, p. 23). The CDBG programme, a centrepiece of the Nixon administration's 'New Federalism,' had the primary objectives to create viable

---

3.   Appalachian Regional Development Act of 1965.

4.   The Appalachian Regional Development Act of 1965 was last amended in 1998 and is scheduled to terminate October 1, 2001

5.   The Department of Housing and Urban Development Act (42 U.S.C. 3532-3537), effective November 9, 1965

housing and living environments and to expand economic opportunities, principally for persons of low and moderate income. Responding to local government complaints about the confusion associated with the proliferation of federal categorical grants, the Nixon administration adopted a funding approach for housing and urban development that created a 'block' of money that would provide formula-based funding and permit local authorities greater discretion in selecting among eligible projects and activities (Jennings et al, 1986, p5).

The 1980s

The Reagan administration came to office in the wake of a twenty-year period of enormous expansion in federal assistance grants and substantial changes in the nature of intergovernmental relations (Jennings et al, 1986, p3). In line with his more general policies to reduce the scope of governmental activity, Reagan attempted to simplify the intergovernmental grant system by consolidating a number of grants into new or revised block grant programmes. All of these new programmes reduced previous funding levels (except the Small Cities portion of the CDBG programme), while providing greater policy discretion and administrative flexibility for state and local officials. However, perhaps the most notable change that came with the new programmes was that Congress designated state governments as the recipients of funding for all the block grants. This shift was especially significant for the CDBG programme, in which states had previously played no formal role (Jennings et al, 1986, pp. 4-5). In essence, Reagan promoted devolution as a means of enhancing programme effectiveness and efficiency. The administration and others felt that programmes operated at the federal level were less responsive to local needs and preferences and were unable to select activities and strategies appropriate to variations in local conditions (Jennings et al, 1986, p. 6). By allowing more priority setting and administrative control at the state level, the Reagan administration believed these community and economic development funds would be more effective and efficient.

The 1990s

By the nineteen nineties, this policy shift toward giving more responsibility to state governments had become a fundamental tenet of federal policy toward distressed regions as well as aid to lower-income individuals. Federal policy toward economic and community development in the 1990s demonstrated a continuation of federal programmes and funding strategies that essentially authorised state and local governments to determine how to best use federal resources. For example, the Clinton administration's Empowerment Zone and

Enterprise Community (EZ/EC) Initiative was and continues to be a key element in America's job creation strategy. Its purpose is to create jobs and business opportunities in the most economically distressed areas of inner cities and the rural heartland. What sets this initiative apart from previous urban revitalisation efforts is that the community drives the decision-making. Residents decide what happens in their neighbourhoods, not federal officials in Washington.[6]

A further shift in the responsibility for and administration of programmes to benefit distressed areas and low-income families came with the Personal Responsibility and Work Opportunity Reconciliation Act of 1996, popularly known as the Welfare to Work Program. This programme places more emphasis on the need to move welfare recipients from welfare to work. Under the Act, the Temporary Assistance for Needy Families (TANF) programme replaced the Aid to Families with Dependent Children (AFDC) programme. Prior to this initiative, welfare policy was almost solely a federal prerogative. With the passage of Welfare to Work legislation, however, states gained new authority in setting policies toward families on welfare. The federal legislation sets broad guidelines, but the law gives state governments broad latitude to meet these requirements.[7]

The federal role today

As we enter a new century, the policy of devolution of policy setting and programme administration to the state level is firmly established. The federal and state level governments have increasingly defined separate roles. Overall, the federal government partially funds economic and community development efforts at the state, regional, and local levels. It sets broad policy guidelines, but leaves priority setting, detailed policy development, and programme administration at the state level. The federal government continues to create new tools to work in conjunction with state and local programmes. The Clinton Administration's Enterprise Zone and Enterprise Community programme and the New Markets initiative are good examples. These are designed not as the major programmatic initiatives of the nineteen sixties, but as parts of a tool kit that would be ineffective without state and local involvement.

---

[6]   U.S. Department of Housing and Urban Development. "Empowerment
       Zone/Enterprise Community Initiative"
       http://www.hud.gov/cpd/ezec/ezecinit.html

[7]   http://www.dol.gov/dol/asp/public/w2w/welfare.htm

Direct federal assistance to stimulate economic development without a state policy or programmatic role has become rare. The federal level Small Business Administration continues to provide direct financing to small businesses that meet federally determined criteria. Even here, however, the Small Business Administration has created a system of technical assistance services to small business that is dependent on state support. And a delivery mechanism heavily promoted by the Small Business Administration, the Small Business Investment Corporations, typically involves some degree of state or local support. With a portfolio of business loans, loan guarantees, and disaster loans worth more than US$45 billion, SBA is the nation's largest single financial backer of small businesses.[8]

Similarly, another federal financing mechanism, the Economic Development Administration, works in partnership with state and local governments, regional economic development districts, public and private non-profit organisations, and Indian tribes. EDA helps communities address problems associated with long-term economic difficulties, as well as sudden and severe economic dislocations including recovering from the economic impacts of natural disasters, the closure of military installations and other federal facilities, changing trade patterns, and the depletion of natural resources. Through grants for infrastructure development, revolving loan funds, technical assistance, and other programme tools, EDA supports rural and urban areas in alleviating conditions of substantial and persistent unemployment or other severe economic distress. Eligibility for EDA programmes typically requires the development of state or regional strategic plans, which EDA must adhere to in its funding decisions (US Department of Commerce, 1999).

The Community Development Block Grant programme remains the premier federal level programme for community and economic development support from the federal government, the nation's largest grant programme and an essential component of federal investment in America's communities. The larger cities in the United States that are designated metropolitan areas receive direct funding from the federal government. Cities have wide latitude in setting policies and priorities and are wholly responsible for programme administration. The smaller cities and counties are funded through programmes administered by state governments, which typically award funds to cities and counties based on competitive applications. Again, the federal government establishes national programme goals and eligibility requirements. State governments, however, are free to set additional policy objectives, establish priorities, develop new programmes funded with block grant funds, and

---

[8]   http://www.sba.gov/aboutsba/

determine what projects will be funded. States are also wholly responsible for programme administration. Supporting both national objectives and local discretion, it provides a flexible source of funding for multifaceted community development and revitalisation activities.[9]

Tax policy

In addition to supporting economic development through programmes and funding, federal tax policy in the United States includes some mechanisms that encourage economic growth and community development. For example, Industrial Revenue Bonds, some of which are tax exempt, allow states and local communities to assist new and expanding industry finance manufacturing, industrial, and pollution controls facilities and/or related new equipment. While the regulations governing bond issuance are a combination of federal regulations and state statutes, tax exempt revenue bonds are appealing to investors because the income derived by the bondholder is not subject to federal income tax. Thus the project financed with revenue bonds can pay lower interest rates on the bonds. These are typically used to finance industrial development projects or lower income housing development, although states have authorised the use of revenue bonds for a variety of commercial and industrial development projects.

Federal policy includes a number of tax credits that are designed to stimulate investment or creation of certain kinds of jobs. The investor or the company hiring new employees receives a credit against federal income taxes. For example, the federal government's Research and Development Tax credit encourages new economic growth by encouraging private sector research and development. Since 1981 the federal government has allowed a credit of approximately 20 percent of incremental increases in qualified research and development (R&D) expenditures. In today's global and increasingly technology based economy, the credit supports the creation of valuable new, high-skilled jobs for American workers, particularly within the software, information technology, and pharmaceutical industries. Other credits include those for hiring welfare recipients, for investment in certain types of technologies, or for investment in housing for lower-income families. President Clinton's proposed New Markets Initiatives will include tax credits for investment in targeted distressed areas.

---

9.   http://www.huduser.org/publications/commedevl/cdbg.html

The rise of state development policies and programmes

In the nineteen sixties to the eighties, while the national and local governments were developing direct programmatic linkages, state governments underwent considerable change and modernisation in their character and management. Many states experienced major constitutional and administrative reforms. Furthermore, changing economic conditions and a changing national political agenda created conditions conducive to reorganising intergovernmental relations. Consequent with the federal policy of devolution, states independently began developing initiatives to stimulate investment in small business, technology, and distressed regions within the state. By the nineteen nineties, state governments had emerged as the principal actors in regional and local economic development. As a result of the federal policy of devolution of programme responsibility to state governments, states had a significant role in the distribution of federal resources to localities (Jennings et al, 1986, pp. 7-8).

While the Housing and Community Development Act of 1974, which created the CDBG programme, did not mention a role for the states, upon renewal of the Act in 1977 Congress did reserve a function for the states. However, Congress then delegated the responsibility for determining what that role should be to HUD. As a result, programme regulations simply included that projects should show how they were consistent with state and regional objectives (Jennings et al, 1986, pp. 26-27). Not until the election of Ronald Reagan, with his view that the federal system needed restructuring, did the idea to transfer the CDBG programme to the states take form. After much debate between local government interest groups such as the National League of Cities (NLC), the National Association of Counties (NACo), and the US Conference of Mayors (USCM) and state groups such as the National Governors Association (NGA), Congress passed the Budget Reconciliation Act of 1981. This Act ultimately allowed the states to assume administrative responsibility of the CDBG programme (Jennings et al, 1986, p. 39). This intergovernmental transfer of policy control was part of a broader set of actions designed to implement President Reagan's vision of a new federal-state relationship. The 1981 federal budget act transferred responsibility for nine major block grants to state governments.

As evidenced by the changes in the 1960s and 1970s and by the administrative transfer of the CDBG programme to the states, the 1980s were a time of significant change for state governments. The nature and extent of the national recession of the late 1970s and early 1980s placed additional stress on state governments. The economic transitions of the nineteen eighties, as major industrial restructuring took place in the United States, placed additional pressure upon state economic development policy makers. Adding to these pressures were changing policy initiatives at the federal level, especially under the Reagan administration, and federal budget deficits that reduced the amount of federal dollars available for programmes (Brace, 1993, pp. 1-2). With the prospect of reduced federal funding, states began to develop their own economic policies to induce private sector growth and prosperity (Redburn and Buss, 1982, p. 251). These pressures essentially forced state governments to set up new agencies and operations for state economic development programmes in the 1980s. Consequently, state funding for economic and community development rose as federal funding declined (Walton and Kraushaar, 1990, p. 276).

Building on the power and control obtained during the 1980s, state and local officials have accelerated efforts to promote economic and community development. They have been innovative in the ways in which they are intervening to assist the private sector in building new businesses and creating jobs. States have expanded the more traditional efforts of providing infrastructure for development and supporting training for industrial development. While these traditional programmes are still a large part of state and local economic development strategy, states increasingly added additional components to promote economic development. Over the last decade, states have added programmes and initiatives that focus on encouraging business start-ups, creating new forms of development finance, stimulating technology development and transfer, fostering expansion of existing businesses, and promoting investment in distressed regions and communities (Smith and Fox, 1990, p. 25). States have also become more aggressive in recruiting investment domestically and internationally, expanding the use of incentives to attract new investment, particularly in distressed regions.

The state role today

Programmes

For decades states have typically had some form of infrastructure development programmes as a common means to stimulate new investment and job creation. Highways and water and sewer systems are the most typical public infrastructure investments. In addition to programmes to provide basic infrastructure in communities, and general transportation development programmes, states typically use targeted investments for industrial sites or specific industrial development projects.

In the emerging information and technology-based economy, state programmes to provide skill training have become increasingly popular. North Carolina pioneered 'customised training' programmes that work directly with employers to develop a customised training programme for the employers' needs, with most costs paid by the state. Now most states have some form of customised training programmes. Education and training programmes increase the profitability of business by increasing the productivity of workers and reducing labour costs. Most training of this kind occurs at state universities and vocational technical schools, although some states have started building specific training facilities to attract companies in targeted recruitment areas. Finally, all states promote themselves as good places to do business. States commonly advertise their most attractive attributes and economic development programmes through newspapers, videos, tradeshows, magazines, and even television commercials (Smith and Fox, 1990, p. 27). In addition, most states have departments or agencies with a myriad of support functions and programmes specifically devoted to economic and community development.

Beyond the more traditional infrastructure and job training programmes, many states also support programmes that encourage small businesses, research and development, and technology transfer. Through small business development centres, states help small and start-up businesses learn good management practices. These centres may also provide financial and training assistance or low-cost space to encourage small business start-ups. States also establish research and development partnerships between universities and private businesses to help identify cutting-edge research with market potential. In a similar capacity, states are providing technical assistance to deliver technology to manufacturing businesses, often using existing capabilities at state universities (Smith and Fox, 1990, p. 32). In co-operation with the federal government, most states have established some form of manufacturing extension programmes to extend the technical services of engineering schools or other technical departments to small and medium sized businesses.

Financing

Perhaps the greatest growth over the last decade has been in state supported financing programmes. States provide many forms of financing to recruit businesses with the expectation of creating jobs and generating additional development. These programmes normally attempt to reduce the cost of financing for the construction of manufacturing facilities or small, start-up technology based companies. Some are particularly targeted to firms starting in or locating in distressed regions of the state. For example, some states offer direct loans and loan guarantees for industrial buildings and equipment. Also, many states offer tax-exempt industrial development bonds or extend the authority to allow local governments to issue them. These bonds exempt bondholders from paying federal income tax on the interest earned, thus reducing the interest that must be paid to attract investors (Smith and Fox, 1990, p. 27).

Many states have also designed programmes to provide financing to risky start-up businesses. For example, a number of states have established venture capital funds to spur the start-up or expansion of businesses that have the potential to boost economic development through rapid growth, but that may have difficulty securing private capital. These are funded variously through direct appropriation of state funds, investment of state employee pension funds, or through special tax treatment for private investment (Smith and Fox, 1990, p. 32).

Tax policy

Most states have tailored their tax policies in some fashion to encourage business location and economic development. Business tax reduction usually takes one of four forms. First, states lower overall tax rates to limit business taxes thus permitting businesses to keep a larger share of their profits. The state taxes that most directly impact on businesses are corporate income, sales and use, and property taxes. While nearly all states impose these taxes on businesses, they do so at widely different rates. Second, states offer tax credits, such as job creation or investment tax credits, to lower tax liabilities. These credits allow the state to direct the tax reduction to industries it deems important to its economic future. Third, states limit the base upon which they levy business taxes. By narrowing the tax base, a state tries to reduce business tax liabilities for a given tax rate, increasing the chances that businesses in the state will be profitable. Some examples of this narrowing include providing sales tax exemptions for manufacturing equipment, deductions to the corporate income tax, and property tax abatement on the real property associated with new manufacturing facilities. Finally, states negotiate tax reductions for certain individual businesses. Using such tax concessions allows a state to attract new businesses or to prevent businesses from leaving a state (Smith and Fox, 1990, p. 26).

Examples of state, regional, and local policies and programmes

There are a variety of economic and community development strategies utilised at the state, regional, and local levels. Some of these include pro-business tax policies, state sponsored enterprise or development zones,[10] state development authorities, state funded non-profits, state operated programmes using federal CDBG funds, direct investment programmes, microenterprise loan programmes, regional partnerships, and locally designed targeted development initiatives. The following examples provide only a snapshot of the various creative and enterprising development tools used across the United States.

Tax policy and tax credits

North Carolina

North Carolina's William S. Lee Tax Credit programme, created in 1996, is designed to make the state more competitive for new and expanding industry, especially in rural and less developed areas. The programme's main strategies include an investment tax credit and a job creation tax credit. The investment tax credit, taken in equal instalments over seven years, is equal to 7 percent of the value, above the applicable investment threshold, of machinery and equipment placed in service in North Carolina by eligible new or expanding firms. The investment threshold ranges from US$0 to US$1 million depending on the level of distress in the county in which the investment is located. Under the act, the state is divided into five enterprise tiers[11] that measure the level of economic distress. All counties in the state are assigned to one of the five tiers, which determines the level of benefit a firm will receive. The credit also involves a 'large investment enhancement' in which large industrial locations can receive additional benefits. A taxpayer is eligible for this enhancement upon certification that it will purchase or lease at least US$150 million worth of real estate, machinery and equipment, or central administrative office property within a two-year period. The job creation tax credit, taken in equal instalments over four years, allows eligible firms with at least five full-time employees to take a credit ranging from US$500 to US$12,500 for the creation of each new full time additional job(s). Like the investment tax credit, the amount of the credit varies by enterprise tier, with the higher credits assigned to the most distressed tier. While the investment tax credit and the job creation tax credit are the most significant incentives, the programme also includes a research and development credit, a worker training credit, and a central administrative office

---

10.   These are different from the federally designated EZ/EC communities.

11.   Enterprise tiers are calculated each year based on each county's ranking in unemployment and per capita income (for the preceding three years) and in percent growth in population.

credit. In line with its aim to create high paying jobs, to receive any of the credits, companies must pay a wage that is at least 110 percent of the county's average annual wage. Companies must also provide health insurance and meet all environmental and workplace safety standards.

Another North Carolina tax policy initiative, the Qualified Business Investment Tax Credit Program, offers investors in certain types of businesses a credit equal to 25 percent of the amount invested, up to a maximum of US$50,000 for individual investors and US$100,000 for institutional investors. For the investor to be eligible for the credit, they must make an investment in a business registered with the state's Securities Division as a 'Qualified Business Venture' or a 'Qualified Grantee Business'. Up to US$6 million of credits are available annually for investments in these businesses.

A Qualified Business Venture is a business organised to engage primarily in manufacturing, processing, warehousing, wholesaling, research and development, or a service-related industry. To be eligible for this designation, the organisation of the business must be the same year in which it applies for registration, or its gross revenues must be less than US$5 million as of its last fiscal year. Furthermore, the business cannot engage to any substantial degree in providing professional services, contracting or construction, selling or leasing at retail, investing, entertainment or recreation, or managing or operating real estate. A Qualified Grantee Business is a business that during the three previous years received a grant or other funding from selected state agencies established to promote new investment. These include the North Carolina Technological Development Authority, the North Carolina Biotechnology Centre, the Microelectronics Centre of North Carolina, the Kenan Institute for Engineering, Technology and Science, or the Federal Small Business Innovation Research Program.[12]

Illinois

Illinois created its Tax Increment Financing (TIF) programme in 1977. TIF helps the state's local governments attract private development and new businesses and helps retain existing businesses that might otherwise find more attractive options elsewhere. It also helps to overcome the extraordinary costs that often prevent development and private investment from occurring on environmentally contaminated and other properties. By and large, new jobs and additional investment created --- private and public --- mean more money for

---

[12] NC Department of Secretary of State. "Qualified Business Tax Credit." www.secretary.state.nc.us/bus_tax/overview.htm

the community. In fact, a 1992 survey of Illinois' TIF municipalities found that the average TIF project produced four dollars of private investment for every dollar of tax increment investment.[13] A tax increment is the difference between the amount of property tax revenue generated before TIF district designation and the amount of property tax revenue generated after TIF designation. As a result, the TIF area improves and property values go up while permitting municipalities to promote economic development without raising local property taxes. Specifically, money for infrastructure improvements and other incentives comes from the growth in property tax revenues generated by businesses attracted by the TIF benefits. Establishment of a TIF does not reduce property tax revenues available to the overlapping taxing bodies. Only property taxes generated by the incremental increase in the value of these properties after that time are available for use by the TIF.[14]

Illinois' programme uses five classifications: Central Business District, Shopping Mall/Commercial, Industrial Mixed Development/Non-Central Business District, and Housing and allows each TIF district to exist for a maximum of 23 years. The programme includes three sets of conditions for qualifying areas as TIFs: blighted conditions, conservation conditions, and industrial park conservation conditions. A blighted area involves factors detrimental to the public safety, health, morals or welfare of the community. These factors include things such as age, dilapidation, deterioration, and overcrowding of structures and community facilities. Vacant land considered blighted involves conditions that that impair sound growth of the area. These might include tax delinquencies, flooding, and deterioration of structures or site improvements on adjacent land. Unused quarries, unused rail yards, rail tracks or railroad right-of-way, unused disposal sites, large areas that have been previously designated as a town centre are all examples of vacant land. An industrial park conservation area includes a municipality with a high unemployment rate with such an area zoned industrial and located within the municipality or within 1.5 miles of the municipal boundaries and annexed to the municipality. A conservation area entails areas with blighted conditions and with at least 50 percent of its structures being 35 years old.

---

13.   Illinois Tax Increment Association. "FAQs." www.illinois-tif.com/faqs.htm#Q20

14.   Illinois Tax Increment Association. "About TIF." www.illinois-tif.com/tif.htm

State sponsored enterprise/development zones

New York

New York's Economic Development Zones Program (EDZ), created in 1987, aims to stimulate economic growth through a variety of financial incentives designed to attract new businesses and to enable existing businesses to expand and create more jobs. The programme designates areas up two square miles in size as EDZs if they are distressed in terms of poverty, unemployment, military base closures, and sudden severe worker dislocations. Businesses making an investment and/or creating new jobs in an EDZ are eligible for a combination of State tax credits and benefits. In addition, municipalities designated as EDZs may offer additional incentives including property tax abatement for improvement to real property in the zone.

Some of the New York's programme's credits and benefits include a wage tax credit, an investment tax credit, a sales tax refund, a zone capital credit, utility rate reductions, and special low-interest loans and priority attention. The Wage Tax Credit is a 50 percent refundable credit for up to five consecutive years for hiring full-time employees in newly created jobs. For employees in special targeted groups, this credit equals US$1,500 a year, with a credit of US$750 a year for all other new hires. The Investment Tax Credit is a refundable credit of 8 to 10 percent, based on investments made in an EDZ, available to certain businesses. An added credit, the Employment Incentive Credit, equalling 30 percent of the investment tax credit, is available to taxpayers employing at least 101 percent of the average number of people employed in the year before taking the investment tax credit. The Zone Capital Credit, a 25 percent credit, is available for the contribution or purchase of shares in a zone capital corporation, for a direct equity investment in a certified zone business, or for contributions to approved community development projects. Many of the states 52 EDZs also have entrepreneurial assistance programmes, low-cost incubator space, small business start-up and micro loan programmes, and one-stop, fast track business assistance services.[15]

North Carolina

North Carolina created its State Development Zone Program in 1998 to target smaller areas in more densely populated municipalities in need of economic

---

15.   Empire State Development, Economic Development Zones Program,
        www.empire.state.ny.us/zones/index.html

growth and to expand the state's William S. Lee Act (discussed above). Therefore, taxpayers located in development zones gain additional tax credit enhancements. A North Carolina development zone is an area comprised of one or more contiguous census tracts, census block groups, or both located in whole or in part in a city with a population of more than 5,000. A zone must have a population of 1,000 or more, and more than 20 percent of its population must be below the poverty level. Development zone tax credit enhancements include: a lower wage standard, no investment threshold, an additional US$4,000 tax credit per eligible job created, and up to a US$1,000 tax credit may be claimed for each eligible worker trained.

State Development Authorities

Connecticut

The Connecticut Development Authority (CDA) offers the state's business access to competitively priced capital for funding business growth and financial incentives for enhancing employee skills. All the authority's investments must fulfil certain economic and development objectives and must satisfy the mission to provide assistance that will retain or increase jobs and provide economic benefits to the state. The idea is that providing creative financial solutions to companies will help generate increased business investment, increase employment, expand the tax revenue base, and prepare a better educated and more highly skilled workforce. To accomplish its goals, the authority works with financial institutions to guarantee or participate in loans made to businesses, provide access to low-cost, tax-exempt industrial revenue bond financing, provide partial reimbursements and prime rate loans to manufacturers that invest in employee training, and enable eligible companies to obtain lower-rate loans under the Small Business Administration 504 programme.[16] CDA also provides direct loans to companies when private lenders are unable to address the total needs of the business and to companies significantly expanding or relocating to Connecticut.[17]

---

[16] The SBA's 504 Certified Development Company (CDC) Program provides growing businesses with long-term, fixed-rate financing for major fixed assets, such as land and buildings. www.sba.gov/financing/frcdc504.html

[17] The Connecticut Development Authority. "About CDA". www.state.ct.us/cda/faq.htm

Through its URBANK programme, CDA provides funds for working capital, machinery and equipment, or real estate of under US$250,000 if the company is in a targeted community. If the company is located outside a targeted community, the Loan Participation or Guarantee Program is available for amounts over US$250,000. Some of the authority's other programmes include a direct loan (up to US$5 million) for manufacturing and economic development projects contributing to the state's economic base or for start-up funds for businesses with strong economic impact potential, an entrepreneurial loan programme (up to US$100,000), and a job training finance programme for partial training grants (up to US$25,000) to manufacturers.[18]

New Jersey

The New Jersey Economic Development Authority (NJEDA) is a self-supporting, independent state financing and development agency serving New Jersey's business community. Founded in 1974, NJEDA has provided more than US$12.7 billion to help eligible businesses and not-for-profit groups. The authority works with businesses of all sizes and types, from sole entrepreneurs to world wide corporations, and has assisted more than 6,000 manufacturers, distributors, service providers and retailers. With the goal of creating and retaining jobs, and strengthening the state's economy, NJEDA helps create public/private partnerships to bridge financing gaps and increase access to capital for small and middle-size businesses and not-for-profit borrowers, arranges low-cost financing, offers loan guarantees and creative financing packages, provides real estate development services, and makes technical support available to strengthen targeted business sectors important to the state's economy.[19]

The authority's Investment Banking Division provides long-term, lower interest rate bond financing of US$750,000 and greater for a wide range of businesses and not-for-profit organisations. Its Commercial Lending Division makes loans and loan guarantees from US$50,000 to US$3 million targeted to small and middle-market businesses. NJEDA also has a Trade Adjustment Assistance Centre that offers professional consulting assistance for manufacturers hurt by

---

18.   The Connecticut Development Authority. "Summary of Programs. " www.state.ct.us/cda/cdaprogs.htm

19.   The New Jersey Economic Development Authority. "Welcome to the EDA". www.njeda.com/intro.htm

foreign competition and certified as eligible for assistance by the federal government.[20]

State operated programmes using federal CDBG funds

In the State CDBG programme, the US Department of Housing and Urban Development (HUD) makes annual grants to states which then use the funds to make grants to smaller communities. States establish their own programmes and rules to govern the distribution of their CDBG funds. While they may implement policies targeting particular geographic areas or giving priority to particular activities, the national programme has eligibility guidelines that limit the states' choices.[21] Eligible activities include housing, economic development, public facilities, social services, land acquisition, and other activities.

New Jersey

The New Jersey Department of Consumer Affairs' (NJDCA) 'Work First New Jersey Welfare-to-Work Program' unites the state wide welfare reform initiative with HUD assisted housing programmes, specifically the Section 8 Family Self-Sufficiency Program. The state has a co-ordinating committee in each of its 21 counties that reflects established partnerships made up of state, county, and local government agencies and representatives of private industry, non-profit agencies, and advocacy groups. This alliance strengthens the programme's goal to assist families seeking to make the transition from welfare recipients to self-sufficient wage earners. The state views this programme as its contribution to the national mobilisation toward self-sufficiency requiring every state to combine local solutions with efficient co-ordination of previously disjointed service providers and agencies.

The implementation of the programme involves administrators establishing action plans for each family to set forth steps to economic self-sufficiency. Participating families receive counselling, referrals, job training, and employment assistance. In addition, the programme establishes a home-ownership escrow account for each wage-earning family. There are now more

---

20. The New Jersey Economic Development Authority. "NJEDA Current Programs. " www.njeda.com/progs.htm

21. US Department of Housing and Urban Development. "State Community Development Block Grant (CDBG) Program. " www.hud.gov/progdesc/cdbg-st.html

than 400 families saving toward homeownership, and the escrow accounts, matched by programme funds, now top US$1.2 million. Sixteen of the 1,200 families volunteering for the programme now own homes, and more than 100 families in the programme no longer need welfare assistance. The backbone of the NJDCA programme is a written contract committing each participating family to specific timetables for attaining their educational, training, employment, and homeownership goals. Overall, the resources of the entire programme network support the families in fulfilling their contract.[22]

Maryland

The State of Maryland's 'Forty at Four' initiative, created in 1997, focuses on stabilising neighbourhoods, conserving existing resources, and providing an interest rate that will attract home buyers to targeted neighbourhoods. The programme, developed in co-operation with 15 local governments, HUD/FHA, community action agencies, local non-profit organisations, neighbourhood associations, local realtors, and lenders, is a way to make home financing more available as part of the state's smart growth policy. Refinanced tax-exempt mortgage revenue bonds pay for the programme. So far, efforts to retire older tax-exempt mortgage revenue bonds and issue new lower-cost bonds have generated US$40 million in proceeds now being made available for 30-year fixed rate home mortgages at a 4 percent interest rate. The programme has reserved 287 loans totalling US$24.8 million. Jurisdictions recommending areas, neighbourhoods and home ownership programmes compete for the funding awards, which may range up to US$5 million. In essence, the programme tests innovative ways to strengthen existing neighbourhoods through several home ownership models including acquisition and rehabilitation projects, purchase of existing homes, and in-fill construction.[23]

---

[22] US Department of Housing and Urban Development. "NJ Consumer Affairs Department Spearheads Housing Self-Sufficiency. "www.hud.gov/bpawards/crownsville.html

[23] US Department of Housing and Urban Development. "Forty at Four' Yelds Smart Growth Through Smart Financing." www.hud.gov/bpawards/crownsville.html

Direct investment programmes

North Carolina

The North Carolina Enterprise Corporation, a group of investment and operating professionals experienced in private equity investing and building successful companies, is the corporate managing general partner of The North Carolina Enterprise Fund, LP. The fund, created in 1990, is a private, institutional, venture capital fund with US$28 million of capital with limited partners including many of the state's more prominent financial institutions, utility companies, major businesses, and pension funds. The fund invests in small to medium-sized, private, North Carolina-based companies that demonstrate significant potential for successful business and investment growth. Typical investment amounts start at US$500,000 and range to US$3 million. While investing in companies in an early stage of business development, preferred investments include firms that require capital to rapidly and profitably expand their business. The fund also invests in appropriate mezzanine financing to include leveraged or management buyouts. Since inception, the fund has committed over US$30 million in capital to 25 companies with the primary objective of investing in businesses able to create lasting shareholder value and have a significant economic impact.[24]

State funded non-profits

North Carolina

The North Carolina Rural Economic Development Centre works to improve economic conditions, support increased entrepreneurial development, and make more and better jobs available in rural areas with a special focus on low-income residents. To carry out this mission, the Centre conducts research and demonstration programmes that test innovative strategies and models such as rural childcare, rural industrial base, natural resources growth, and financing infrastructure. Significant outreach efforts such as reports, workshops, seminars, and conferences, communicate findings from projects and programmes that aim to support rural development. Through its Community Development Corporation, Supplemental Grants, NC Microenterprise Loan, and Capital Access programmes, the Centre fosters entrepreneurial development

---

[24]. The North Carolina Enterprise Corporation. "The North Carolina Enterprise Fund, L. P.". www.ncef.com/index.html

helping to improve lagging rural economies. In addition to its research and finance programmes, the Centre conducts training for rural leaders to increase their knowledge of rural development strategies and sharpen leadership skills.

Kentucky

Kentucky's Kentucky Highlands Investment Corporation (KHIC) is a community development corporation focusing on venture capital and economic development. The firm, founded in 1968, invests in start-up and expanding non-retail business enterprises located (or to be located) in a nine-county area of south east Kentucky. KHIC backs high precision manufacturers, as well as relatively low technology, labour-extensive companies, considering investment opportunities that have the potential for developing into a profitable business. Maintaining a mullet-million capital pool and numerous investments in its portfolio ranging from US$100,000 to over a million dollars, the company is also the administrator of the Kentucky Highlands Empowerment Zone (KHEZ). Businesses located within the Empowerment Zone area of Jackson, Clinton and Wayne Counties may take advantage of advantageous financing and substantial federal tax credits.

KHIC also operates Mountain Ventures, Inc., the Appalachian Capital Corporation, and the Kentucky Highlands Real Estate Corporation. Mountain Ventures is a small business investment company with several million dollars of available investment capital for venture capital situations. The Appalachian Capital Corporation makes below market rate financing available to viable businesses located in or locating in Southeast Kentucky. The maximum loan used to finance the purchase and/or construction of fixed assets (land, buildings, and equipment) or working capital, is 75 percent of the project, not to exceed US$150,000. Finally, the Kentucky Highlands Real Estate Corporation maintains an inventory of available industrial sites and buildings. This corporation also develops industrial buildings and sites, and sells or leases them to related investees and others.[25]

---

[25]   Kentucky Highlands Investment Corporation. "Kentucky Highlands
         Investment Corporation."www.ezec.gov/homepages/rural/kentucky/khic.htm

Microenterprise loan programmes

North Carolina

The North Carolina Microenterprise Loan Programme, administered by the North Carolina Rural Economic Development Centre (discussed above), provides loans and business services to self-employed individuals and other small firms placing specific emphasis on providing services to rural, low-income, female/minority participants. The programme, serving all 85 rural counties in the state, essentially fosters self-sufficiency by providing the opportunity for self-employment and small business growth through loans for start-up or expansion by individuals who do not qualify for conventional loans. Eight local lending sites operate group-based lending programmes in which entrepreneurs participate by forming groups of four to ten people. Once certified, the group makes credit decisions for its members. All loans must be current in order for the group to consider making additional loans. Group lending, based on a tiered lending structure, allows an initial loan of up to US$1,500 per individual within the group. When the group pays off that, the next loan may be for up to US$5,000 and the next for up to US$8,000.

The individual lending programme uses a referral network to provide access to capital. Referrals direct loan requests to a credit committee reviews the loan application and makes a loan decision, making loans for up to US$25,000 based on demonstrated need. In addition, one local site operator, NC REAL Enterprises, provides individual based loans in conjunction with a training programme. REAL provides loans up to US$25,000 to youth and adults who complete an entrepreneurship course at a participating high-school or community college and completes a comprehensive business plan.

Utah

The Utah Microenterprise Loan Fund (UMLF), founded in 1993, is a tax-exempt, non-profit corporation representing a broad-based partnership of local banks, industrial loan corporations, and private and public enterprises. Funded by private donations and loans from local financial institutions, there are no tax dollars involved and each financial institution retains a proportionate share of every outstanding loan. Because many entrepreneurs do not have formal training or education, they may be unable to secure conventional credit for business ventures because they do not have sufficient capital, credit history or collateral. Therefore, the UMLF makes loans to start-up and existing firms located in Salt Lake County who do not have access to traditional funding sources, especially those who are socially or economically disadvantaged. The fund provides a secured form of financing (up to US$10,000), with terms up to five years, with a fixed interest rate of prime plus 3 percent.[26]

Regional partnerships

Mountain Association for Community Economic Development

In 1976, ten community development organisations in Central Appalachia region created the Mountain Association for Community Economic Development (MACED) as a provider of technical assistance to community-based groups. Through the years MACED has worked with people and organisations to improve life in this region's mountain communities, particularly for low-income people. Engaging in both community development and business development, the partnership works closely with local players ranging from grassroots community organisations to bankers. In addition, MACED regularly collaborates at the state, regional and national levels with other organisations in the community development field.[27]

Having lent and leveraged more than US$24.7 million creating more than 2,000 direct jobs, MACED's business development programme finances projects which have the potential to provide jobs to low-income people but which private banks typically will not finance. These projects employ from two to 300 persons in industries ranging from concrete contracting to technically advanced tool and die manufacturing. In 1994, MACED sharpened its focus on sustainable development through the sustainable communities programme and the Central Appalachian Sustainable Forestry Program. These programmes work to ensure that development addresses the importance of economy, ecology, and equity in sustainability. Finally, MACED sponsors a new, national organisation called 'Communities by Choice' which provides a communications and resource network for community-based groups, regional intermediaries, and community foundations working on sustainable development issues.[28]

---

[26]   Utah Microenterprise Loan Fund. http://www.umlf.com/

[27]   Mountain Association for Community Economic Development. "Overview."www.maced.org/overview.html

[28]   ibid

All of North Carolina's 100 counties belong to one of seven regional economic development partnerships. The partnerships enable regions to compete effectively for new investment and to devise suitable economic development strategies based on regional opportunities and advantages. The idea is that counties have a better chance of retaining current industries and attracting new industries if they pool their economic development resources as part of a region.[29]

Each of the seven partnerships works to create a variety of resources that will be helpful to business in the area. For example, the AdvantageWest Partnership, located in the western NC mountains, offers information on several targeted industries that benefit from the area's location and resources, profiles of the area's communities, a directory of economic developers, utilities, chambers of commerce, and tourism organisations, and answers requests for business relocation information.[30] AdvantageWest also has a certified industrial site programme that accelerates business start-up to save companies time and money. Another of the state's partnerships, North Carolina's Southeast, provides information on available sites and buildings, financial advantages to manufacturers, a regional data book, and detailed information about the region's industrial parks.[31]

County and municipal programmes

Charlotte, North Carolina

'City Within A City' (CWAC) is the City of Charlotte North Carolina's approach to meeting the economic development and quality of life issues in its older urban neighbourhoods and business districts. Since its inception in 1991, the programme has provided a framework for discussion and implementation of appropriate strategies to accomplish community redevelopment goals in inner-city neighbourhoods. The principles of the programme focus on

---

29.   North Carolina Department of Commerce. "Partnerships for Regional Economic Development." www.commerce.state.nc.us/contacts/

30.   Advantage West. "Advantage West: Western North Carolina Regional Economic Development Commission." www.awnc.org/

31.   North Carolina's Southeast. "North Carolina's Southeast: The Regional Economic Development Organisation for South-eastern North Carolina." www.ncse.org/

neighbourhoods, empowerment, capacity building, sustainability, partnerships, collaborative service delivery, and neighbourhood accountability. The programme works with neighbourhoods and business districts to find active ways to address their goals and needs and support individuals, families and organisations to enable them to make positive changes in their lives.[32] By providing information and training, CWAC helps residents and neighbourhood organisations identify problems and implement sustainable solutions that will have long-term impacts and stabilise individuals, families and neighbourhoods while focusing service delivery on targeted neighbourhoods and business areas.

Summary and Conclusions

The last several decades have seen the beginning of a significant federal role in regional and local development, followed by the gradual but consistent devolution of that role to state and local government. At the same time, independent of federal actions, state governments have assumed more responsibility for state, regional and local economic development policy. States have increasingly used their own resources, whether through investments, direct funding, or tax policy, to finance job creation and investment.

In the decade of the seventies and early eighties, the devolution was principally a result of transfer of federal funds and programmatic responsibilities to the state governments. Beginning in the mid-eighties and continuing today, states themselves undertook numerous programmes to stimulate state and regional economies. In the nineteen eighties, most of these initiatives were driven by the restructuring of the manufacturing sector in the United States and the perceived need to stimulate more entrepreneurial development and technology transfer. In the nineteen nineties, both of those policies continue. In addition, however, states are increasingly concerned with their overall competitiveness in a global economy and with the need to develop distressed regions and inner cities within otherwise healthy economies.

The decade of the nineties has seen a period of unparalleled expansion in the United States economy, which this month set a new record for the longest period of expansion in the nation's history. All states have shared in that economic growth, with most states recording record levels of low unemployment and rising prosperity. Yet the economic restructuring that accompanied that growth has had significant negative consequences for some regions and communities that lack the qualities to compete in the new economy,

---

32.   City of Charlotte, North Carolina. "City Within a City."
        www.ci.charlotte.nc.us/cicouncil/focus_areas/cwac.htm

and for individuals who lack the education and skills for the new jobs. Thus state policy has focused more directly on job creation in distressed regions and communities.

Several observers have referred to states as 'laboratories of democracy', because individual states can pioneer and test programmes which, if successful, are then copied in other states. Thus the Middle Atlantic States, which suffered significant job losses in the late seventies and eighties, pioneered many technology transfer and business development programmes that are widely copied today. Similarly, southern states pioneered many of the business recruitment programmes that most states now have to some degree.

Currently, there is a wide array of tools that support a complex array of strategies…from industrial recruitment to entrepreneurial development to microenterprise development to large scale commercial or community development projects. Sophisticated tax policies encourage investment in machinery and equipment, in venture capital, in low-income housing, and investing in distressed areas or inner cities. Financing techniques include various types of bonds, revolving loan funds, development banks, and incentives for private investment in riskier enterprises. These programmes are delivered through a mix of institutional structures, including development authorities, non-profit organisations, state agencies, and regional organisations.

There are excellent examples that can be usefully studied and adapted to different regions, states or countries. This paper has briefly reviewed the history of these policies and briefly profiled a number of programmes. Further information on those programmes is available through the sources in the bibliography and the web sites cited in the endnotes.

SECTION FOUR

CONCLUSION

CHAPTER 10

CONCLUSION

A more devolved economic development paradigm is required

The principal message of this book is that the combined forces of devolution and globalisation are creating a new paradigm for economic development policies. This new paradigm is based on promotion of endogenous development through locally-tailored policies designed and delivered by city and region governments and their partners. Policymakers need to recognise that devolution and globalisation are changing the way that cities and regions need to design and deliver economic development policy. This book seeks to highlight some of the implications and potential responses.

Globalisation involves increased international flows of capital and technology and increasingly international markets and competition. This is creating a need for more rapid and deeper economic adjustment than in the past. At the same time, the performance of city and regional economies appears to be less tied to the fortunes of their national economy and more affected by international developments. Globalisation is therefore changing the rationale for public intervention in terms of how the economy is regulated and how economic policies are put into place.

One of the principal impacts on economic policymaking has been a weakening of the effectiveness of traditional macro-economic policies in securing economic adjustment. Macroeconomic policy is increasingly constrained by economic openness such that national governments have less scope to manage economies through monetary and fiscal policies than they have had in the past. Furthermore, macroeconomic policy is not well adapted to helping individual regions and cities to respond to those international shocks that affect them particularly strongly, or to build up a long-term economic base that will secure their competitiveness in global markets.

The impact of increased openness on macro-economic policy instruments and their limited capacity to support economic adjustment in cities and regions suggests that there is an increasingly important role for micro-economic policies in securing economic development. This also fits with an increased focus on building endogenous strengths, which has been one of the most important trends in economic development in recent years. It is now increasingly recognised that 'bottom-up' support for endogenous development can be highly effective in supporting long-term development though measures to support entrepreneurship and develop human capital.

However, in the past, micro-economic policy interventions in OECD countries have tended to operate through top-down sectoral instruments. These are less well adapted to securing economic adjustment than devolved policies designed and delivered by cities and regions. Devolution to cities and regions helps tailor micro-economic policies to local needs, helps create an integrated policy offer and helps mobilise local partners to increase the leverage of government interventions. In particular, city and region governments and development agencies have the possibility to introduce distinctive and innovative micro-economic policies adapted to their own needs and opportunities. In the globalising economy, devolved governments can improve on top-down policies that are not differentiated according to local circumstances, resulting in more efficient and more effective policies. Furthermore, by bringing government closer to the people affected, devolution is also likely to increase the acceptability of policies.

In recognition of these benefits, we are currently witnessing an important trend towards devolution of responsibilities for designing and delivering economic development policies. The establishment of the new Scottish Parliament is one example, but there are many others across the OECD countries. Together, devolution and globalisation are creating a new environment giving regions a new opportunity to create a niche for adding value economically in global markets, based on distinctive and innovative policies.

Devolved development strategies should build competitiveness and cohesion

Policymakers in city and region governments and development agencies should be clear about the objectives of the interventions they develop. These objectives should essentially be two-fold. Firstly, there is a need to underpin city and region economic competitiveness in the global economy. Secondly, it is important to combat the social exclusion that can be associated with globalisation. Cities and regions need policies in both of these domains.

In terms of underpinning economic competitiveness, there are a number of key issues to address. In terms of neoclassical economic theory, city and region competitiveness can be thought of as depending on the availability of three key factors of production - financial/physical capital, labour and human capital and land/resources - and on how productively these factors can be employed. The productivity of factors is in turn influenced by considerations like the mobility of labour and capital, the extent of external economies including local networks and associations between firms and institutions, and the environment for innovation. This implies that policymakers need to concentrate both on expanding the availability of the factors and working on the wide range of influences that affect the productivity with which they are employed. In this book we have concentrated on the role of cities and regions in supporting entrepreneurship and human capital development. This is because these are two areas where recent success stories suggest that policymakers can have important impacts on city and region economic growth. Both have a pervasive impact on factor productivity and help attract and build capital. Measures in these areas can help create a healthy local environment for competition in the global economy although other potential measures such as support for innovation should not be neglected.

City and region governments and development agencies should also adopt an explicit strategy for combating social exclusion within their area. Globalisation presents tremendous opportunities for improving quality of life for people and communities through economic growth. However, in the globalising economy, the benefits of economic growth tend to be distributed unevenly between places and people. People with relatively few skills and people living in distressed urban and rural areas appear to be the main losers in the ongoing processes of economic restructuring. Their problems are often, although not always, associated with the loss of traditional jobs. The issue that policymakers need to face is that whilst some localities are being very successful in creating new jobs and wealth others are experiencing heavy job loss and long-run economic decline. Moreover, throughout the economy, the people obtaining high quality jobs tend to be those with the highest skills and mobility. People with few skills, with special needs or living in distressed areas need special actions to help overcome worklessness and other forms of exclusion. We should not assume that social exclusion will automatically be addressed by economic growth.

One of the paradoxes of globalisation is that high spatial concentrations of poverty and unemployment often exist adjacent to areas of great wealth and economic activity. This is particularly true in major metropolitan areas. Indeed, in periods of economic expansion, policymakers often realise that solving the problems of the poorer areas can be important to enabling continued economic growth in a city or region as its economy nears overheating. But the main reason for developing policies for social cohesion is to ensure that everyone has a place in the economy, not just those who are highly skilled and in the most dynamic areas. Cities and regions should therefore design initiatives to promote social cohesion at the local level, complementing initiatives pursued at the national level. In doing this, city and region governments are called to make choices about what paths of development to promote in the economy. They should seek to invest in creating good quality jobs and in supporting access to those jobs, whilst recognising that certain constraints exist of course in the extent to which taxes and business costs can be increased in the context of increasing capital mobility.

Furthermore, although this publication has not looked specifically at environmental policies, it should be recognised that sustainable development and environmental protection is also a critical principle of territorial development, together with economic development and social cohesion.

New institutional arrangements are needed

Together with meeting peoples' demands for self-government, one of the principal aims of devolution is to help adjust governance to changes occurring in the globalising economy. It is therefore important that the new institutional structures created are appropriate for the new economic environment. Globalisation is associated with increasingly complicated and rapidly-moving economic development problems and the need for cities and regions to develop endogenous strengths in order to exploit niches within the global economy. Institutional arrangements are therefore required that permit both the local tailoring of policy and enhanced cross-cutting between different public activities.

Traditional civil service arrangements have not proved very effective in achieving either cross-cutting or local tailoring of policies. This partly reflects poor information flow on policy needs because of the separation of policy conception (at central level) from policy execution (at local level) and poor co-ordination between the different units of administration responsible for activities in different sectors. Devolving responsibilities for policymaking to the city and region level can be a way of addressing these problems. However, in the process of devolution there is a danger that cities and regions could themselves recreate ineffective centralised or top-down policy design and delivery at their own level, copying the structures traditionally used by central government.

Devolution should therefore be seen as involving more than a simple central-local transfer of power. In order to achieve real innovation, tailoring and cross-cutting, cities and regions should reach out to other local organisations, from local governments, the social partners and civil society. The key feature of this sort of approach is the design and delivery of policy by networks of local actors rather than by a single agency working on its own. They may even wish to adopt a more experimental system where various local stakeholders are given the chance to develop and benchmark different approaches, with co-ordination from the centre. In this book, Sabel and O'Donnell have referred to this model as the 'democratic experimentalism'. It involves a new form of public administration that is neither a formal bureaucracy nor an informal network, where governance is by strategic coalitions of stakeholders. The OECD's work on local partnerships demonstrates how this type of model can be organised practically.

Building local networks within a city or region has a number of important advantages for policymaking:

- It enhances the integration and co-ordination of policy between different sectors and activities.

- It re-establishes the link between the conception and execution of policy and improves information flow on policy needs.

- It brings in new stakeholders to the policy process, including community sector organisations for example.

With the shift to devolution of policies towards the city and region level and the use of the local networking approach, the central government role in the management of economic development is therefore evolving, but it retains some very important functions. Central government is becoming less an initiator of policies and more a body that balances policies developed locally by setting an overall national framework. Central government therefore needs to change from seeing itself as the controller of city and region governments and agencies towards seeing itself as their partner. Central government nonetheless retains key co-ordination functions in particular.

One of the functions that central, nation-state, government still needs to perform in the context of devolved economic development management is the regulation of competition between territories. Questions of competition between cities and regions can arise because some of the policies that cities and regions may wish to develop could be incompatible in the long-term with those that others are seeking to develop. For example, policies addressing social exclusion, if implemented in one area only, could set into motion movement of people from one area to another. Similarly, subnational bodies could compete with each other by offering tax and other incentives to attract and retain business investment. Some type of framework is therefore needed at national level that gives cities and regions the freedom to develop the sorts of strategies they want to pursue but at the same time prevents the emergence of significant conflicts between areas.

A second key function for central government is to co-ordinate a certain level of redistribution of funds between rich and poor cities and regions so that all areas have a critical mass of funding for economic development projects. Without such redistribution, it is likely to be impossible to ensure any real equality of opportunity at national level. This is because, without co-ordination, some regions are likely to experience a virtuous circle of economic growth, increasing taxes and increasing investment local infrastructure and environment whilst others are likely to experience the opposite - a vicious circle. This redistribution function of central government is contentious and also appears to be becoming more difficult with increasing mobility of capital, however it would appear to remain critical to approaches that rely on triggering endogenous development.

A final major consideration underlined in this book on institutional arrangements for devolved economic management concerns the need to avoid a recentralisation of policy control in the city or region. Decentralised local networks seem to be right for current conditions, but there can sometimes be a resistance to sharing power from core institutions in the city or region because the message behind devolution is not understood. City and region governments should recognise that devolution offers them the best prospects for enhanced economic and social development if they involve new players and partners in finding and resourcing innovative policies. Indeed, this innovation could be particularly strong where a large number of players are involved and where parallel, often overlapping, sets of institutions are allowed to develop. It is often seen as a natural instinct to resist duplication and seek economies of scale and scope in policy provision, but this could stifle innovation. Instead, it may be better to allow a certain amount of rivalry to flourish, whilst organising clear goals and performance measures to evaluate and benchmark different approaches and to support and disseminate the best approaches as the system learns and innovates. Thus rather than creating a centralised unit for policy design and implementation, this framework-setting and benchmarking function may prove to be the key role of city and region governments.

The OECD Territorial Development Service is examining these issues further in its ongoing work on governance.

Cities and regions hold important policy tools

City and region governments and development agencies have many of the best
policy instruments available to respond to the economic and social development
challenges of globalisation. At the same time as the development potential of
traditional macroeconomic policies and central government sectoral initiatives
are being questioned, cities and regions are developing important micro-
economic tools for supporting endogenous development. In the globalising
economy, cities and regions need policies that will create a competitive local
environment. Policies for stimulating entrepreneurship and building human
capital are particularly important in this respect. Cities and regions also need
policies for promoting social cohesion, so that people and places are not
excluded from economic and social activity.

It is important that cities and regions make use of these tools by introducing
innovative development strategies that are genuinely tailored to the needs of
their area and that draw out synergies between the different activities promoted.
They should focus strongly on exploiting the endogenous strengths that will
enable the city and region to compete in global markets. In doing so, it is
necessary to look outward for market opportunities and for opportunities to
bring in complementary capital and technologies as well as to look inward at the
resources and capabilities that exist locally.

One of the critical determinants of competitiveness in the emerging economic
environment is entrepreneurship. The creation of new businesses and the
innovation in products and markets that is associated with entrepreneurship
increases the ability of the economy to adjust to changes in technologies and
market demand and to use production factors efficiently. Many of the best
policy instruments to encourage entrepreneurship are to be found at the city and
region level, such as credit guarantee associations, venture capital support,
extension and information services, business incubators and science parks and
the promotion of business networks. These tools for the promotion of
entrepreneurship are not limited to the market sector, however, but can also be
used to encourage social entrepreneurs to create non-profit sector enterprises
with social goals.

Clustering approaches are a classic example of how cities and regions can
intervene in order to promote entrepreneurship. These initiatives seek to
promote collective working by firms and institutions in the same or related
sectors and to improve the local environment for the success of those sectors.
The public sector interventions aim to address market failures and stimulate
innovation by maximising externalities between local firms and institutions, by
supporting localised learning, by providing public goods infrastructure in the

sectors concerned and by rectifying co-ordination failures. The specific policy actions, however, will be very different according to the cluster concerned. For example, in collaboration with the private sector and other players, city and region governments and development agencies might provide information on local and overseas market opportunities, support equity finance, encourage the creation of customised training facilities and so on.

In developing cluster approaches, there are certain guidelines that the public sector should follow.

- It should be recognised that cluster development is essentially a market process. The world-famous clusters in the north of Italy emerged with virtually no direct policy support. The public sector can facilitate these processes, but it is likely to be difficult or impossible to create entirely new clusters of firms. In this context, one of the most important activities that the public sector can undertake is the simple act of bringing players together so that they can begin to see the opportunities for collective working.

- Policies must not be too narrowly focused on one or two typical headline clusters, for example in high-technology industry, because there are dangers in excessive regional specialisation and because these sectors may be inappropriate for the area in question. The general tenet that policy should be tailored to local conditions is very pertinent here. Policymakers need to be very sensitive to local conditions in designing cluster approaches and resist taking cluster initiatives 'off-the-shelf' from other areas.

- There should be a focus on encouraging innovation within the chosen sectors. Clusters need to react to changes in markets and technologies or they will decline. Some areas have been more successful than others at this.

- Clusters should not be viewed in isolation. It is important to promote internal and external links with other sectors and with other policy initiatives.

A second critical determinant of competitiveness in the emerging economic environment is human capital. It is widely recognised that globalisation is associated with the emergence of a knowledge economy in which investment in human capital is increasingly important. Businesses require a more skilled workforce and people need more skills for employment and income improvement. Technical skills increasingly need to be combined with more generic skills such as flexibility and entrepreneurialism. And skills need to be more frequently updated.

In this knowledge economy, cities and regions must secure a sufficient qualified workforce. In many OECD Member countries, the availability of finance for training is not the main barrier to achieving this. What is important is encouraging the take-up of training and ensuring that the training is delivered with the right kind of organisational approach. The changes in the nature of skills associated with globalisation and the knowledge economy affect the ways in which training needs to be delivered. In particular, the new approaches need to develop active knowledge. Training policies designed and delivered at the city and region level have a number of advantages over centrally-driven programmes in this respect. They are better placed to promote local partnerships between employers, local governments and unions. They are also better placed to promote approaches that are based around real problem-solving projects, that alternate between training and that tackle the various other social and economic issues that affect whether or not training is successful.

Partnerships, in particular, are a very important feature of successful local approaches to skills development. Certain guidelines are referred to in the book on how city and region governments and development agencies should manage partnerships, namely make policy goals consistent at central level, adapt the strategic framework for the partnership to the needs of the partners, strengthen the accountability of partnerships and provide flexibility in the management of public programmes. Furthermore, with the current proliferation of partnerships in many areas it may be important to co-ordinate their work, as is done in the Netherlands by PITT for example.

Cities and regions also need policies for social cohesion, which reattach people and places that otherwise could become victims of the economic restructuring associated with globalisation. One important challenge is to address problems in distressed urban and rural areas, where many excluded people are concentrated. To a large extent, the problems of these areas are related to the decline of the old economy and obstacles to finding a place in the new economy by attracting and developing growth industries. The policies developed by cities and regions therefore need to address these underlying problems.

This book has highlighted some of the many policy instruments that cities and regions can use to attract and grow investment in distressed areas and to provide the kind of training and support that will help excluded people to access these opportunities. The initiatives that cities and regions should seek to develop include tightly-targeted tax credits, infrastructure provision, local active labour market policies, community financing and support to the social economy. In the context of devolution and globalisation, there is also a need to ensure that the necessary infrastructure, including information and communications technology infrastructure, is provided in distressed areas so that local enterprises remain competitive and able to access external markets. This support to distressed areas should emphasise building long-term endogenous capacities rather than simple income redistribution.

Devolution is an opportunity for institutional and policy innovation

This book has set out a vision of devolved economic development policies capable of responding to the challenges of globalisation. The key features in this vision are flexible and networked institutional arrangements and integrated and locally-tailored development strategies using tools for entrepreneurship, human capital development and social cohesion among others. Devolution is an opportunity for cities and regions to innovate in their economic development approaches. The opportunity should be seized to acquire greater flexibility and improved capacity to change at the local level, because globalisation is associated with a more dynamic and competitive economy.

One of the principal messages of the book is that devolution is more than just a transfer of power, it is also a new spirit of co-operation and networking. For policy to be successful in the complex and rapidly-changing environment of globalisation, there is a need to build greater confidence between the various public, non-profit and private actors that are so important to economic and social development. City and region administrations should therefore act in partnership with all the other institutions of their territory in order to plan, co-ordinate and implement development policies. These devolved institutional networks should be seen as a critical part of the institutional capital of cities and regions that require nurturing and investment.

The second principal message of this book is that cities and regions should develop distinct strategies that are really adapted to their special circumstances. Cities and regions should use devolution to build up their own competitive advantages with innovative economic development policies that are adapted to their own local circumstances. Different cities and regions can choose to take very different trajectories of development, depending on the choices of local people and on the opportunities available. In this context, it is very important to understand the territorial economy and the drivers of change at global level as well as to evaluate the impact of policies and the alternatives available.

In seeking to develop appropriate strategies and governance arrangements in an era of devolution and globalisation there is a strong demand at local level for policy analysis and best practice information. The OECD's Forum on Cities and Regions was therefore created at the Glasgow conference, on which this book reports, as a framework for international comparative analyses of city and region economic and social policies. The Forum disseminates information and analysis on the drivers of change in the globalising economy and on the policy responses that city and region governments and development agencies can make.

ANNEX 1

THE OECD FORUM ON CITIES AND REGIONS

The purpose and activities of the Forum

The OECD Forum on Cities and Regions (FCR) was inaugurated in Glasgow at the conference on 'Devolution and Globalisation: Implications for Local Decision-makers' on 28-29 February 2000. It aims to stimulate international comparisons between members of the OECD LEED Partners Club on the design of city and region development strategies and instruments capable of responding to the challenges of the globalising economy.

The Forum has a programme of work that covers the entire range of issues that city and regional governments and development agencies need to address to promote economic competitiveness and social cohesion in this increasingly dynamic and complicated environment. Key work areas include promotion of innovative and effective economic development and social policy tools, assessment of what should be included in comprehensive and integrative development strategies, analysis of how to design appropriate governance and policy delivery mechanisms and examination of how cities and regions can best finance their development activities. The FCR is also developing a programme of entrepreneurship policy reviews in case study cities and regions. These reviews will explore how cities and regions can bring together a wide range of policies to create a healthy environment for entrepreneurship. All the work of the Forum has a strong focus on making concrete recommendations that can be taken up by members and an active exchange of information on best practices and policy results.

The FCR organised three events in 2000:

- An international conference on 'Devolution and Globalisation: Implications for Local Decision-makers', held in Glasgow on 28-29 February in collaboration with Scottish Enterprise and the Glasgow Development Agency.

- An experts seminar on 'The Role of Culture in Local Development and Job Creation' held in Paris on 25 September.

- An experts seminar on 'Environment, Employment and Local Initiatives' held in Paris on 23 October.

Subject to availability of funding from members, future activities and events include:

- A major cross-national study on inward investment and local development, identifying best practice policies for inward investment attraction, aftercare and retention, long-term embedding and response to closure. Cities and regions are invited support a case study in their area.

- A seminar in London in December 2001 on making strategies for cities and regions in the global economy.

- A summit on smart growth and sustainable development strategies in Toronto in 2002.

- A study on new methods of financing local development, including public-private partnerships, municipal bonds and other instruments.

- A series of local reviews of entrepreneurship, which, using a common methodology, will explore how cities and regions can put in place comprehensive programmes to support a healthy local environment for entrepreneurship. Cities and regions are invited support an entrepreneurship review in their area.

Cities and regions interested in joining the Forum can obtain further information from Jonathan Potter at the OECD LEED Programme.

Jonathan Potter
Administrator
LEED Programme
OECD
2, rue André-Pascal   Telephone: ++ 331 4524 8977
75775 Paris Cedex 16   Fax: ++331 4524 1668
France   E-mail: jonathan.potter@oecd.org

ANNEX 2

THE CONFERENCE PROGRAMME

'DEVOLUTION AND GLOBALISATION - IMPLICATIONS FOR LOCAL DECISION-MAKERS'

International conference, Glasgow, Scotland, 28-29 February 2000

Organised by the OECD LEED Programme, Scottish Enterprise and Glasgow Development Agency

Objective: 'To bring together development agencies and experts from different OECD cities and regions to debate the opportunities created by delivering economic development policies within a devolved framework in a globalising economy.'

Monday 28 February, 2000 at the Trades Hall, 85 Glassford Street, Glasgow

Chair of morning sessions: Paul Cullen, Chair of the OECD LEED Directing Committee and Department of Enterprise, Trade and Employment, Ireland

Session 1: The implications of devolution and globalisation for economic development policy in OECD cities and regions

9.15-9.30	Opening address, Bernard Hugonnier, Head of OECD Territorial Development Service
9.30-9.35	Welcome from Scottish Enterprise, Charlie Woods, Director of Strategy, Scottish Enterprise, Scotland
9.35-10.00	Devolution and globalisation: trends and challenges for OECD cities and regions, Jon Potter, OECD LEED Programme

10.00-10.15	Devolution, globalisation and new economic development strategies for Scotland, Nicol Stephen, Scottish Deputy Minister for Enterprise and Lifelong Learning
10.15-10.35	General discussion
10.35-11.00	Coffee break

Session 2: Institutional innovations *(Rapporteur: Sylvain Giguère, OECD LEED Programme)*

11.00-11.20	Managing economic development policy within the context of devolution and globalisation, Professor Charles Sabel, Columbia University, United States
11.20-11.30	Decentralisation of economic development policies in North Rhine Westphalia: Michael Deitmer, Head of Structural Development, Ministry for Economy, SMEs, Technology and Transport, North Rhine Westphalia, Germany
11.30-11.40	Response by Ging Wong, Human Resources Development Canada, Canada
11.40-12.15	General discussion
12.15-12.25	Report-back by Rapporteur and close of morning session by Chairman
12.25-13.30	Lunch

Chair of afternoon sessions: Paavo Saikkonen, Vice Chairman of the OECD LEED Directing Committee and Ministry of Labour, Finland.

Session 3: Innovations in policy tools *(Rapporteur: Alistair Nolan, OECD LEED Programme)*

13.30-13.50	The Scottish Clusters Approach: Charlie Woods, Director of Strategy, Scottish Enterprise, Scotland
13.50-14.00	Response by Alessandro Cavalieri, IRPET (Regional Institute for the Economic Programming of Tuscany), Italy and Andrea Balestri, Secretary of the International Club of Local Clusters and Italian Club of Industrial Districts, Italy
14.00-14.30	General discussion

14.30-14.45	Local programmes to promote economic development in distressed areas in the United States, by Rick Carlisle, Secretary of Commerce, State of North Carolina, USA
14.45-14.55	Response by John Evans OECD Trade Union Advisory Council
14.55-15.20	General discussion
15.20-15.45	Coffee break
15.45-15.55	Local policies for skills and training in knowledge economies, by P Keulers, Director, Partners in Training and Technology, Netherlands, an employer-led training initiative and OECD Business and Industry Advisory Council
15.55-16.05	Response by Professor Xavier Greffe, University of Paris I Panthéon-Sorbonne, France
16.05-16.35	General discussion
16.35-16.40	Report back by Rapporteur

Session 4: Lessons for future *(Rapporteur: Josef Konvitz, Head of Territorial Development Policies and Prospects Division, Territorial Development Service, OECD)*

16.40-17.50	Round table discussion with city mayors and region ministers.
	Chair: Fabrizio Barca, Chairman of the OECD Territorial Development Policy Committee and Head of the Department for Development and Cohesion Policies, Treasury Ministry, Italy
	Panellists: Carlo Magri, Deputy Mayor of Milan, Italy; Mr Tauno Moilanen, Mayor of Imatra, Finland; Mrs Maravillas Rojo, Deputy Mayor of Barcelona, Spain; Tanya Mattheus, Ministry of Employment, Flanders region, Belgium.
	How OECD cities and regions have introduced new economic development approaches designed to respond to the changing environment of devolution and globalisation
17.50-18.00	Report back by Rapporteur and closing remarks by the Chairman

20.00   Evening dinner reception given by the Lord Provost of
                 Glasgow in the City Chambers

Tuesday 29 February, 2000 at The Lighthouse, 11 Mitchell Lane, Glasgow

                 Chair: Sergio Arzeni, Head of the OECD LEED
                 Programme

9.30-11.30   SCOTTISH ROUND TABLE

                 Round table discussion on how Scottish economic
                 development policy can respond to the changing
                 environment created by devolution and globalisation.

                 Panel chair: Gerry Rice, World Bank.   The panel
                 members: Alan McGregor, Training and Employment
                 Research Unit, University of Glasgow; Anne Brooks,
                 Economic and Community Development, Glasgow; Josef
                 Konvitz, OECD; Stuart Gulliver, Glasgow Development
                 Agency; Stephen Hill, Welsh Development Agency.

                 Questions proposed by the Chair for discussion by the
                 panel followed by questions from the floor and open
                 discussion.:

                       –   What are the key lessons and messages that
                           the panellists have gained from the previous
                           presentations and discussions?

                       –   In the light of the new environment, how
                           can   future   economic   development
                           approaches be made more effective?

11.30-12.00   Coffee break

12.00-12.25	LAUNCHING OF THE OECD FORUM OF CITIES AND REGIONS

12.00-12.25   **LAUNCHING OF THE OECD FORUM OF CITIES AND REGIONS**

Presentation of the aims, structure and activities of the OECD Forum of Cities and Regions by Sergio Arzeni, Head of the OECD LEED Programme.

Presentation of forthcoming Forum events by Forum members.

Signing of the Charter inaugurating the OECD Forum of Cities and Regions.

12.25-12.30   Closing statement by Sergio Arzeni, Head of the OECD LEED Programme

12.30-13.30   Buffet Lunch

13.30-15.30   **TOUR OF GLASGOW ECONOMIC REGENERATION SITES**

Coach visits to selected economic development and regeneration projects in Glasgow including the Crown Street project and the Glasgow Science Centre and Media Park. Theme explored: how the Glasgow has achieved a transition from a traditional industrial based economy to a modern diversified economy.

BIBLIOGRAPHY

Amin, A. and Robins, K. (1991) 'I Distretti Industriali e lo Sviluppo Regionale: Limiti e Possibilità', *Studi & Informazioni*.

Anastasia, B. and Corò, G. (1996) *Evoluzione di un'economia regionale. Il Nordest dopo il successo*, Ediciclo Editore.

Arrow, K. (1974) *The Limits of Organisation*, W.W. Norton & Co.

Aucoin, P. (1995) *The New Public Management: Canada in Comparative Perspective*, Institute for Research on Public Policy: Montreal.

Balestri, A. and Ricchetti, M. (1999) 'Valuing the Italian Dream', in G. Malossi, Volare, *The Icon of Italy in Global Pop Culture*, The Monacelli Press.

Barro, R. (1998) *Determinants of Economic Growth*, Cambridge MA: MIT Press.

Bassanini, A. and Scarpetta, S. (2001) 'Does human capital matter for growth in OECD countries? Evidence from pooled mean-group estimates', OECD Economics Department Working Paper No. 289, OECD, Paris.

Becattini, G. (1978) 'The Development of Light Industry in Tuscany', in *Economic Notes*, No. 2-3.

Becattini, G. (1989) 'Riflessioni sul distretto industriale come concetto socio-economico', in *Stato e Mercato*, n. 25.

Becattini, G. (1998) *Distretti industriali e Made in Italy*, Bollati Boringhieri.

Becattini, G. and Rullani, E. (1993) 'Sistema Locale e Mercato Globale', *Economia e Politica Industriale*, n. 80.

Bellandi, M. (1992) *Decentralised Industrial Creativity in Dynamic Industrial Districts*, UNCTAD/GTZ Symposium, Geneva.

Berger, S. and Dore, R. (1996) *National Diversity and Global Capitalism*, Cornell Un. Press.

Berryman, S.E. and Bailey, T.R. (1992) *The Double Helix of Education and the Economy*, The Columbia University Press, New York.

Birch, D., Haggerty, A. and Parsons, W. (1997) *Who's Creating Jobs*, Cognetics Inc., Cambridge, Massachusetts.

Blanchard, O. and Katz, L. (1992) *Regional Evolutions*, Brookings Papers in Economic Activity, 2, Brookings Institute, Washington DC.

Boldrin, M. and Canova, F. (2001) Inequality and convergence in Europe's regions: reconsidering European regional policies, *Economic Policy*, April 2001, pp 207-253.

Brace, P. (1993) *State Government and Economic Performance*, The Johns Hopkins University Press, Baltimore, Maryland.

Braczyk, H., Cooke, P. and Heidenreich, M. (Eds) (1998) *Regional Innovation Systems*. UCL Press, London.

Bramanti, A. e M.A. Maggioni (a cura di) (1997) *La Dinamica dei sistemi produttivi territoriali: teorie, tecniche, politiche*, Franco Angeli: Milan.

Brown, A., Buck, M., and Skinner, E. (1998) *Business Partnerships: How to Involve Employers in Welfare Reform*, Manpower Demonstration Research Corporation, Washington.

Burton-Jones, A. (1999) *Knowledge Capitalism*, Oxford University Press, Oxford.

Cabinet Office (1999) *Professional Policy Making for the Twenty First Century*, London: Cabinet Office, report by the Strategic Policy Making Team.

Cabinet Office (2000a) *Wiring it Up: Whitehall's Management of Cross-Cutting Issues*, London: Stationery Office.

Cabinet Office (2000b) *Reaching Out: the Role of Central Government at Regional and Local Level*, London: Stationery Office.

Campbell, C. and Wilson, G. (1995) *The End of Whitehall: Death of a Paradigm?* Oxford: Blackwell.

Castells, M. (1996a) *The Rise of the Network Society*, Oxford, Blackwell.

Castells, M. (1996b) *End of Millenium*, Oxford, Blackwell.

Cavalieri, A. (1995) *L'Internazionalizzazione del processo produttivo nei sistemi locali di piccola impresa in Toscana*, Franco Angeli: Milan.

Christmann, G. (1999) 'Challenges for Managing Rapid Structural Changes in the Economy', in *Economic and Cultural Transitions towards a Learning City: The Case of Jena*, OECD, Paris.

Conti, G. and S. Menghinello (1997) 'L'internazionalizzazione produttiva dei sistemi locali', in *Rapporto sul commercio estero*, ICE.

Corò, G. and S. Micelli (1998) 'Distretti industriali ed imprese trasnazionali: sistemi alternativi o percorsi evolutivi convergenti?', I processi innovativi nella Piccola Impresa, University of Urbino workshop.

Davenport, E. (1989) 'From Boston to Britain: The Development of Compact' in *Local Work Monthly Bulletin*, April, No. 7, Centre for Local Economic Strategies, Manchester.

Dicken, P. (1998) *Global Shift. Transforming the World Economy*, Third Edition, Paul Chapman Publishing Ltd, London.

Dunsire, A. (1993) 'Modes of Governance', in Kooiman, J., *Modern Governance: New Government-Society Interactions*, Sage Publications, London.

European Commission (1999) *Guide for Setting Up a Second Chance School*, Brussels.

European Commission (2001) *Governance in the European Union*, Cahiers of the Forward Studies Unit, Luxembourg: Office for Official Publications of the European Communities.

Eurostat (1997) *Youth in the European Union from Education to Working Life*, No. 11, Luxembourg.

Eurostat (1998) 'From School to Working Life: Facts on Youth Unemployment,' in *Population and Social Conditions*, No. 13, Luxembourg.

Fabiani, S., Pellegrini, G., Romagnano, E. and Signorini, L.F. (2000) 'Efficiency and localisation: the case of Italian industrial districts', in M. Bagella and L. Becchetti (Eds) *The Competitive Advantage of Industrial Districts: Theoretical and Empirical Analysis*, Physica Verlag, Heidelberg.

Ferrucci L. and Varaldo, R. (1993) 'La natura e la dinamica dell'impresa distrettuale', *Economia e politica industriale*, n. 80.

Florida, R. (1995) 'Towards the Learning Region', in *Futures*, 27, pp. 527-536.

Fortis, M (1998) *Il Made in Italy*, Il Mulino.

Fujita, M., Krugman, P. and Venables, A. (1999) *The Spatial Economy: Cities, Regions and International Trade*, Cambridge, Mass. MIT Press.

Gertler, M.S. (1999) 'Globalisation, Regional Economic Transition and Learning: Restructuring, Renewal and the Role of Culture', in *Economic and Cultural Transitions towards a Learning City: The Case of Jena*, OECD, Paris.

Grandinetti R. (1993) 'L'internazionalizzazione sommersa delle Piccole Imprese', *Rivista Italiana di Economia, Demografia e Statistica*, n. 3-4.

Greffe, X. (1993) *Rapport général sur le développement de l'apprentissage et des formations en alternance*, Ministry of Labour and Ministry of Education, Paris.

Greffe, X. (1994) *Sociétés postindustrielles et redéveloppement*, Hachette, collection Pluriel, Paris.

Greffe, X. (1995) *La formation professionnelle des jeunes*, Anthropos-Economica, Paris.

Greffe, X. (1999a) *Gestion Publique*, Dalloz, Paris.

Greffe, X. (1999b) *A Pilot Action on Local Partnerships in Europe: Final Recommendations*, European Commission DG V, Brussels.

Hastings, T. (1999) 'Economic and Cultural Transitions towards a Learning City: The case of Jena', Summary Report, in *Economic and Cultural Transitions towards a Learning City: The Case of Jena*, OECD, Paris.

Hirst, P. and Thompson, G. (1999) *Globalisation in Question. The International Economy and the Possibilities of Governance.* Second Edition. Polity Press, Cambridge.

IMD (1998) *The World Competitiveness Yearbook 1997*, IMD Press.

Jennings, E.T. Jr., Krane, D., Pattakos, A N. and Reed, B.J. (1986) *From Nation to States: The Small Cities Community Block Grant Program*, State University of New York Press, Albany New York.

Keating, M. (1998) 'Territorial Politics in Europe. A Zero-Sum Game? The New Regionalism. Territorial Competition and Political Restructuring in Western Europe'. European University Institute Working Paper RSC No. 98139, European University Institute, Florence.

Laidlaw, B., and Layard, R. (1974) 'Traditional versus Open University Methods: A Comparison', in *Higher Education*, 3.

Le Galès (1998) 'Government and governance of regions: structural weaknesses and new mobilisations', Chapter 14, 239-267 in P. Le Galès and C. Lequesne (eds) *Regions in Europe*, Routledge, London.

Leicester, G. and Mackay, P. (1998) *Holistic Government: Options for a Devolved Scotland*, Edinburgh: Scottish Council Foundation.

Leyshon, A. (1996) 'Dissolving difference? Money, disembedding and the creation of "global financial space"', Chapter 5, 62-80 in P. Daniels and W. Lever (eds) *The Global Economy in Transition*, Longman, Harlow.

Liautard, (1999) 'L'environnement logiciel des systèmes d'accréditation', in *L'accréditation des compétences dans la société cognitive*, World Bank - European Union Symposium, Marseille, 2-3 February 1998, Editions de l'Aube.

London Development Agency (2000) *Draft Economic Strategy*, London: London Development Agency

Markusen, A. (1996) 'Sticky places in slippery space: A typology of industrial districts', *Economic Geography*, Vol. 72, 293-313

Marshall, A. (1919) *Industry and Trade*, Macmillan.

Martin, R. and Tyler, P. (2000) 'Regional Employment Evolutions in the European Union: Empirics and Policy Implications', Paper presented to the Regional Studies Association Conference, Aix en Provence, France, 14-16 September 2000

Mistri, M. (1998) *Culture locali e processi di globalizzazione: il caso dei distretti industriali*, AISSEC Conference, 3-5 June, Siena.

Mistri, M. (1993) *Distretti industriali e Mercato Unico Europeo, Istituto Guglielmo Tagliacarne*, Franco Angeli: Milan.

Morgan, K. (1997) 'The Learning Region: Institutions, Innovations, and Regional Renewal', in *Regional Studies*, Vol. 31, No. 5.

OECD (1990a) *Implementing Change. Entrepreneurship and Local Initiative*, OECD: Paris.

OECD (1990b) *Enterprising Women*, OECD, Paris.

OECD (1996a) *Ireland. Local Partnerships and Social Innovation*, OECD: Paris.

OECD (1996b) *Networks of Enterprises and Local Development*, OECD: Paris.

OECD (1996c) *Transitions to Learning Economies and Societies*, OECD: Paris.

OECD (1997a) *Managing Across Levels of Government*, OECD: Paris.

OECD (1997b) *Globalisation and Small and Medium Enterprises, Volume 1, Synthesis Report*, OECD, Paris.

OECD (1998a) *Fostering Entrepreneurship*, OECD: Paris.

OECD (1998b) *Micro-financing and Local Development*, OECD: Paris.

OECD (1998c) *Local Management for More Effective Employment Policies*, OECD: Paris.

OECD (1999a) 'Preparing Youth for the 21st Century: The Policy Lessons from the Past Two Decades', Conference Background Paper, OECD Directorate for Employment, Labour and Social Affairs, Paris.

OECD (1999b) *The Local Dimension of Welfare-to-Work*, OECD: Paris.

OECD (1999c) *Social Enterprises*, OECD: Paris.

OECD (1999d) *Decentralising Employment Policy. New Trends and Challenges*, OECD: Paris.

OECD (1999e) *Business Incubation: International Case Studies*, OECD: Paris.

OECD (2000a) 'Small and Medium-sized Enterprises: Local Strength, Global Reach', Policy Brief series, OECD, Paris.

OECD (2000b) *OECD Economic Outlook*, OECD, Paris.

OECD (2000c) *Government of the Future*, OECD, Paris.

OECD (2001a) *Cities for Citizens: Improving Metropolitan Governance*, OECD: Paris.

OECD (2001b) *Local Partnerships for Better Governance*, OECD: Paris.

OECD (2001c) *Putting the Young in Business. Policy Challenges for Youth Entrepreneurship,* OECD: Paris.

OECD (2001d) *The Well-Being of Nations: The Role of Human and Social Capital*, OECD: Paris.

OECD (2001e) *Women Entrepreneurs in SMEs: Realising the Benefits of Globalisation and the Knowledge-based Economy*, OECD: Paris.

OECD (2001f) *Enhancing SME Competitiveness. The OECD Bologna Ministerial Conference*, OECD, Paris.

OECD (2001g) *OECD Territorial Outlook*, OECD, Paris.

OECD/DATAR (2001) *World Congress on Local Clusters, Proceedings*, OECD/DATAR, Paris.

Ohmae, K. (1995) *The End of the Nation State. The Rise of Regional Economies*, New York: The Free Press.

Perri 6 (1997) *Holistic Government*, London: Demos.

Peters, B.G. and Pierre, J. (2001) Developments in intergovernmental relations: towards multi-level governance, *Policy and Politics*, 29.2, 131-5

Piore, M. and Sabel, C. (1984) *The Second Industrial Divide: Possibilities for Prosperities*, Basic Books: New York.

Porter, M. (1990) *The Competitive Advantage of Nations*, Basic Books: New York.

Porter, M. (1998a) *On Competition*, HBR Press, Cambridge: Massachusetts.

Porter, M. (1998b) Clusters and the new economics of competition, *Harvard Business Review*, November-December, pp. 77-90.

Porter, M. (1990) *The Competitive Advantage of Nations*, MacMillan: London.

Putnam, R.D. (1993) *Making Democracy Work; Civic Tradition in Modern Italy*, Princeton University Press.

Redburn, F.S., and Buss, T.F. (1982) *Public Policies for Distressed Communities*, D.C. Heath and Company, Lexington, Massachusetts.

Reigner, H. (2001) Multi-level governance or co-administration? Transformation and continuity in French local government, *Policy and Politics*, Vol. 29.2, pp. 181-192.

Reynolds, P. Hay, M. Bygrave, W. Camp, S. and Autio, E. (2000) 'Global Entrepreneurship Monitor', 2000 Executive Report, Kauffman Centre for Entrepreneurial Leadership at the Ewing Marion Kauffman Foundation, Kansas City, Missouri, USA.

Reynolds, P., Storey, D.J. and Westhead, P. (1994) 'Cross-national comparisons of the variation in new firm formation rates', *Regional Studies*, Vol. 28.4, pp. 443-456.

Rhodes, R.A.W. (1997) *Understanding Governance*, Buckingham: Open University Press.

Rolle, F. (1997) 'Une expérience de formation locale : le CUCES', in *Revue Française de Sociologie*.

Rosenfeld, S. (1996) 'United States: Business Clusters', in OECD, *Networks of Enterprises and Local Development*, OECD: Paris.

Rullani, E. (1995) 'Contesti e varietà nell'economia di impresa', XXXVI Riunione scientifica annuale della Società Italiana degli Economisti, Firenze,.

Saxenian, A. (1994) *Regional Advantage, Culture and Competition in Silicon Valley and Route 128*, Cambridge MA, Harvard University Press.

Scarso, E. (1998) 'Processi di Internazionalizzazione e Traiettorie di Sviluppo dei Sistemi Produttivi Locali', I processi innovativi nella Piccola Impresa, Università di Urbino workshop.

Schmidt Braul, E. (1998) 'Approche socio-politique de l'économie des filières de la production culturelle et de ses effets sur la dynamique sociale et sur la cohésion sociale', paper at symposium on publishing, CEFRAC, Paris.

Schumack, P. and Greffe, X. (1997) *Enterprise Culture and Job Creation in the European Union*, LEDA Programme, Commission of the European Union, DG V, Brussels.

Schweke, W. (2000) 'The methods and uses of regional and local economic benchmarking. A snapshot of US practice', Paper presented to the 36th session of the OECD LEED Directing Committee, OECD LEED Programme, Paris.

Schweke, W., Rist, C. and Dabson, B. (1994) *Bidding for Business: Are Cities and States Selling Themselves Short?* Corporation for Enterprise Development, Washington.

Scott, A. (1998) *Regions in the World Economy,* Oxford University Press, Oxford.

Sforzi F. (1999) 'Italie: Systèmes locaux de petites et moyennes enterprises et mutation industrielle en Italie' in OECD, *Réseaux d'enterprise et Développement local*, Paris.

Smith, T.R. and Fox, W.F. (1990) 'Economic Development Programs for States in the 1990s', *Economic Review*, Federal Reserve Bank of Kansas City, Vol. 75, Number 4.

Stöhr, W. (1990) *Global Challenge and Local Response. Local Initiatives for Economic Regeneration in Contemporary Europe*, Mansell Publishing, London.

Stoker, G., Hogwood, B., Bullman, U., Osei, P. and Cairney, P. (1996) 'Regionalism', A Local Government Management Board Research Paper, Luton.

Storper, M. (1997) *The Regional World*, Guilford Press, New York.

Storper, M. and Scott, A.J. (1995) 'Market forces and policy imperatives in local and global context', *Futures*, Vol. 27.5, pp. 505-526

The Copenhagen Centre (1999a) *New Employment Partnership in Europe : Innovative Local Employment Strategies*, Copenhagen.

The Copenhagen Centre (1999b) *Partnership Alchemy*, Copenhagen.

Tiberi Vipraio, P. (a cura di) (1997) *Problemi e prospettive dei distretti industriali in Friuli-Venezia Giulia*, Udine.

Treptov, R. (1999) 'On the Concept of the Learning City and Region: Pre-school, Out-of-school and Adult Education Activities', in *Economic and Cultural Transitions towards a Learning City: The Case of Jena*, OECD, Paris.

United States Department of Commerce (1999) *Economic Development Administration Fact Sheet*, January.

Uturaud-Giraudeau, M. (1997) 'La culture d'entreprise au lycée pilote innovant du Futuroscope', in Schumack, P, and Greffe, X., *Enterprise Culture and Job Creation in the European Union*, LEDA Programme, Commission of the European Union, DG V, Brussels.

Vickery, G. (1996) 'The globalisation of investment and trade', Chapter 4, 83-117 in J. de la Mothe and G. Paquet (eds) *Evolutionary Economics and the New International Political Economy*, Pinter, London.

Wagner, L. (1982) *The Economics of Educational Media*, Macmillan, London.

Walton, M. and Kraushaar, R.A. (1990) 'Ideas and Information: The Changing Role of States in Economic Development', *Economic Development Quarterly*, Vol. 4 No. 3.

Wanieck, R. (1993) 'A new approach towards decentralisation in North-Rhine Westphalia', *Regional Studies*, 27.5, 467-495.

Wells, H.G. (1934) *Experiment in Autobiography*, Golland & Cresset, London.

Welsh Development Agency (2000) *Entrepreneurship Action Plan for Wales*, Strategy Document, Welsh Development Agency, Cardiff.

Wollman, H (2001) 'Germany's trajectory of public sector modernisation: continuities and discontinuities', *Policy and Politics*, 29.2, 151-170

OECD PUBLICATIONS, 2, rue André-Pascal, 75775 PARIS CEDEX 16
PRINTED IN FRANCE
(04 2001 18 1 P) ISBN 92-64-19656-0 – No. 52183 2001